Close Your Wealth Gap!

Close Your Wealth Gap!

Financial Lessons to Upgrade Your Life

Rob Luna

WILEY

Published by John Wiley & Sons, Inc., Hoboken, New Jersey.
Published simultaneously in Canada.

For general information on our other products and services or for technical support, please contact our Customer Care Department within the United States at (800) 762-2974, outside the United States at (317) 572-3993 or fax (317) 572-4002.

Wiley also publishes its books in a variety of electronic formats. Some content that appears in print may not be available in electronic formats. For more information about Wiley products, visit our web site at www.wiley.com.

Library of Congress Cataloging-in-Publication Data is Available:

ISBN 9781394195602 (Hardback)
ISBN 9781394195626 (ePDF)
ISBN 9781394195619 (ePub)

COVER DESIGN: PAUL MCCARTHY

SKY10053965_082523

*I dedicate this book to everyone who is trying
to improve their life and the lives of their families.
Education is the greatest equalizer I know.
Please use this information to take action.*

Contents

Acknowledgments

All glory to God because through Him all things are possible.

I want to thank **my wife Sabina**, who is always my biggest fan. Thank you for helping me balance my passion about business and investing with my blood pressure levels. Your love and support mean everything to me. I couldn't imagine my life without you. #Godsplan

To **my daughter Bella**, I am so proud of the young woman you are becoming. Your wisdom is beyond your years. I look forward to watching all the greatness that lies ahead of you. You are such an incredible person. I am very blessed to have you in my life.

I want to thank my business partner **Luis Galdamez** for all the hours helping me gather and proof check all the data that is used in the book and on the book's site. You are not only a great business partner, but you are also an amazing friend! I couldn't have met my deadlines without you!

To **Charles Payne**, thanks for allowing me uncensored access to your audience each week. You inspire me both professionally and personally. I share your relentless commitment to help people get their own slice of the American dream, no matter how hard people try to keep it from them. You are an absolute legend.

To **Kenny Polcari**, the first time I saw you on TV as a 20-year-old Wall Street rookie, I said, "That is exactly who I want to be when I grow up," and today we are friends. Such a small world. You are a rockstar!

To **Neil Cavuto**, after the first time I appeared on your show, a handwritten card showed up at my office from you thanking me for being on the show. I was shocked you even knew my name, let alone took the time to write me. Your humility is what makes you so great in my eyes and is a lesson to us all to check your ego at the door. Thank you.

To **Professor Jeremy Siegel**, thank you for inspiring my passion for financial markets. What that inspiration has done for me and my family is more than you will ever know.

To **Tim Grover**, you are a beast. You are consistent, authentic, and one of the few people I chase daily. From the moment we were introduced, I knew I still had a long way to go. I strive to perform at your level one day.

Finally, to **everyone who purchased this book**. Thank you for helping me continue to live my dream. I wasn't supposed to be here. God is good.

Introduction

Warning: this book is going to provide you with a plain-English and very specific financial roadmap that will show you how to significantly improve your life. The problem is that this knowledge will shatter any excuses you had up to this point, cause you to act more strategically, and force you to deploy discipline into every aspect of your financial life. Furthermore, once you see how easy it is, you will want to kick yourself hard for not learning and implementing this stuff sooner! With all that said, I think you can handle it, and I can't wait to hear your success story.

What Is Financial Literacy?

Financial literacy is a major buzz word that grabs a lot of attention these days. If you ask five different people what it means to them, you will probably get five different answers. For the purposes of this book, we are going to define *financial literacy* in this way:

> Financial literacy is gaining and/or accessing the knowledge that is required to optimize all the financial decisions you will need to make during your lifetime. By consistently making wealth-maximizing decisions, it will allow you to achieve your highest quality of life in the fastest possible timeframe.

That is what this book is all about: living your best life as soon as possible and providing you with the knowledge and means to sustain that lifestyle throughout your lifetime. No matter what type of dreams you have, they require money. I have yet to meet a dream that is completely free. Becoming financially literate means having the knowledge to pay for those dreams so that they may become a reality in your life.

In this book I am going to teach you both conventional and nonconventional methods to increase your financial literacy and upgrade your life. Some of this information you may have heard before, and some I promise will be completely new and even controversial. I don't care about any of that. I only care about changing your life, and to do that, I need to make financial literacy more approachable, multidimensional, and executable no matter where you stand academically or where you rank on the socioeconomic ladder today. That in a nutshell is my mission.

What we won't be doing in this book is diving into the dirty details needed to become a financial analyst. You won't have a lot of academic theory thrown at you, or pages upon pages of financial diagrams with Greek letters attached to them. The truth is that, unless you are looking at becoming an analyst as a career, it is completely unnecessary to dive that deep just to build personal wealth.

What I am going to do in this book is hand you the CliffNotes version of everything you need to do to become the CEO of your own financial future and upgrade your life. I will make things as simple as possible but not so simple that it won't provide you the vital information that you do need to succeed. Even though I am going to simplify this as much as possible, it is still going to be new and somewhat challenging information. I want to set clear expectations up front that financial freedom requires a commitment, so be prepared to put in the work. You may need to read some of this information three or four times and work through it on a spreadsheet or piece of paper. There will be no extremely complex math, so a calculator, pad of paper, and a pencil will be just fine.

You may also want to spend some time on the www.close yourwealthgaptools.com website to work with our tools to figure out your own situation. We have taken the complex work of putting together spreadsheets and done that work for you so that you just need to plug in your info. I do promise you, though, that if you are willing to put in the work, this information will be your fastest and most sustainable path to achieving your dream lifestyle.

I'm Just Like You

Let me first tell you a little about myself. I want you to know who I am primarily so you can understand I am not exceptional, I was not given an advantage over you, and if you follow what I teach you in this book, I am confident you will be more successful than you have ever imagined.

My name is Rob Luna. I am a Cuban/Italian American who grew up in Los Angeles, California, during the 1980s and early 1990s in a predominantly Hispanic neighborhood. My mother was addicted to drugs, and my older brother got caught up in heavy gang violence that dominated southern California during the late 1980s and 1990s. He was eventually imprisoned, leaving me to navigate a very tough environment alone. I had many close friends who were killed by drive-by shootings, and, in short, my life was purely about survival as a child and teenager—survival in the sense of not only dodging gunshots daily, but also having to feed and clothe myself from about 11 years of age on.

From the perspective I have today, it was a tough life. There was no running water at times, our electricity turned off usually for a few days each month, and we moved from apartment to apartment just to dodge eviction notices.

Financial literacy was obviously not a hot topic of conversation in my house. What necessity taught me though was the fine art of entrepreneurism, which delivered some of the best financial and economic lessons of my life at a very early age.

As a young "entrepreneur" I was constantly hustling. I would negotiate a broker fee with neighborhood kids to sell their old bicycles on consignment, I peddled five-dollar candy bars door to door, washed cars, cut lawns, and picked up whatever job people needed done to earn a buck.

As I grew closer to adulthood it seemed as though the gang violence in my neighborhood was increasing daily. I avoided much of it by staying involved in sports—baseball, then boxing, and finally wrestling. It was sports that offered me an opportunity to get out of Southern California at 18 and go to Arizona where my coach was able to secure a job for me, money for college, and a chance to wrestle. He told me simply "this is your one chance don't F it up"! I took that to heart. My wrestling career was short lived, but it was an education that saved my life and put me on a path to achieve a lifestyle that I still sometimes must pinch myself about.

They say that we make plans and God laughs at us. My life is a testament to that. My plan in my freshman year at college was to become a child psychiatrist. I was hired by a company working with at-risk youth. This allowed me to get experience in the field, pay my bills, and attend school in the evenings. Within a very short period of time the company filed for bankruptcy, and I needed to find something to be able to make my rent payment. At the time, the newspaper was still the first place to go for job ads. I opened the paper and immediately spotted a big ad that read "Hiring Stockbroker Trainees." I had no idea what that meant, but I had seen the movie *Wall Street* and knew that stockbrokers made a lot of money. Even though I was broke, I always aspired to achieve the "better things" in life. I also understood those high aspirations would take a lot of money to realize. I applied for the job with about 100 others. I was one of the lucky few selected. I was told by the hiring manager Pat Donovan, who had a heavy Brooklyn accent, that I was hired because I had the best tie, so they were going to give me a "shot." Funny thing is that it was a tie I could barely afford at the time, but it turned out to be my best investment ever. Thank you, Nordstrom!

I was all-in on this career because I truly knew it was my one opportunity that may not come again. I spent every hour I could soaking up financial content, earned numerous designations, more degrees, and read every book I could get my hands on, with my favorite being *Stocks for the Long Run* by Jeremy Siegel. Dr. Siegel's book took me to the Wharton School where I enrolled in an investment analyst program. This experience fueled my passion for higher education and helped me take my wealth management firm Surevest to the next level. I built Surevest from my bedroom on credit card debt. The firm grew tremendously over the years and allowed me to do financial planning and manage money for some of the nation's wealthiest people. I was invited weekly to speak on national media, I was named a *Forbes* Best-in-State Wealth Advisor, and eventually built my company into a multimillion-dollar business that I sold to a publicly traded company and finally exited at the beginning of 2023. In a strange way I also was able to fill many of my earlier dreams, using my psychology education over those 20+ years to consult and console my clients through personal ups and downs and to manage the emotions that come with investing.

I tell you my personal story because I want you to forget any preconceived notions that you have been using for not becoming financially literate and living a better life. In this book, I am going to give you the same roadmap I use for myself today and have used for hundreds of multimillionaire clients over the past 25 years who have paid me millions of dollars for this information. I want you to throw away any excuses that will keep you and generations of your family from experiencing a better life. I want you to have no justifiable reason for not reaching your full potential.

It's Up to You

The problem, from my experience, is that I also know that even after I give you proven step-by-step instructions on how to put yourself in a better financial position, many of you will fail. That is not because the information isn't good (I am living proof that it is), but because you refuse to execute it. You refuse to be accountable to what it takes to break the mold of mediocrity. You refuse to adopt a different mindset—a winner's mindset, a wealth-maximizing mindset. Some of you, however, will use this information to exponentially change the trajectory of your lives. You will live in the house you always wanted, eat at the restaurants you enjoy, go on the vacations you dreamed of, but most importantly you will empower yourselves with wealth's greatest gift of all, choice. Wealth provides the freedom to do things because you want to do them, not because you are financially forced to do them. I bet you would like to be able to say that in your own life.

When we talk about having the wealth necessary to stop working, I do not like to use the word *retirement*. That word conjures up the image of a couple of old people playing bridge in a nursing home in Florida. I call it "work optional." The definition of work optional is working because you enjoy what you are doing, not because you must. My goal is by the end of this book for you to be on a path to making work optional as soon as possible. What I mean by that is for you to clearly know what your ideal lifestyle will cost, how much you need to save, how to invest, and where to find resources to stay on track to get it done.

As I mentioned, however, the ultimate accountability will be left in your hands. If you really want to change, this book will show you how to do it step by step.

Part I

All About the Wealth Gap and Your Relationship to Money

Chapter 1
The Wealth Gap

There is a major problem in our country that our education system and government unfortunately are not getting any closer to solving. It is well publicized that the rich are getting richer and the poor are getting poorer, which is squeezing out the middle class. This is not an uncommon problem in other countries where you have the ultrawealthy living alongside people experiencing extreme poverty. I have seen it in my travel abroad to places like India. The difference is that in America, we don't have caste systems. We are born with the ability to be who and what we want to be—a freedom by the way that we must continue fighting to preserve each day.

Figure 1.1 illustrates how the wealth gap has been widening since the 1990s. In 1990, the total household wealth in the United States was $21.17 trillion of which the top 0.01% of households owned $1.83 trillion, while the bottom 50% owned only $0.77 trillion combined. This means that the wealthiest households owned about 2.4 times more wealth than the bottom 50% of households. Fast-forward to 2022 where the total household wealth in the United States was $135.33 trillion of which the top 0.01% of households owned $16.93 trillion, while the bottom 50% owned $4.52 trillion combined. That means the wealthiest households' share increased to 3.7 times more wealth than the bottom 50% households.

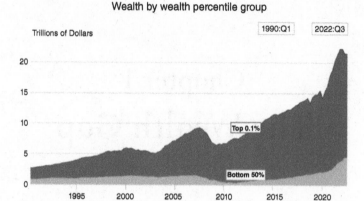

Figure 1.1 The wealth gap, illustrated.
SOURCE: Survey of Consumer Finances and Financial Accounts of the United States, Federal Reserve.

Imagine for just a moment if the wealth gap had remained the same in 2022 as it was in 1990. That would mean that the bottom 50% of households would be expected to have a combined wealth in 2022 of about $7.12 trillion. That is $2.6 trillion more wealth than the actual figures, which is more than the $2.1 trillion gross domestic product (GDP) of Italy in 2021.

Of course, the point is not to keep the wealth gap the same, but rather to shrink it.

The missing link for many to change their own future is the right information to do so. I continue to be astonished by the high degree of financial illiteracy in our country. CNBC said that in 2022 15% of Americans lost at least $10,000 in that year alone due to financial illiteracy.[1] The average person lost $1,800. Financial illiteracy I believe is the primary driver of the increasing wealth gap we are witnessing in America.

---

[1] Sarah O'Brian, Lack of financial literacy cost 15% of adults at least $10,000 in 2022. Here's how the rest fared, CNBC, Jan 19, 2023. https://www.cnbc.com/2023/01/19/heres-how-much-people-say-lack-of-financial-literacy-cost-in-2022.html

The top 0.1% of the households that own most of the US wealth are not necessarily smarter than everyone else. They just acquired the knowledge to do a few simple things that drive wealth creation. They have learned to purchase appreciating assets. Figure 1.2 illustrates the total amount of dollars invested in stocks and mutual fund shares by the top 0.01% and the bottom 50%. It is a staggering difference, and the gap between the two groups is widening. In 2022 the top 0.01% owned $6.89 trillion of stocks and mutual fund shares, while the bottom owned only $0.19 trillion.

The top 0.01% of households also own privately held businesses. I have said for a very long time that the way to build generational wealth is by becoming a business owner. Figure 1.3 clearly illustrates how much wealth is concentrated in private businesses by the top 0.01% and how little wealth is held by the bottom 50% in privately held businesses.

If you pay close attention to Figures 1.1, 1.2, and 1.3, you will notice they move in tandem. That is because household wealth is driven by owning appreciating assets such as stocks, mutual funds, and private businesses.

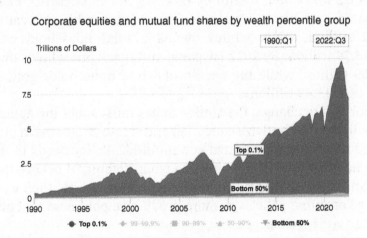

Figure 1.2 The investing gap, illustrated.

SOURCE: Survey of Consumer Finances and Financial Accounts of the United States, Federal Reserve.

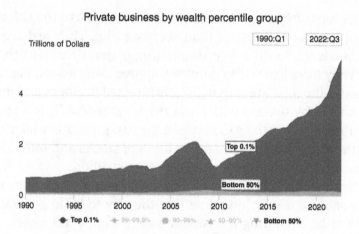

Figure 1.3　The business owner gap, illustrated.
SOURCE: Survey of Consumer Finances and Financial Accounts of the United States, Federal Reserve.

Who the Gap Affects

This wealth gap is impacting everyone, but disproportionately, it is minorities who are feeling the greatest sting. Figure 1.4 breaks down US household wealth by race. As you can observe, in 1990 Hispanic and Black households owned a combined wealth of $1.32 trillion, while whites owned a total household wealth of $18.79 trillion. By 2022 Hispanic and Black households owned $10.59 trillion, while the wealth of white households grew to a total of $111.49 trillion.

For this to change, the United States must adopt the appropriate policies to incentivize education and create awareness in underserved and underrepresented communities. Policy needs to move from handing out "fish" to incentivizing "fishing." I believe that if we can help underserved communities create wealth, then we can change enabling policies to more productive polices so that everyone can rise together.

For example, encouraging minorities to own their own home can have a drastic impact on wealth creation. Figure 1.5 shows the amount of wealth held in real estate by race, and it is clear to see a

Wealth by race

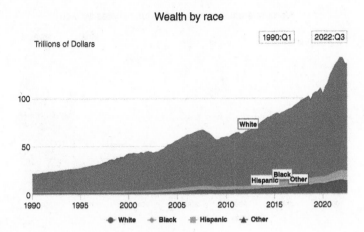

Figure 1.4 The wealth gap by race.
SOURCE: Survey of Consumer Finances and Financial Accounts of the United States, Federal Reserve.

Real estate by race

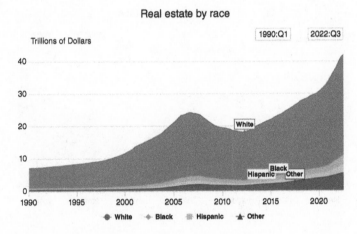

Figure 1.5 The wealth gap of real estate holdings by race.
SOURCE: Survey of Consumer Finances and Financial Accounts of the United States, Federal Reserve.

direct correlation between household wealth (Figure 1.4) and real estate ownership. We also want to encourage stock and mutual fund share ownership (Figure 1.6) and private business ownership (Figure 1.7). In other words, we need to motivate minorities to own appreciating assets.

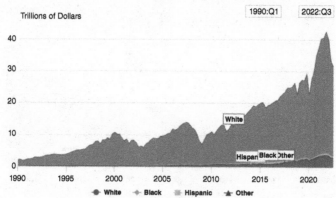

Figure 1.6   The wealth gap of investment holdings by race.
SOURCE: Survey of Consumer Finances and Financial Accounts of the United States, Federal Reserve

Private business by race

Figure 1.7   The wealth gap of business ownership by race.
SOURCE: Survey of Consumer Finances and Financial Accounts of the United States, Federal Reserve.

I have seen this play out my whole life, starting with myself. Education and wealth change politics and political views. They changed me. For our country to prosper over the long run and remain the greatest country in the world, we must help lift everyone through empowering and educating , not by enabling through agenda-driven government policy. Free market capitalism works if people understand and can participate in its essence. I am living proof of that. I came across this knowledge by luck. Luck is not a reliable enough strategy to count on changing our country and creating a more optimistic and prosperous America, though. We must take a strategic and intentional approach to closing the wealth gap.

Unfortunately, I don't currently see an awful lot being done to change this wealth gap, which is why I have made it my mission in the second half of my career to do my part in helping close the gap.

The way I see it, you basically have two choices. You can become a statistic and use the "wealth gap" as your excuse to live a subpar lifestyle, or you can use it as motivation to have change begin with you. When you change yourself, it not only improves your life, but it sets up your kids and future generations for a much better life.

Our schools are still not teaching basic financial literacy, and most teachers themselves don't even understand the foundational elements of what a solid financial plan should look like. I have even spoken to economics majors who never learned personal finance in any of their classes.

What You Can Do About the Gap . . .

As mentioned, in this book, I am not going to give you a very detailed description of cash flow analysis, stock valuation models, cap rate analysis, or modern portfolio theory. There are books specifically dedicated to that, and, unless your goal is to become a financial analyst, that is not the level of information you need to upgrade your life.

Instead, what I am going to provide you with is the CliffNotes version of all the actionable lessons that I have learned, from 25 years of experience, and from three of the top business schools in the world. These are the real-life lessons I have implemented for myself and I have implemented for others as a wealth manager working with people who had a minimum of $5 million of investable assets. I already know this information works, and I have been paid millions of dollars in my career to help others execute this exact information I am now sharing with you.

This is not some random academic theory or some get-rich-quick scheme. I will teach you the exact framework that has been proven to work, and I will break it down into simple steps that you can use to upgrade your own life. These lessons have significantly changed people's lives and given them access to a world that they believed was reserved for people other than them.

I am here to tell you that everything you want is achievable. I am living proof. You just need the knowledge and drive to go after it. At the end of this book, you will be armed with that knowledge. You will not only understand what you are doing, but also, importantly, when, why, and what the outcome should be. Unless you understand the destination, you will never have the right map to get you there. Most people spend their lives going in circles because they lack that type of clarity. I want to change that for you. I want to provide you the clarity you need to begin to operate strategically and with purpose daily toward improving your life.

...And How This Book Will Help

To make things easy to understand, I am going to take you through a financial journey that will strategically walk you through the most important concepts you will need to master to gain control of your financial life.

First, in Chapter 2, we will identify your relationship with money and why it is so important to clearly understand what that is early on in our journey. Next, in Chapter 3, we will jump into your financial boot camp where you will go through a basic training in financial literacy to give you a solid foundation in which to begin putting the pieces of your financial life together.

We'll continue with your bootcamp in the next three chapters. In Chapter 4, you are going to build the dashboard for your financial life. This dashboard will give you clarity and transparency over your financial life like you have never had before. After you have that transparency, in Chapter 5, you are going to clearly identify the areas you need to improve on. No worries—I will show you some actionable strategies that you can begin to improve your financial results right away no matter what financial position you find yourself in today.

Now that we have assured addressing all the low-hanging fruit, it's time to get to work building your financial roadmap in Chapter 6. This roadmap is going to take your from where you are at today and build an action plan for you to achieve your ideal lifestyle. I will also share with you my "Magic Shortcuts" that take some very extremely complex issues and make them as easy to implement as two plus two. Once you have your plan dialed in, it's time to learn how to invest. I am going to share with you a bucketing system that I have used for high-net-worth people in my practice for more than 20 years. You are going to be amazed at how simple it is to use and how much more control and certainty you will have over the investments that you make. No more guess work. This is the solution that you have been looking for.

Once you begin to see your investments and your income grow, you are not going to want to hand over all that hard-earned money to Uncle Sam! In Chapter 8, I will show you some smart and importantly legal ways that you can reduce your tax bill and keep more of what you earn.

Two of the most misunderstood and misused tools I have seen in financial planning has been life insurance and annuities. In Chapter 9, I will fill you in on everything that you need to know to avoid making any mistakes.

Now that you have maximized what you are doing today, in Chapter 10 I will teach you what I call the *wealth-maximizing mindset*. All that I have learned over decades working with some of the world's wealthiest people comes down to some very key things that you can start doing right away to start thinking as the wealthy do. You will be amazed at what this way of thinking will do for upgrading your lifestyle.

In Chapter 11 it will be time to act. We will go through building your action plan. We are going to make sure that this is not one of those books that you read and then do nothing. This will be your roadmap to start taking action.

We will finish with age-based advice and a case study to show you exactly what you need to be doing to achieve your dream life. By the time you are done with this book, you are going to feel like a new person with an improved outlook and much more confidence about upgrading your life!

You will be able to use this book both as a source of foundational knowledge and as a resource you can always come back to if you have questions.

You can also access the book's website, www.closeyour wealthgaptools.com, to find updated tools and resources to guide you on your journey.

I don't care how young or old you are. I don't care how far behind you think you are. These are things that you can and must start doing immediately to begin moving yourself up the ladder and avoid living a second-class life. I truly believe that financial literacy is the key to closing your own personal wealth gap. If I can help you do it with this information, I know that we can begin to solve the much larger problem our nation is facing. I will ask you to use this information to empower not only yourself but also your family, friends, and others. This information has been life changing for myself, my family, and my clients. The goal is to demystify and simplify finance and make this information accessible to everyone so that millions of people can upgrade their own quality of life with these financial lessons.

Chapter 2

What Is Your Relationship with Money?

It is important to understand your relationship with money. Every time I see the lottery prize get to $500 million or more, I buy 10 tickets. I play not because I believe that I'll win, but because the idea of winning that size of a prize provides me the entertainment value of being able to dream big for a day or two before being hit with the reality that I once again hit zero out of six numbers. For me, when the jackpot is less than half a billion, it isn't enough to overcome my logical side and the knowledge that I have a nearly 100% chance of just throwing my 20 bucks into a bonfire each time I play. Unfortunately, that logic is thrown out the window at a half billion! My greed drive overrides my logical brain at that sum. Those-sized dreams are worth the odds! This is an obvious example, although extreme, of where I have attached money to doing or achieving the things I really want in life.

What Do You Dream Money Will Do for You?

When you play the lottery, daydream about a long-lost relative leaving you millions, or like most people, getting a promotion, earning a fat commission check, or building a business that creates wealth, what is it that you believe that wealth will do for you? What are the things that you dream of?

I ask this because I know that the behavioral part of money and investing is more important than any of the financial rules and lessons I will teach you. Unless I can get you to first understand your relationship with money, eliminate any limiting beliefs about money, and understand why money matters to you, then you will find very little purpose in the lessons I'm about to teach you. Without purpose, there is little chance that you will even have the motivation to finish reading this book. You will certainly not retain the information because you do not possess the appropriate belief system that will allow you to execute on the information. However, once you realize how this information can put you on the path to achieving your dreams, it all takes on greater meaning. Your odds of not only finishing the book but executing on this information improve tremendously when you are able to tie actions to your real purpose for money.

I want to show you how money can become the tool that helps you achieve your highest level of potential. I submit that most people will settle for a life that is some subpar version of what it can be without this information. They typically subscribe to some arbitrary benchmark of mediocrity just because they have been told by parents, teachers, friends, and their own inner voice that this is our personal ceiling. This is what people "like them" are worth.

From my experience, the people who achieve great wealth do not possess these limiting beliefs or surround themselves with that type of mentality. They believe strongly that they are worthy of achieving their dreams no matter how lofty. They do not diminish their own value, and they have extreme clarity about what money means to them and have laid out a clear roadmap to accomplish their financial goals. They also have accountability to keep them on track and prevent excuse overload from paralyzing them every time things get a bit difficult.

Money Questions to Ask Yourself

So, before we begin the lessons, I need to get you to stop and make sure you write down your "whys" about money. When you do that, these lessons will become more valuable and more actionable for you. Start by writing down your answers to the following four questions:

1. How will money make things better for you?
2. What void or problem is in your life today that can be solved simply by having more money?
3. What do you believe is the single greatest thing money will do for you?
4. Do you believe you can be a billionaire?

My Answers to the Money Questions

I will share my own personal response with you just to give you a perspective of what one individual's relationship with money looks like. I expect your answers to be completely different, but this should shed some light on how to approach the questions.

Question 1: How Will Money Make Things Better for You?

My Answer: It will afford me more time to spend with loved ones and causes that are most meaningful in my life.

    Thoughts behind my response: Earlier in my life, there was so little time allocated to those things. Most of my time was spent grinding to earn a dollar. The more wealth that I have accumulated, the more time I am able to spend on what is important in my life. To me, that is the power of wealth.

Question 2: What Void or Problem Is in Your Life Today That Can Be Solved Simply by Having More Money?

My Answer: Providing more opportunities for people.

Thoughts behind my response: As an entrepreneur, I have become addicted to creating opportunities for people. My professor at Wharton, Adam Grant, said, "There is no such thing as true altruism." I believe that to be true. Creating opportunities for people, in which you get to play a part in seeing them achieve their own financial dreams, is very addictive and rewarding.

Question 3: What Do You Believe Is the Single Greatest Thing Money Will Do for You?

My Answer: It will provide choice.

Thoughts behind my response: Anyone who has studied psychology or been through therapy will tell you that a lot of who we are today is a direct result of our childhood. This is exactly the case with money. Another reason I told you a little about my childhood was to bring a human component to our lessons that you could identify with. Having had little to no choice as a child, I wanted to change that. Money has been my tool to provide myself with choice. To me, money holds a very powerful grip on my life. I work so hard because I never want to relinquish choice again.

What do you think money will provide you with that you don't have now? Or is there something you have and are afraid of losing that money may help secure for you? A relationship, a lifestyle?

Question 4: Do You Believe You Can Be a Billionaire?

My Answer: Yes, I know I can.

Thoughts behind my response: Although I firmly believe I can become a billionaire, which is the most important part, I also understand the sacrifices my family and I would need to make to achieve that. Everything I need, want, or desire requires less than a billion dollars fortunately!

Now, you must decide for yourself what sacrifices are worth the type of wealth that you are striving for. Bill Gates, for example, believed being a billionaire was worth the sacrifice it took to get there because of greater purpose than himself. His drive was a greater purpose of bringing healthcare to remote places in the world—in other words, changing lives beyond his own. These types of ambitions are billion-dollar ambitions that he personally believed were worth the sacrifice. You may think similarly or completely different about the trade-offs.

Knowing Your Why

There is no right or wrong answer to any of these four questions. What is most important in this exercise is that you first believe you can do anything that you set out do. That type of mindset will be necessary for you to use the lessons in this book to upgrade your life.

Equally important to the previous four questions is that you clearly identify and understand why you are doing it. Why are you taking time to even read this book? Why will you invest? Why will you start a business or work countless hours? What is the purpose of becoming financially secure? What does upgrading your life mean to you? Write down your whys and bring your greater purpose with you along on our journey so that you can begin to associate a plan with these new tools to achieving your bigger purpose and allow your why to become reality in your life.

Part II

Financial Boot Camp

Chapter 3
Starting Today

When I wrote this book, I wanted to make sure it wasn't just one of those great movie trailers that teases you just enough to buy the film but then leaves you with an abrupt and disappointing ending. I wanted the information in this book to make an immediate impact in your and your family's lives. The great thing about this book is that it is going to culminate in an action plan for you to apply. Specifically, I will be showing you the things that you need to go out and do depending on your stage in life as specifically as I can without holding back any "secrets."

Before we get to those action plans for you to take away and execute, I am going to put you through a comprehensive financial boot camp. Just as it is in the military, before you can hit the battleground and execute, you must first be trained on the basics to prepare yourself for action. By the time you are done with boot camp, you are going to have a significantly stronger foundation in which to execute all the action items that I will give to you in our age-based action plans. Unlike a lot of books or gurus who teach hypothetical strategies or motivate you to act but leave you void of actionable steps, I am going to give you step-by-step directions as specifically as possible so that you can go out and execute on your own, with this book as your guide.

You will have this book as an ongoing reference, but you will also be able to access the books website www.close yourwealthgaptools.com, where you can access free tools and resources that we will be continually updating to support your journey and share your success with me.

Remember what I said at the beginning of the book? I am going to leave you with no choice other than to throw all your excuses away and begin executing no matter where you are at today. If this book becomes just one of many books that you cracked open, skimmed, put on the shelf, and took no action on, then shame on you. Your ability to begin changing your life is in the pages to come. I promise you that.

To clarify, this information really will change your life, but only if you understand it and act on it. Reading this book and taking just one simple step that I provide you will start to become addictive and will lead to more positive steps and result in an upgrade of your entire life.

Start Today, Not Tomorrow

Your new financial life must start today, not a week from now or two years from now—right now! You have procrastinated long enough, and you are losing valuable time every hour that you wait to get started. The one thing I will not be able to provide you with in this book is more time, so you need to start acting with a sense of urgency because you have a lot of work ahead of you.

It's too easy and far too typical for us to make excuses about our finances. Have you caught yourself, a friend, or maybe your parents say this: "It's too late; I'm just going to have to work forever." It seems like I have heard that one a million times. It would be great if we could all do that, but our bodies and mental prime prevent that from being a viable option, so throw that one away. Burying your head in the sand unfortunately will not make up for lost time, but acting now can put you on a path toward achieving your goals faster than you probably think.

Thinking you are too young or that you have too little money to begin is also a big mistake. "I won't retire for years, so I am not going to worry about retirement now." Throw that mentality out the window also. The habits you create when you are young will follow you throughout life. People who overspend and save too little when they are young do the same thing when they are old; sorry to break that bad news to you. The excuses just start to pile up and sound far more pathetic as you age. The same thing goes for procrastination. Developing healthy money habits now is crucial to enhancing your potential to build wealth later. I have a saying: data kills emotions, and it also does not lie. Let me share with you some stats to drive home just how important it is to stop procrastinating and get started now.

The Cost of Waiting

For many people, becoming a millionaire is a big goal of theirs. Whether or not that is the right number for you will be largely dependent on the type of lifestyle that you want to live. No matter what your magic number is, the longer you wait, the more frustrating it is going to become. Each year that you postpone getting started represents a much larger number that you will need to invest each year.

For example, if you have a 30-year time horizon (meaning you're 30 years old and want to retire at 60), you will need to put away about $5,500 a year starting today. Waiting just a few years makes a huge difference. Figure 3.1 shows that when you wait just three years, you need to save 36% more each year! If you wait 10 years, that amount almost triples! So, the moral of the story is get started now.

The Cost of Waiting to Invest

Goal $1,000,000 30 Years from Today

Annual Return	10.0%

When Do You Start	Amount You Need to Invest Every Year
Now	$5,527
In 3 Years	$7,507
In 5 Years	$9,244
In 10 years	$15,872

Start of Year		Today	In 3 Years	In 5 Years	In 10 Years
Today	$	5,527	–	–	–
1	$	11,606	–	–	–
2	$	18,293	–	–	–
3	$	25,649	$ 7,507	–	–
4	$	33,740	$ 15,765	–	–
5	$	42,641	$ 24,848	$ 9,244	–
6	$	52,432	$ 34,840	$ 19,412	–
7	$	63,201	$ 45,831	$ 30,597	–
8	$	75,048	$ 57,921	$ 42,900	–
9	$	88,080	$ 71,220	$ 56,434	–
10	$	102,414	$ 85,849	$ 71,321	$ 15,872
11	$	118,182	$ 101,940	$ 87,697	$ 33,332
12	$	135,527	$ 119,641	$ 105,710	$ 52,538
13	$	154,606	$ 139,112	$ 125,525	$ 73,664
14	$	175,593	$ 160,531	$ 147,321	$ 96,903
15	$	198,679	$ 184,091	$ 171,297	$ 122,465
16	$	224,074	$ 210,007	$ 197,670	$ 150,584
17	$	252,008	$ 238,514	$ 226,681	$ 181,515
18	$	282,735	$ 269,873	$ 258,592	$ 215,539

Figure 3.1   The cost of waiting, with a goal of $1 million.

19	$	316,535	$ 304,367	$ 293,695	$ 252,965
20	$	353,716	$ 342,311	$ 332,309	$ 294,134
21	$	394,614	$ 384,049	$ 374,783	$ 339,420
22	$	439,602	$ 429,960	$ 421,505	$ 389,234
23	$	489,088	$ 480,463	$ 472,899	$ 444,030
24	$	543,524	$ 536,017	$ 529,433	$ 504,305
25	$	603,403	$ 597,125	$ 591,620	$ 570,608
26	$	669,270	$ 664,345	$ 660,026	$ 643,541
27	$	741,723	$ 738,286	$ 735,272	$ 723,768
28	$	821,422	$ 819,622	$ 818,043	$ 812,017
29	$	909,091	$ 909,091	$ 909,091	$ 909,091
30	$	1,000,000	$1,000,000	$1,000,000	$1,000,000

Figure 3.1 (Continued)

Not only does procrastination make it harder to get started, it also significantly impacts the amount of money that you will have in the future. For example, let's say you invest $6,500 a year (which is also the IRA contribution limit for 2023). As shown in Figure 3.2, when you wait just three years investing the exact same amount each year, you go from having nearly $1.2 million to less than $900,000, a difference of $300,000! If you wait 10 years, the amount you'll have is only $409,000! That's a whopping $800,000 less than if you start today. As Nike says, just do it!

Now that you understand how important it is to get started right away, you also need to know where to begin.

Where Are You at Today?

The first step to getting started is understanding exactly where you are today. Part of changing your financial future is getting a good and honest assessment of where you are today to put yourself on the path to get where you want to be tomorrow. I completely

The Cost of Waiting to Invest

| Annual Investment | $6,500 | | | |
| Annual Return | 10.0% | | | |

Start of Year	Start Today	Start in 3 Years	Start in 5 Years	Start in 10 Years
Today	$ 6,500	$ –	$ –	$ –
1	$ 13,650	$ –	$ –	$ –
2	$ 21,515	$ –	$ –	$ –
3	$ 30,167	$ 6,500	$ –	$ –
4	$ 39,683	$ 13,650	$ –	$ –
5	$ 50,151	$ 21,515	$ 6,500	$ –
6	$ 61,667	$ 30,167	$ 13,650	$ –
7	$ 74,333	$ 39,683	$ 21,515	$ –
8	$ 88,267	$ 50,151	$ 30,167	$ –
9	$ 103,593	$ 61,667	$ 39,683	$ –
10	$ 120,453	$ 74,333	$ 50,151	$ 6,500
11	$ 138,998	$ 88,267	$ 61,667	$ 13,650
12	$ 159,398	$ 103,593	$ 74,333	$ 21,515
13	$ 181,837	$ 120,453	$ 88,267	$ 30,167
14	$ 206,521	$ 138,998	$ 103,593	$ 39,683
15	$ 233,673	$ 159,398	$ 120,453	$ 50,151
16	$ 263,541	$ 181,837	$ 138,998	$ 61,667
17	$ 296,395	$ 206,521	$ 159,398	$ 74,333
18	$ 332,534	$ 233,673	$ 181,837	$ 88,267
19	$ 372,287	$ 263,541	$ 206,521	$ 103,593
20	$ 416,016	$ 296,395	$ 233,673	$ 120,453

Figure 3.2 The cost of waiting, showing the difference between starting now versus later.

21	$ 464,118	$ 332,534	$ 263,541	$ 138,998
22	$ 517,030	$ 372,287	$ 296,395	$ 159,398
23	$ 575,233	$ 416,016	$ 332,534	$ 181,837
24	$ 639,256	$ 464,118	$ 372,287	$ 206,521
25	$ 709,681	$ 517,030	$ 416,016	$ 233,673
26	$ 787,150	$ 575,233	$ 464,118	$ 263,541
27	$ 872,365	$ 639,256	$ 517,030	$ 296,395
28	$ 966,101	$ 709,681	$ 575,233	$ 332,534
29	$1,069,211	$ 787,150	$ 639,256	$ 372,287
30	$1,176,132	$ 865,865	$ 703,181	$ 409,516

Figure 3.2   (Continued)

understand for most of you this may be a difficult assessment. It is much easier to ignore your financial situation than it is to stare it in the face. The truth is, you will never make the changes in your life necessary to change your financial future unless you face your own reality.

No matter where you are now financially, if you make the commitment to learn and improve, I promise you that you will accomplish more than you believe. The goal of this book is to arm you with the knowledge to get your financial house in order and keep it there for the rest of your life. This all starts with accepting reality and understanding that you probably have not always made the wealth-maximizing decisions in your life. That's okay, because most people including myself haven't. We have all bought stuff we couldn't afford, didn't work as hard as we could have, and wasted money on things we can't even find today. In short, we didn't value money or the knowledge to earn and grow that money as much as we should have. If you are like most, you probably used excuse after excuse to justify why you couldn't save or invest the amount you should have by now.

The important part is that today you realize it's time to change that way of thinking. It is time to change your behaviors. I want to provide you with the knowledge to eliminate those excuses and make the changes necessary to begin your journey to a better life. Financial illiteracy and lack of commitment and discipline are the primary things that are keeping you from achieving your goals today. Make the commitment to end the excuses today, take inventory of your situation no matter how painful that may be, and let's put you on the path to upgrading your life.

In the next chapter, we will discuss the framework you will follow and provide you with the tools to start documenting and acting on this important information.

Chapter 4
Managing Your Financial Life in a Dashboard

W hat does your financial house look like today? When I meet with new people, the first question most people always want to know is what should I invest in? My answer is always the same and it usually surprises them. It is, I have no idea. I first need to know where exactly you are at today and where you are trying to go to give you the appropriate advice.

When you start investing without clearly understanding where you are and where you need to go, it almost always ends poorly. Investing without a plan is exactly what most people do. Investing without a plan is like trying to build your dream home without blueprints. It just doesn't work out well. You either end up taking too much or too little risk. You have too much or not enough liquidity.

Just think about it. If you had huge amounts of credit card debt that you were paying 15% interest or more on, why would you invest in stocks that are only going to return 9% or 10% or bonds earning 5%? It would make much more sense to put your extra cash into paying down that high interest debt first. By making that wealth-maximizing choice, you are automatically earning a guaranteed 15%, which is higher than you could expect from both stocks and bonds.

What if you were saving for a new home that you wanted to purchase in 12 months? Would it make sense to invest that money in stocks? Sure, stocks go up over time and deliver a very good return, but in any one-year or two-year period, they could easily be down 10% or more. Knowing that, do you think it would make sense to invest in stocks for the down payment you need on a home in a year if there was a real possibility you would have less money when it was time to buy? Wouldn't a one-year CD at 4% make more sense if you knew it was guaranteed to be there and earn more interest than you could earn in your savings account for the next year?

Those are just a few examples of why investing should be tied directly to your personal financial situation. Most people I have seen though do not do it that way. Most people make investments and hope for the best. Hope is a reliable investment strategy and certainly not one that you are going to depend on going forward. You are going to make sure that your investments are directly tied to where you stand personally today and where you want to be tomorrow to achieve maximum success.

Getting an honest assessment of where you are today and maintaining control of your financial life in the future is going to consist of understanding, building, and continually managing three things. These three things will be the core of what will be called your financial dashboard. They all work hand in hand, so I want you to be thinking about how each one impacts the other as you read this. You should start to see and understand a correlation between each of the three components. When one of these changes, it will always impact the other two, either positively or negatively. It's important that you understand that correlation.

The following three components will make up your dashboard:

1. Balance sheet
2. Net worth statement
3. Cash flow statement

Your financial dashboard is all set for you to begin plugging in all your own numbers at www.closeyourwealthgap tools.com. This chapter will walk you through the three components.

Managing your dashboard is the key to having control and visibility, which are the essential components of managing your financial future. Just like operating your car, your financial dashboard will tell you if you're running too hot or cold, too fast, or too slow, and by maintaining the right levels on your odometers, it will allow you to operate at peak performance. I cannot stress the importance of getting your arms around all three of these metrics.

Understanding this information and continually managing it is the number-one duty you now have as the CEO of your own financial life. These are the things that you can control. A lot of what I will teach you is to focus on what you can control and pay little attention to what you cannot. There are plenty of things that will impact your finances that you will not be able to control such as stock market returns, inflation, interest rates, recessions, and so forth. Instead of worrying about the uncontrollable, let's identify and learn what you can control and commit to taking decisive action to manage those things instead. That is a much more constructive strategy than wasting time worrying about the things you have no control over.

Do not worry if these terms within the dashboard are initially unfamiliar to you. There is nothing that you need to be intimidated by. I will help break everything down into easy steps where you don't need to be a CPA or a finance major to understand it. Anyone with a high school education can do this, I promise. Gaining and maintaining control of your financial life becomes very liberating once you really understand how this information will allow you to improve your entire life.

Balance Sheet

Let's start with your balance sheet. Your balance sheet is comprised of all your assets and all your liabilities.

Assets

Your *assets* are things like your 401(k), savings account, equity in your home, CDs, stock portfolio, or anything that you can sell and turn to cash.

Some assets you have are considered liquid, which are things like stocks, cash, and savings account. What those assets have in common is that you can normally withdraw the amount in those accounts within 24–48 hours. Having most of your assets in those types of investments and accounts is called having *liquidity*.

Other assets such as real estate, private businesses, and automobiles are considered to be illiquid.

Illiquid assets are also part of your balance sheet, but they cannot as easily be turned into cold, hard cash. For example, you can sell your home, but it requires much more than 24–48 hours to complete that transaction today. You must first find an agent, list it, then find a buyer. Then, depending on how long that takes, it still is normally another 30–60 days in order to finish the transaction and receive the funds.

It is important to have the right combination of liquid and illiquid assets. How much liquidity will depend on many things that we will address later in the book when we start to build out your financial buckets in Chapter 7. Right now, I just want you to understand the difference between the two.

Liabilities

Most people who have assets also have *liabilities*. Liabilities are the opposite of assets. Remember this saying: "Assets earn, and liabilities burn."

You always want to have more assets than liabilities. Assets are a positive on your balance sheet, whereas liabilities are negative.

Examples are your mortgage balance, credit card debt, student loans, and car payments. These are things that take away from your earnings and or your assets. If you lose your job and stop earning, then you must rely on your assets to pay your liabilities. If there are not enough assets to cover your payments, then it's game over. You want to make sure that never happens to you, so you need to be smart about having the right balance of assets and liabilities to protect yourself.

Net Worth Statement

When you add up all of your assets and then subtract all of your liabilities, that your *net worth.*

Assets – Liabilities = Net worth

Where do you stand when you do this exercise? You can plug all the details of your assets and liabilities into your financial dashboard at www.closeyourwealthgaptools.com to automatically have the number populate for you.

Your net worth can vary from negative, when your liabilities are more than your assets, to very high when your assets exponentially exceed any liabilities. You may have heard that someone has a high net worth, which means they have assets that significantly exceed their liabilities. A person could also have a low net worth, where their assets barely exceed their liabilities. Someone can even have a negative net worth, meaning their liabilities exceed their assets. Unfortunately, many people in the United States find themselves in the later situation because of credit card debt, auto payments, and student loan debt.

The following are three examples of net worth statements to give you an idea of how it all comes together: high, low, and negative. Where do you stand today?

Example: High Net Worth

Maria is a 45-year-old business owner who is single. Maria started her own restaurant right out of college, and now she owns several locations. After opening her third restaurant, Maria began to contribute the maximum amount to the company's 401(k) plan. Now she has accumulated $2 million, of which $500,000 is in a taxable trust account and $1,500,000 is in the 401(k) plan. A few years ago, Maria sold her first home and purchased a bigger house that has a current value of $2.5 million with a mortgage balance of $1.9 million. Maria recently worked with a business consultant to help value her business, and after the analysis, they determined that her enterprise is worth $5 million.

Figure 4.1 shows Maria's net worth statement with some additional details of her net worth.

Balance Sheet | High Net Worth

Assets	Amount
Liquid	
Checking Account	$ 50,000.00
Savings Account	$ 75,000.00
Emergency Account	$ 250,000.00
Investment Accounts	$ 500,000.00
Retirement Accounts (i.e. 401(k))	$ 1,500,000.00
Illiquid	
Home	$ 2,500,000.00
Private Business	$ 5,000,000.00
Automobiles	$ 350,000.00
Total Assets	**$ 10,225,000.00**

Liabilities	Amount
Mortgage Balance	$ (1,900,000.00)
Credit Card Debt	$ –
Automobile Loan	$ –
Student Loans	$ (50,000.00)
Total Liabilities	**$ (1,950,000.00)**

Net Worth	$ 8,275,000.00

Figure 4.1　Example of high net worth.

Maria has accumulated a considerable net worth, with a large part of that being in the business that she has built. For most entrepreneurs, this is common to see. This is especially true in the early years where a large part of their net worth is tied to their business due to the time and often monetary investment in their business. For most who are successful, it eventually becomes their largest asset.

Even though Maria has some debt, the only debt that she carries is what I consider good debt. You will learn more about this later in the book when we discuss good versus bad debt in Chapter 5. Maria has done a great job in diversifying her wealth into a retirement plan, taxable investments, and emergency fund. This is a very solid balance sheet that she has built, especially for her age.

Example: Low Net Worth

Anthony and Carla are in their mid-30s with three children. They are both teachers at their local elementary school, and they recently purchased their first home. Anthony and Carla are now starting to focus on their personal finances, and they've began to put money away in their retirement accounts. They also want to focus on paying down the debt that they accumulated over the years.

Figure 4.2 shows Anthony and Carla's net worth statement with some additional details of their net worth.

Anthony and Carla currently have a low net worth, so they need to focus on increasing their assets and lowering their liabilities. The first thing they need to do is increase their emergency fund, because without an adequate emergency fund, they are in a very vulnerable position if they hit a rough patch.

Once they have established an adequate emergency fund, they should look to pay off their high-interest credit card debt. Credit card debt is about the single worst type of debt that you can carry.

Balance Sheet | Low Net Worth	
Assets	**Amount**
Liquid	
Checking Account	$ 2,500.00
Savings Account	$ 1,500.00
Emergency Account	$ 1,500.00
Investment Accounts	$ 800.00
Retirement Accounts (i.e. 401(k))	$ 3,500.00
Illiquid	
Home	$ 450,000.00
Private Business	$ –
Automobiles	$ 20,000.00
Total Assets	**$ 479,800.00**
Liabilities	**Amount**
Mortgage Balance	$ (425,000.00)
Credit Card Debt	$ (20,000.00)
Automobile Loan	$ (20,000.00)
Student Loans	$ (10,000.00)
Total Liabilities	**$ (475,000.00)**
Net Worth	**$ 4,800.00**

Figure 4.2 Example of low net worth.

It is not deductible, it has very high interest rates, and, even worse, it has a floating rate note, which means the rate is not locked and could go even higher. Never carry credit card debt if you can afford to pay it off.

Next, there should be a balance of systematically building up their investment account, which will give them growth and liquidity. Anthony and Carla should also look to regularly contribute to their retirement accounts. Simultaneously, they should begin to reduce the auto and student loan debt in that specific order.

Example: Negative Net Worth

Adam is a single 25-year-old with no children. He is a barista at the local coffee shop and has not given his personal finances much thought. He hesitated to put money away in his company's 401(k) plan but reconsidered after he learned that his employer matched his contributions. Adam does not have much in assets aside from his used 2012 Toyota Corolla. He loves concerts and going out with his friends and has used his credit cards to help sustain his lifestyle.

Figure 4.3 shows Adam's net worth statement with some additional details of his net worth.

Balance Sheet | Negative Net Worth

Assets	Amount
Liquid	
Checking Account	$ 500.00
Savings Account	$ 1,000.00
Emergency Account	$ –
Investment Accounts	$ –
Retirement Accounts (i.e. 401(k))	$ 1,500.00
Illiquid	
Home	$ –
Private Business	$ –
Automobiles	$ 5,000.00
Total Assets	**$ 8,000.00**

Liabilities	Amount
Mortgage Balance	$ –
Credit Card Debt	$ (20,000.00)
Automobile Loan	$ –
Student Loans	$ (7,500.00)
Total Liabilities	**$ (27,500.00)**

Net Worth	**$ (19,500.00)**

Figure 4.3   Example of negative net worth.

Adam has a negative net worth, but at least he is making the step of contributing to his 401(k), which is a great start. He could be doing so much more, though, which you'll learn about when building your financial dashboard starting in the next section.

Most concerning to me is that Adam has no emergency account. This is the only thing I always recommend before making any investment or even paying off high-interest credit card debt. Having an emergency fund is non-negotiable; everyone must put it as their first financial objective.

After the emergency fund, the credit card debt, which many times exceeds 20%, must start to be tackled in a systematic way. The moral of the story is don't be an Adam! Please use this as the example of what you never want your personal balance sheet to look like. If it currently looks a bit too familiar, help is on the way!

Now that you have created a balance sheet and seen three different examples of net worth statements, I think you are starting to realize that we are all trying to look a lot more like Maria than we are like Adam. The great news is, by the time you complete this book, you will know how to build a roadmap that places you in that direction. You will learn the tools, mindset, and strategies that the wealthy use to build intentional wealth. All of the mystery will be taken out of the equation for you.

Cash Flow Statement

Now that you have a balance sheet and know what your net worth is, you can begin to focus on your cash flow statement. Your cash flow statement is very important because this is what ultimately allows you to improve or destroy your balance sheet, which, as you have seen, directly impacts your net worth. If you cannot control your cash flow, you will never be able to put yourself on a sustainable path to easing financial stress.

Understanding your cash flow is a simple process. You will simply take your income minus your expenses.

Income − Expenses = Cash flow

Once you do that, you will ideally be left with a positive number. If not, this will show us the deficit that we need to solve for. The larger you can get your number to be on the positive side, the more you will be able to contribute to the asset side of our balance sheet and grow your net worth.

Let's break down the cash flow statement below to see where you stand.

How much do you earn? List all your income *sources*. This would be the income from your job, any interest, rent payments, or dividends you receive from savings or investments, or any other source of income that you can count on consistently coming in.

How much do you spend? Now, let's list all your *expenses*. The worksheet provides you with a good idea of the most common expenses, but if there is something you don't see here, make sure that you include it so that we can accurately capture all of your expenses.

What is left? Subtract your income minus your expenses. If you have downloaded our financial dashboard spreadsheet, this is automatically done for you and is the number listed as *cash flow*. This number will either be a positive or a negative. If the number is negative, then the first thing you need to do is focus on turning that to a positive before we go any further. If your number is positive, then a percentage of this is the money you should be investing toward your goals. The key to increasing your net worth and upgrading your life is to first focus on increasing your positive cash flow and then building your net worth through investing a portion of that excess cash. The higher the excess cash, the more you can save and invest. The more you can put away, the sooner you will achieve financial freedom and make becoming work optional a reality.

Managing Your Dashboard Means
Controlling Your Life

Now that you have completed this exercise of creating a dashboard for yourself, with your balance sheet, net worth statement, and cash flow statement, you should have a good idea of where you stand.

You should be able to answer these questions:

- What is your net worth?
- Is it positive or negative?
- Are there things that you need to do such as pay off credit card debt to strengthen your balance sheet to improve your net worth?
- On your cash flow statement, are you making more than you are spending?
- Do you need to cut expenses, increase income or maybe both?

You are probably starting to realize that everything on your financial dashboard is all interconnected and changing one thing impacts all three either positively or negatively. More expense or more debt, the impact is going to be negative. Greater cash flow and less expenses will impact it positively. It is very liberating once you realize how powerful this is. This is the first step of gaining control of your financial future. This is the clarity that you need to combine with accountability and action to begin to improve things.

Chapter 5
Improving Your Financial Dashboard

N ow that you have built your dashboard, let's break it down a bit more and learn how to effectively manage and improve on each of these components for the rest of your life.

Improving Your Balance Sheet

The balance sheet consists of all your assets and all your liabilities. There are a couple of simple rules to note about your balance sheet: (1) All assets are good, some much better than others, but in general you want to load your balance sheet with high-quality assets. (2) Pretty much all liabilities are bad with a few exceptions. Let's discuss how to maximize this balance.

Decreasing Your Liabilities

We will start with liabilities because that is a much quicker and a bit simpler lesson than assets. A *liability* is defined as some amount that you owe to someone else usually with some certain payment terms. To simplify, let's refer to liabilities as *debt*. With debt, there is "bad debt" and "good debt." You need to understand the difference between the two.

Bad Debt

There are some debts that you should avoid at all costs. These are what we call *bad debts*. These debts have extremely high interest rates, have too much risk, or are not associated with assets. In many cases, they contain all the aforementioned features. You must steer clear of bad debts at all possible costs. Here are the 10 most important bad debts to avoid:

1. Credit card debt
2. Payday loans
3. Balloon payments
4. Floating rate mortgages
5. Negative amortization or interest-only mortgages
6. Borrowing from family and friends
7. Auto loans unless you have business purpose for them and can deduct the expense
8. Home equity lines and loan unless used to make equity improvements to the property
9. Margin debt
10. Gambling debt, clearly!

Good Debt

Contrary to popular belief, not all debt is bad debt. I bought my first home when I was 19 and took out a mortgage to buy that home with just 3% down. Home ownership, as young as possible, I believe is one of the quickest ways to begin building wealth. For the vast majority of Americans, the largest percentage of their net worth is their home equity. Owning instead of renting for the same payment allowed me to personally build equity, which I later rolled into a larger home, which I then rolled into an even larger home, and eventually rolled again into another home. This time when I sold my home it was much more than enough money for the next property. I also had excess cash to begin making other investments outside of real estate as well. It all started from taking on that first piece of "debt." It was that single piece of debt that allowed me to get started building my assets.

Here are some types of debt that may make sense and are normally considered wealth maximizing if used properly, instead of wealth destructing like our bad debts. You will notice there are far fewer on our good-debt list than there are on our bad-debt list.

- Mortgages
- Student loans
- Home equity loans
- Low-rate debt consolidation loans

Increasing Your Assets

Now that we've gone through liabilities, let's get into assets. Buckle in because this is a much longer and slightly more complicated journey to understand the different types of assets that you can invest in.

First, what is an *asset*? Anything that has current or future value is considered an asset. That is a very broad description, though, and we must get just a bit more granular for you to really understand the power of assets and how to build them strategically to support your lifestyle.

When you read a book about investing, what is the entire book about? The book is usually about assets, whether the book is about investing in real estate, stocks, bonds, businesses, franchises, precious metals, currencies, collectibles, and the list goes on. These are all assets that you can acquire.

Everyone has their own thoughts about which asset is superior to another, but they all work well when used strategically to accomplish your personal goals. Most professionals break down assets into four core categories. For our purposes we will also break things down into those same four major asset classes that you need to know. I want to stick with the four core asset groups to simplify things for you but also because these four assets make up the vast majority of what is owned inside the portfolios I have managed for most wealthy investors. If you understand these four assets, you will know all that you really need to know about the major investments for accumulating wealth. The first three—stocks, fixed income, and real estate—should be the majority of what you invest in until your portfolio exceeds $1 million. That may seem like a big number, but consistent investing will get you there quickly.

Stocks

The first book I ever read about investing was *Stocks for the Long Run* by Jeremy Siegel. I had the privilege of learning from Professor Siegel during my time at Wharton and professionally when I was on the advisory board at Wisdom Tree. There is nobody I have ever met who is more passionate and knowledgeable about investing in stocks than Dr. Siegel.

In Dr. Siegel's books he says that "the percentage of your portfolio that you should hold in stocks depends on your individual circumstances, but based on history, an investor with a long-term time horizon, you should keep an overwhelmingly large part of their portfolio invested in stocks."[1] I have had conversations with Dr. Siegel, and he practices what he preaches. A large portion of his own investments are in stocks, and that should be the same for most people, because they require very little management when chosen correctly and have delivered very good returns over long periods of time.

This is primarily because stocks have done a remarkably good job at keeping up with inflation over time, which protects your purchasing power. Over time, good companies have been able to pass along rising costs to consumers through price increases. That ability to pass along rising costs through price increases has allowed them to keep their profits well above their costs and increase earnings that they can then pass along to you the shareholder. That is done in the form of increased dividends, increased share price, buybacks, and many times all three.

---

[1] Jeremy Siegel, *Stocks for the Long Run,* 5th edition, McGraw-Hill, 2014.

When you buy a stock, you are buying a percentage of the company it represents. This means that you have a stake in all the profits that the company generates.

Dividends versus Capital Appreciation

An investor in a stock has two primary ways to get paid. The first is through dividends, and the second method is via capital appreciation. When a company sells its product or service, it collects revenue from its customers. Associated with those revenues are the cost the company must pay, such as the office space, employee salaries and the many other expenses needed to keep the company running, including taxes. What's left is called net profits (revenue minus expenses). At this point, management must make a decision to return the profits to shareholders, reinvest the profits back into the business to grow it, or a combination of both.

When a company decides to return net profits to its shareholders, it usually will do it via a dividend. A dividend is just profits being returned to its owners. A dividend is typically stated in a percent relative to the price of the stock and it's referred to as a dividend yield. It's done this way to allow investors to quickly compare multiple companies that may pay a different dividend amount. For example, if a Company A is trading at $50 per share and it pays an annual dividend of $2.00 per share, the stock is said to have a yield of 4% ($2 divided by $50). On the other hand, if Company B is trading at $30 per share and it pays a dividend of $1.50 per share, the stock would have a dividend yield of 5% ($1.50 divided by $30). If an investor wanted a higher dividend and only focused on the dividend amount ($2 vs. $1.50), that investor would have incorrectly chosen Company A when in fact Company B is paying a higher dividend relative to the price of the stock.

If a company does not pay a dividend because it either does not have a net profit or is investing all of the net profits back into the business, then the only way to make money as a stockholder is to sell the stock at a higher price than the purchase price. For example, if you buy a stock that does not pay a dividend at $100 and sell it for $120, then your gain is 20% ($20 gain divided by the $100 purchase price).

Some investors prefer companies that pay a dividend, while other investors prefer the company to reinvest profits back into the business. As you will see later in this book, there is a strong case to be made for both approaches.

Market Capitalization

Market capitalization (market cap) is a quick way to gauge the size of a company. Market capitalization equals shares outstanding times the stock price per share. For example, if a company is trading at $75 per share and there are 250 million shares outstanding, then the company is said to have a market cap of $18.75 billion ($75 times 250 million). It is useful to understand if you are buying a small-, mid-, or large-cap stock because, in general, stocks within their respective category tend to trade in tandem with other companies of similar size. That's because companies of similar size tend to share similar risk characteristics.

Generally speaking, here is a breakdown of market cap:

- Small-cap stocks have a market cap of less than $1 billion.
- Mid-cap stocks have a market cap between $1 billion and $10 billion.
- Large-cap stocks have a market cap between $10 billion and $25 billion.
- Mega-cap stocks have a market cap greater than $25 billion.

Domestic/Foreign Stocks

Another way to categorize stocks is by the country in which the company is headquartered. This type of classification allows for an investor to quickly understand the systemic risk associated with all companies in a given country. For example, when the Federal Reserve lowers or increases short-term rates, it affects all companies in the United States in a similar fashion. Take Apple, Inc. (Ticker: AAPL) as an example. This company is headquartered in Cupertino, California, United States, and therefore it is said to be a domestic stock to an investor located in the United States. However, Alibaba Group Holding Limited (Ticker: BABA) is a Chinese multinational technology company specializing in e-commerce, retail, the Internet, and technology and would be considered a foreign stock to a US investor.

Typically, a US investor who wants to purchase a foreign stock would have to do it via American Depository Receipts (ADRs). This type of security allows US investors a means to gain investment exposure to non-US stocks without the complexities of dealing in foreign stock markets and foreign currencies.

Fixed Income

Fixed income is another name for bonds. When someone purchases a bond from a company or government, the investor is lending money to that organization. In return, the organization promises to pay the investor their money back and pay interest for the time the money is borrowed.

For example, say that you want to buy a bond issued by Ford Motor Company (Ticker: F). You would go to the Fixed Income section of your brokerage account and look up what bonds are available. If you found a bond for $10,000 with a coupon of 5% that matures December 31, 2027, and you bought it, you would in essence be lending Ford $10,000, and in return, the company promises to pay you $500 every year in interest (in reality, bonds pay semi-annually, so every six months you would get paid $250) and on 12/31/2027, Ford would return your initial $10,000 investment.

When you purchase a bond, you become a creditor of the company. Unlike buying a stock, when you buy a bond, you are not an owner of the company, which means you are not entitled to any of the profits. At the same time, if the company goes bankrupt, as a bond holder you are higher up on the capital structure, so you are more likely to recover some of your investment.

Fixed income securities are considered less risky than stocks, so their prices typically fluctuate less when compared to stocks. If you hold a bond until maturity, you are expected to get your principal back; however, if you decide to sell your bond before it matures, you will receive a different amount depending on the market conditions.

Bond prices move up or down depending on interest rates. When interest rates move up, the value of your bond decreases and when interest rates move down, the value of your bond increases. The best way to understand this relationship is by looking at the $10,000 Ford Motor Company bond that has a 5% coupon and matures 12/31/2027. This bond will pay $500 annually and return the initial principal at maturity, but let's say nine months from today interest rates have moved up and Ford wants to borrow more money. Now Ford will be forced to issue new bonds at a higher coupon, say it's 6%. Now if someone is looking to buy a Ford bond, they will look at your bond that only pays $500 annually and a current new issue bond that pays $600 annually and this investor will decide to buy the new issue bond because it pays more. To make your bond attractive to this potential buyer, you will have to sell your $10,000 bond for less to make up for the fact that your bond pays $100 less annually.

The mechanics of how to calculate the new price of your bond is outside the scope of this book, but the most important takeaway is that the value of your bond is now lower because interest rates moved up. The opposite is also true; if interest rates had moved down to 4%, your Ford bond would be more valuable because it pays $500 annually, while new issue bonds only pay $400 annually. Therefore, someone would have to pay you a premium for your bond that yields more.

Real Estate

Most people are familiar with real estate, and for many individuals, their primary home is the largest asset that they own. However, there are many different type of real estate classes that you can own such as retail, office space, self-storage, industrial warehouse, and single-family housing.

In addition to selecting the type of real estate that you can own; you can also diversify your holdings by spreading it out geographically into different properties in different geographical, locations. As an investor, you are looking to purchase real estate with the greatest income and highest potential for appreciation. That real estate may or not be in your own back yard. Be willing to look outside to find better value. Typically, areas with the fastest population and job growth are the areas that are most attractive for investment dollars. For most, accumulating a large, diversified portfolio of real estate is difficult and their needs to be a certain level of expertise to acquire, renovate, and manage properties.

Now anyone can gain access to real estate by purchasing a real estate investment trust (REIT). These types of securities can be purchased in a brokerage account, and you don't need a lot of money to get access to many real estate classes. REITs are diversified portfolios of real estate that is professionally managed for you. Adding real estate to your investment portfolio is a great way to increase the diversification of your investments.

Real estate also has various tax advantages in owning it, and many like the idea of owning a physical versus paper asset. It has been a good long-term investment, and I recommend that everyone has some exposure to real estate.

Start by owning your own home. I started with a $56,000 home with 3% down, which was my first investment in building my personal wealth. It was one of the best decisions I ever made. For most people, owning a home is the wealth maximizing decision.

Alternatives

A fast-growing category, alternative investments represent all asset classes that are neither stocks, bonds, cash, nor real estate. Usually, alternative investments are private and illiquid, which means it's more difficult to sell the asset compared to something like a stock or bond that have massive liquidity inside public markets. Some examples of alternative investments are private equity, private credit, private real estate, collectible automobiles, and luxury watches.

Investing in the alternative space requires a more sophisti-cated investor who understands how to value the asset and has the means to take on additional risk for a potential higher return. I have seen both people who hold alternative assets and those who don't be successful. The key is the proportion of your portfolio that is invested here. For the alternative part of your portfolio, I would never recommend more than 20% of your total investable assets in this segment.

As I mentioned at the beginning of this chapter, alternatives are what I consider optional in building wealth. It's better to wait until your portfolio exceeds $1 million and you are comfortable with the illiquidity and risk associated with these investments.

Improving Your Net Worth Statement

The great thing about this lesson is that your balance sheet directly ties to your net worth statement, so you get to acquire two new pieces of knowledge for the price of one. Your net worth statement is simply the net calculation of your balance sheet, which is your assets minus your liabilities and is automatically calculated for you on your dashboard if you're plugging that information into the books website. Otherwise, it is simply adding all your assets, then adding all your liabilities and subtracting the liabilities total from the asset total. That sum is your net worth.

When you improve your balance sheet, you automatically increase your net worth. The corollary is that when your balance sheet deteriorates, so does your net worth. The way that you improve your balance sheet is to increase your assets and reduce your liabili-ties. To do that, you just need to build more and borrow less. Things really are that simple. Greater assets and less debt are always going to keep you moving in the right direction toward increasing your net worth.

If you want to be a high net worth individual, it starts with building excess cash flow and then intelligently allocating that excess cash flow toward reducing your liabilities and increasing the quality assets on your personal balance sheet.

Controlling Your Cash Flow

Everything begins and ends with your cash flow. Just like a business, your success or failure financially will be largely dependent on your ability to successfully manage your cash flow. Businesses don't fail because of bad ideas or dumb marketing; they go out of business because they run out of cash. This is the same for individuals. Cash flow is king.

Since cash flow is king, this is what we are going to spend most of our time on. If you can improve your cash flow, good things will start to happen. The first step is to get yourself to a positive cash flow number. This means you must make more than you spend. It sounds simple, but the reason we have such a financial crisis in the world is because most people live beyond their means. They spend more than they make by doing things like taking on credit card debt and "paymenting" themselves into poverty.

Avoid Paymenting Yourself into Poverty

Paymenting means making lots of small payments on Netflix, phone bills, iCloud storage, dating apps . . . the list goes on. Before you know it, all these little payments start to take up a huge amount of your monthly income leaving you with nothing to save. Unfortunately, people don't look at the total cost of things anymore; they just look at whether they can afford that one new payment. This is a broken mindset that you must leave behind to start generating wealth.

This book is about upgrading your life. My philosophy about life and wealth is different from other gurus out there. I am not here to tell you to eat ramen noodles, live in a 600-square-foot house, and drive an old beater car; there are other guys to go to for that strategy. Personally, I discourage all those things unless you really like eating ramen noodles! I want you to live the life of your dreams and not settle for less.

I believe that having a broken mindset—meaning always coming from a place of scarcity versus abundance—will almost guarantee that you never reach your full financial potential. This type of mindset will drive you toward achieving mediocrity instead of excellence. This mindset will keep you in budget hotels, mediocre neighborhoods, average restaurants, and continually have you accepting a second-class lifestyle. I don't care who you are or how modest you believe you are. Everyone—I repeat, *everyone*—likes nice stuff. Prime steak is better than select, five-star is better than two-star, and comfort is better than cramped. Whether you prefer a new pickup or a Ferrari doesn't matter, but having the best of what you love does matter. Settling for some second-rate version of what you want and deserve in life is not acceptable.

All that said, we all must earn a seat at the table to afford those nicer things. I don't believe in fake it until you make it. I believe in just make it. The world owes us nothing. We must go out and earn it the right way so that once we reach our goals, we can sustain them. This is not about getting rich quick and going broke even faster. This is getting to the place you want to be in life and staying there forever.

Decreasing Your Spending

A big part of controlling cash flow is understanding your expenses. Look at all your expenses. I want you to break all your expenses down into two categories: core and discretionary expenses. This is segmented on your financial dashboard for you at www.closeyourwealthgaptools.com.

- Your core expenses are the things that are difficult to escape such as food, shelter, transportation, healthcare costs, utilities, and so forth.
- Your discretionary expenses are things such as eating out, vacations, gym memberships, and so forth.

It is important to break these things down because no matter what happens in life, your core expenses are something that you will have a difficult time eliminating. Discretionary expenses, on the other hand, are the things you can eliminate or reduce if the going gets tough. While doing this exercise, make sure you go through every credit card, bank statement, PayPal or Venmo account, to make sure that you capture everything. I say this because I can't tell you how many times I have had clients do this exercise and they came back to me with statements such as "I thought I canceled that years ago" or "I had no idea that it cost this much."

Also, unless you can really understand what you are spending, it will be impossible to create the financial roadmap that you need to achieve your goals. Remember what I said about burying your head in the sand? Those days are over. You are going to start making this a monthly exercise as part of taking inventory and improving your financial life. After this initial assessment of organizing everything, 30–45 minutes a month is all it should take to maintain it. You will find tools like the expense worksheet calculator on our website to help you organize everything.

Figure 5.1 shows an example of the expense worksheet calculator using the national average of expenses, which are roughly $66,928. The inputs shown here are a sample calculation of that total.

Eliminate the Low-Hanging Fruit

Part of checking your dashboard monthly is looking at all your expenses carefully. Were you double charged for something? Was there a subscription that should have been canceled that you are still being charged for? Did you get that refund for the stuff you shipped back to Amazon? Is there a monthly bank fee that shows up that you never knew you were paying?

The low-hanging fruit on improving your cash flow is eliminating inaccurate expenses and checking your charges monthly. You will start becoming more strategic and catch a lot more errors than you would think when you start to practice this routine monthly.

Expense Worksheet

Item	Expense Type	Monthly Expenses	Annual Expenses
Household Expenses			
Utilities (Water, Gas, etc.)	Core	$ 200.00	$ 2,400.00
Mortgage/Rent & HOA(s) Dues	Core	$ 2,222.50	$ 26,670.00
Cable, Internet, Phone	Core	$ 150.00	$ 1,800.00
Home, Landscape, etc.	Core	$ 100.00	$ 1,200.00
Food & Beverage			
Groceries	Core	$ 438.25	$ 5,259.00
Dining Out	Discretionary	$ 252.50	$ 3,030.00
Vehicle Expenses			
Car Payment	Core	$ 555.25	$ 6,663.00
Gasoline and Tolls	Core	$ 179.00	$ 2,148.00
Maintenance	Core	$ 125.00	$ 1,500.00
Parking, SiriusXM, etc.	Discretionary	$ 54.17	$ 650.00
Medical Care			
Deductibles, Co-pays, etc.	Core	$ 454.33	$ 5,452.00
Children's Expenses			
Tuition and Childcare	Discretionary	$ 102.17	$ 1,226.00
Sports, Clothing, etc.	Core	$ 146.17	$ 1,754.00
Recreation			
Vacations & Travel	Discretionary	$ 297.33	$ 3,568.00
Subscriptions, Clubs, etc.	Discretionary	$ 100.00	$ 1,200.00
Gym, Spa, Yoga, etc.	Discretionary	$ 54.50	$ 654.00
Apparel			
Clothing, Shoes, etc.	Core	$ 146.17	$ 1,754.00
	Total Expenses	$ 5,577.33	$ 66,928.00
	Core Expenses	$ 4,716.67	$ 56,600.00
	Discretionary Expenses	$ 860.67	$ 10,328.00
National Average Annual Expenditures		$66,928.00	

Figure 5.1 Worksheet calculator.

SOURCE: BLS Reports. Consumer Expenditures in 2021, US Bureau of Labor Statistics, January 2023. www.bls.gov.

Shop Around for the Best Deals

Once you have broken everything down and cleaned up your accounting, I want you to do a competitive analysis of all your expenses. What I mean by that is take a look at things like your wireless bill. Are you on the best plan? Shop it around with other carriers; look at something like changing to a family plan or a reduced cost plan with your current provider.

Insurance is another expense that I regularly see people save a lot of money on. Have an independent insurance agent give you a free quote on your insurance. Insurance is a very competitive business and prices are always changing. See if it makes sense to switch carriers or change your coverage.

The exercise is about thoughtfully going through each expense to see if there is a better plan, deal, service, or provider. Many times you can lower costs without even cutting anything out. I have even been able to upgrade things at times by just calling and looking for better prices. Once people know you are shopping them, it's amazing how deals and discounts suddenly appear.

I recommend doing this routine once per year. I normally do it each December when things slow down for the holidays and I have some time to get on the phone to make the calls. You almost always get better deals on the phone or in person than you do online or through email. Talk to somebody and lower your expenses.

Do I Really Need This?

Part of increasing your financial literacy is understanding the trade-off between buying stuff and investing toward a better life. When you take the time to evaluate your expenses each month, it gives you the opportunity to reflect on all the outflows that you have each month. These are all the things that are holding you back from reaching your goals in the fastest possible timeframe.

Now, some expenses are probably absolutely worth it. For example, if you have a gym membership that you use regularly, it is a great investment in your health. If you show up just once a month, though, you are probably much better off buying a few pieces of equipment to use at home and taking a jog around the neighborhood each day. That will be a better decision for both your health and your wallet.

Speaking of health, how much money are you spending on Door Dash or Uber Eats? When you look at the charges that are added to your bill, I was shocked that I was almost paying double for my Burrito Bowl from Chipotle. Not only is that a colossal waste of money, but is Chipotle really upgrading my life? I am not here to tell that you will get rich by skipping Starbucks and making coffee at home because the truth is it will not. All I am saying is you may be unnecessarily wasting your money on things that you could get for the same or many times higher quality for less. Too many times I have seen people pay far more for inferior quality and service than they should have.

Make sure you are getting the maximum quality and value for your dollars. Don't pay more for less.

Paying Monthly Is Usually Not Best

One final tip I will give you is that paying monthly is usually not the best wealth-maximizing decision for most of your expenses. Take insurance, for example. When you pay monthly, they charge you a finance charge versus paying annually where there is none. The worst part is that the finance fee is usually double digits!

Most subscriptions are the same way. Many times with subscriptions you can save as much as 20% by paying annually. One thing I would caution is that if a discretionary expense like Netflix is being paid monthly instead of annually where you would receive a discount, the truth is you probably do not need it. That is a good personal checks and balances system to implement for yourself to see if it is something you can afford.

Anytime you find that you have to take a payment plan option, which is not the most wealth maximizing decision, I need you to have the discipline to say that this is something I do not need. Wait until you are able to purchase it at the most cost-effective price before you pull the trigger. It's a small simple step, but those small steps done consistently yield large results over time.

Increasing Your Earnings

Now that you have your expenses organized and accounted for, it's time to look at what you have on the income side of the equation.

The goal is always to increase your income and lower your expenses. As you upgrade your life, it's natural that your expenses also upgrade for things such as nicer vacations, nicer homes, and better cars, but you can only upgrade your lifestyle as you upgrade your income.

Start by entering all your income into your dashboard. This will be everything that you earn from working; any interest or dividend income that comes in; if you have rental properties, enter the rents collected. Remember on rentals, you must accurately account for the expenses such as repairs, mortgage, insurance, and so forth.

I gave you some suggestions on categorizing and reducing your expenses. Now I am going to provide you some simple ways to improve your income, as well as a longer-term perspective on increasing your income that you probably have never heard before.

I could easily dedicate an entire book to ways to earn extra income. I bring up side hustles and other ideas here because I consider them the gateway to entrepreneurism and a great way to start improving your cash flow to create money to start investing. They help you abandon the excuse of "I have no money to invest." If that's true, then you're not working hard enough.

Beware of Zero Interest Savings

First, start by leaving no money in your bank savings or checking account except for what you need to pay your bills monthly. Most banks pay you next to nothing in interest. Your money sits there earning zero while they invest it and earn the interest themselves. Part of what you need to do is start holding your money accountable—meaning, is your money working for you? Money sitting in your sock drawer or in a zero-interest bank account is absolutely not working for you. Wealthy people don't allow their money to be lazy. They make it work hard.

There are numerous reputable online accounts available today such as American Express, Marcus by Goldman Sachs, and Capital One just to name a few that you'll find if you enter a Google search for high-interest savings. These banks pay very attractive rates. The difference in interest that you earn could possibly be enough to pay your cable bill or even your car payment or your mortgage as it increases. These accounts are very convenient because they link right to your primary checking account so that you can very easily move the money back and forth when you need it.

Side Hustle It!

Next, consider a side hustle. There are several different side hustles out there that you can do to earn extra income, and it doesn't matter which one it is. For example, drive for Uber or Lyft. Beyond that, today so many people are becoming part of the gig economy. Websites like Upwork.com or Fiverr.com are sites where entrepreneurs can match their services with the needs of customers who are looking for work. Just about any skillset that you have probably has a demand on one of those sites. Give it a try.

Pet lover? Look at sites like Rover.com where you can sign up and turn your love for pets into cash. Signing up to watch dogs or cats in your home can quickly earn you a few hundred extra dollars a week. This is easy money for something that probably doesn't even seem like work to you.

Of course, there is the old-school, part-time job path. Working just a couple nights or weekend days can bring extra income that you may need to get to the next level and begin building your investment portfolio.

If I can get you to start with a side hustle, it will do a couple of great things. First, it will improve the surplus on your cash flow statement, and second, I am almost certain it will flip your entrepreneurial switch. Whether your side hustles stay as that or become money printing machines, increasing your income will always do good things for your financial future. Make it your goal to start a side hustle this year and please share your success stories with me.

Sell Your Unwanted Used Items

I will give you a very easy one that anyone can do as an example. Consider selling things online or at auctions sites such as eBay. I have done this myself when I started my business to make some cash on the side as things ramped up, and I have had several friends and clients do this successfully over the years. I used to go to discount warehouses that would sell designer clothes at huge discounts. I would look to see what brands were selling on eBay and then buy up a few items and resell them. If the items sold fast, I would go back and grab what was left.

I have seen friends shop yard sales and estate sales to find deals they can resell. You would also be surprised at how much money is probably just laying around your house right now that is stuck in items that you no longer even use or want. The point is, it's easy and I have seen it work as a quick way to enhance your cash flow. There is no substitute for experience, so give it a try. Search your house and list something online. Just a couple hours a week and you could easily pick up enough to fund your Roth.

Start Your Own Side Business

Maybe selling things online isn't for you. If you want to be a bit more entrepreneurial, there is an easy way to come up with an idea for a business. Consider surveying everyone you know for the number one problem they have. Once you find out what it is, ask them how much it would be worth to them if you could solve it for them. After you survey a few dozen people, I bet you'll get a couple of good ideas for side hustles.

Start small, and if it begins to gain traction, continue to focus more effort and energy on it. If it doesn't work, don't be afraid to scrap it quickly and repeat step one again. Most very successful entrepreneurs that I work with had a few "bad" ideas before they finally found that one big idea. That includes me. I was going to manage the career of rappers when I was 20 years old. I thought that would be my calling for a few good weeks one summer. That ended poorly if you consider one client who never paid me. That experience led me to where I am today, though, so it was worth it. You must start somewhere. Put yourself out there. You may have that next big life-changing idea.

Calculating Your Breakeven Expenses

After reading this I know what some of you might be saying to yourself: "This all looks great but what a hassle for me to grab all this information and enter it." I am sorry, but I am not going to let you off the hook that easily. As I mentioned at the start of this book, I don't want anyone to make an excuse for why they don't have their financial house in order. That is why I'm going to share with you a quick way to determine your expenses without having to spend too much time gathering all of the information.

All you must do is take your gross income, which you can easily do by looking at your last pay stub of the previous year or however your income was collected for the previous year. You then need to subtract the taxes you pay which may already be done on your paystub or W2, and then subtract any savings you've made. That's it! Note that if there were no savings, then you know that you are spending everything that you are earning.

So let's review this again to make sure you have it: Gross income – (Taxes + Savings) = Expenses

What is left is what you've spent. When you make money, you must pay taxes, so that must be subtracted to arrive at your net pay. From there you subtract what you save, and the rest was spent. You see what you make must go either to taxes, savings, or spending. As simple as this is, I've used this exercise with many people to help them realize that they are spending more money than they thought. You will probably discover the same thing yourself.

Here is a quick example:

Annual Expense Calculation		
Salary	$	65,000.00
Taxes	$	(16,250.00)
Savings	$	(5,000.00)
Expenses	$	**(43,750.00)**

Chapter 6
Building Your Financial Roadmap

At this point you have learned the important fundamentals of building your personal financial profile. You understand where you stand financially and the things you can do now and will do in the future to improve on your current situation. Now, its time to move on to an extremely important topic—your financial roadmap.

The major question you need to answer when investing is, what are you investing for? Is this a short-term goal or a long-term goal that you need to fund?

I am always perplexed when people ask me, "Rob, what stock should I buy?" or "Should I purchase real estate or invest in the stock market?" I reply to the same way to everyone: "I don't know." I usually get a blank stare and I know what they are thinking at that moment: "Rob, I thought you were an investment expert, so why don't you know what I should buy?" The answer is quite simple: to know what investment to make, I need to have a good idea of a person's current financial situation and what they are trying to accomplish financially. In other words, we need to create a financial roadmap that lays out a clear path for a person to reach their goal in the most efficient way possible. That means minimizing the possibilities of mistakes and maximizing the potential for return in each investment decision you make.

Creating a financial roadmap will point out what's going on financially in your life. Your roadmap will outline what you are investing for: retirement, college, a new car, a new home, a once in a lifetime trip or whatever goals that you have which will require funding. The more clarity that you have in terms of your dashboard, and the costs, timeframe, and so on, that are tied to your future goals, the easier it will be to match the right strategy and investments to those goals. Your roadmap should dictate your investments, not the other way around.

Let's put some perspective around why it's important to identify what you are investing for before acquiring assets. Imagine if one day I were having dinner at a restaurant and a young person approached me and asked, "Rob, I have $2,500 to invest. What should I buy?" What if I told this person the latest stock I just bought and the next day she buys it too? What can go wrong? After all, I bought the stock because I think it has potential for a good return. Well, what if I later find that that this young person had a 3-year-old child and another one on the way and that she was working two jobs just to make ends meet? What if this person was a single mother with no savings? Would buying the same stock I just bought be the right thing for this woman? No, it would not be the right thing. There are probably certain things that would need to be addressed before she makes a stock investment. I don't know what those things are until we develop a financial roadmap.

In this roadmap I would want to know if she had an emergency account and if she does, is it sufficient? Does she have life insurance to financially protect her children? If she does, is the coverage sufficient? Does she have a formal document that states who would be legally responsible for her children if she were to pass away? Does her current job offer a retirement plan with a company match? I can go on and on with the questions I would ask to get a good understanding of her situation. However, once we develop the financial roadmap, we can quickly get to work by setting actional steps and setting milestones along with an accountability process. This framework will give this woman the highest chance of achieving her financial goals.

The truth is that you really don't need to spend countless hours trying to develop your financial roadmap, and you certainly don't have to pay someone thousands of dollars for a basic financial plan. I want to share with you some simple but effective tools to help begin your financial roadmap. I call them the Magic Shortcuts, and they do an excellent job at providing clear financial goals for your investments.

Once you put this together with the financial buckets that you will learn about in Chapter 7, you will be on your way toward being a strategic investor. If you still feel like you need some help piecing it all together don't fret, this book culminates with some very specific age-based recommendations and mini case studies so that you will be well on your way to success.

The Magic Shortcuts

For most people it's not necessary to have an elaborate plan, but it is very important to identify what you are investing for before you invest. Progress over perfection is something that I constantly preach to my team and my investors. I have seen so many people wasting time attempting to come up with the "perfect" plan on paper, but when it comes time to execute, they become paralyzed, and the complexity of their plan prevents it from being executed in the real world.

The following are a handful of some simple rules that I use regularly for myself and my clients. I think you will also find these rules helpful in putting together a roadmap for your own goals. There is a shortcut for quick budgeting rule, a shortcut to determine how long it will take you to double your money, a shortcut to figure out the number you need to retire (or as we say, make work optional), a tool to make sure you are getting the return you need for the risk you're taking on, a way to become an instant millionaire, and I even threw in a way for you to simplify how to use life insurance to help protect your plan.

The 60/30/10 Rule

This quick budgeting tool answers the question "How much should I spend and save annually?"

If you want a great hack to building a proper budget, start implementing the 60/30/10 rule. With this strategy, you spend 60% of your earnings on *needs* like food, clothing, insurance, and mort- gage payments. Thirty percent of your earnings goes to *wants* like travel and entertainment, and the final 10% goes to your savings and investments. If you can save 10% of what you earn and invest that money wisely, I assure you that you will be on a great path to achieving long-term wealth. Want to see how this works?

Let's say you are 40 years old, and you earn $100,000 per year for simple math. This means you are currently living off that $100,000, including taxes and potential savings. If you were born after 1960, 67 is your full retirement age where you can get full Social Security.

Based on $100,000 per year, that means you would save $10,000 per year. If you invest $10,000 per year or $833 monthly and earn 10% until retirement, you will have accumulated $1.2 million. This assumes you have zero in investments today; you never get a raise and never increase your savings. Based on $1.2 million at a 5% with- draw rate, that gives you $60,000 per year plus your Social Security, which is expected to be $36,000 (in today's dollars). The portfolio distribution and Social Security are expected to provide $96,000 in today's dollars, which means you would be expected to keep a simi- lar standard of living in retirement

Essentially, as long as you invest 10% consistently, you should be in good shape to replace your income. Of course, the goal is to always invest more, but what I have preached all along is action— progress over perfection. Everybody can and should do 10%. The best way is to set it up to be deducted automatically from your pay- check or checking account so that you don't even miss it.

Not everyone is making six figures a year yet. If you are just starting out and maybe earning $35,000 per year, it is still the same principle, but you will need to make some adjustments to this math. The reality is, you will probably need a roommate or spend a year or two more at home if that's an option for you. Your discretionary budget will need to be cut a bit, and before worrying about investing, I want you to focus on building up your emergency fund and paying off any high-interest credit card debt that you may have. Once that is done and your earnings increase, you will make the shift to the 60/30/10 rule.

The Rule of 72

This magic shortcut answers the question "How long will it take to double my money?"

Want to know how long it takes to double your money? The rule of 72 is a great way to do it. Simply take 72 and divided it by the expected return you can get from investing. For example, we said stocks over the long run provide about a 10% rate of return. If you take 72 and divide it by 10, you get 7.2. That is 7.2 years to double your investment. More conservative bonds return about 4%. If you divide 72 by 4, you get 18. That's 18 years! This is why when you're younger, you want to invest more in stocks than in bonds. Your money will double twice as fast.

The 20X Rule

This magic shortcut answers the question, "How much do you need to save to stop working?"

Curious how much money you need to be work optional? There are a lot of ways to get there, but the truth is you can get a very close estimate of what you will need by using the 20X rule in a couple of minutes with your smartphone calculator.

Let's say that you need $100,000 a year before taxes to live on. If you take $100,000 multiplied by 20, you get $2 million. Using a 5% withdrawal rule, which means that you take out 5% of the principle balance of the account each year, with the goal to sustain those payments for your lifetime, that $2 million you have accumulated times the 5% gives you the $100,000 to replace your income and cover your expenses. So you see, the $2 million lump sum is the exact amount you need to accumulate in order to replace your income and make work optional.

Again, just add up what you spend each year and multiply that by 20, and that will tell you how much money you need to accumulate through saving and investing. Pretty cool, right?

The best part is that it only takes third-grade math to figure it out. Once you know this info, how crazy is it that people have a better idea how the pyramids were created than they do on the amount of money that they will need to retire on.

Make $100,000 × 20 = $2 million
$2 million × 0.05 (your withdrawal rate) = $100,000 to replace the income

The 10-Year Bond Rule

This magic shortcut answers the question, "How much should I be earning?"

The 10-year Treasury bond is something that is quoted daily on all financial websites. This is considered the risk-free rate for investors. Essentially, what this tells you is the rate of return that you can receive from the US government over the next 10 years without any risk. Any investment that you make should always be carefully compared to this yield. You want to make sure that the riskier the investment is, the higher the return is that you will receive *above* the 10-year bond.

For example, if the 10-year rate is at 4%, a bond you purchase from a big company like Coca-Cola should be something higher, like 5%. If it's a loan you're giving to your family member, though, it should probably be at least 8% because we all know that the odds of them paying you back are much lower than from Coke or the US government!

This is also why when you look at stocks or real estate over the long run you see returns in the 7–10% range. When the 10-year bond ticks higher and gets closer to those returns, it becomes competition for those assets. Why would you take the risk in stocks or real estate when you can do nothing and be assured a return close to the same? When rates are lower, there is much less competition, so you will see that stocks and real estate tend to do much better. In short, always look at the 10-year bond yield before investing.

The 30-Year Rule to Becoming a Tax-Free Millionaire

This magic shortcut answers the question, "How can I become a millionaire by 48?" (Make sure every 18-year-old you know gets this information to be a millionaire by 48.)

Now, this is something that I believe every high school student should know how to do. Becoming a millionaire by 48 is something that everyone should easily be able to achieve. Over the long run, the stock market earns about 10%. The key is time in the market, and, as we discussed, you need to get started early to fully benefit from the benefits of compound interest. We talked about several side hustles where you should easily be able to earn an extra $125 a week part time. By earning that ($6,500 a year) and investing that in a low-cost index fund like SPY, you would have accumulated $1,176,132 after 30 years. If it was invested in a Roth IRA, that would be tax free!

The point is that knowledge is power, and the idea of being a millionaire to some seems so far out of reach. By doing just this one simple exercise, though, you can see that its very achievable to just about anyone, as shown in Figure 6.1.

The 10X Life Insurance Rule

This magic shortcut answers the question "How much life insurance coverage should you get?"

My insurance philosophy is very simple. I think proper life insurance is important when there is an insurable need and term insurance is more effective than permanent insurance. Life insurance death proceeds are used to help maintain the beneficiary's

Annual Investment	$6,500	
Annual Return	10.0%	
Age	Investment Value	
18	$ 6,500	
19	$ 13,650	
20	$ 21,515	
21	$ 30,167	
22	$ 39,683	
23	$ 50,151	
24	$ 61,667	
25	$ 74,333	
26	$ 88,267	
27	$ 103,593	
28	$ 120,453	
29	$ 138,998	
30	$ 159,398	
31	$ 181,837	
32	$ 206,521	
33	$ 233,673	
34	$ 263,541	
35	$ 296,395	
36	$ 332,534	
37	$ 372,287	
38	$ 416,016	
39	$ 464,118	
40	$ 517,030	
41	$ 575,233	
42	$ 639,256	
43	$ 709,681	
44	$ 787,150	
45	$ 872,365	
46	$ 966,101	
47	$ 1,069,211	
48	$ 1,176,132	

Figure 6.1 Investing $6,500 a year.

standard of living because of an unforeseen death of the insured. I don't believe life insurance should be used as an investment vehicle.

When you break out life insurance and investment vehicles, you can get a more efficient and less costly outcome. A simple way to determine proper life insurance is by applying the 10X rule. Say you make $60,000 annually and you want to make sure your 5-year-old son is protected financially until the age of 25. You would simply multiply $60,000 by 10, which means you need a 20-year term life insurance policy with a $600,000 death benefit. If you were to prematurely pass away, the $600,000 would be invested and replicate your net income, which would allow your child to continue to live the same lifestyle as if you were still alive.

Summary of the Shortcuts

The key is acting. There are several fancy formulas that I can teach you over a few years that will also work well. You probably do not have a few years to learn this information, though, and it is not at all necessary. Our goal is to get you 90% of the way there as soon as possible. If we can do that, the other 10% can come in time, and that is not really the part that will improve your lifestyle very much anyhow.

You now have a simple budget with the 60/30/10 rule. You also know how much you need to save in order to stop working based on what it will take to support your lifestyle with the 20X rule, when you begin investing toward your goals, and you have the 10-year bond rule to make sure you aren't taking on too much risk. Looking for how much life insurance you need to protect your family? You can now calculate that amount in seconds with the 10X rule.

There is no excuse not to be a millionaire. I showed you a very simple way to get there starting today even if you aren't making hundreds of thousands of dollars a year. There is a lot more to come here in the book, but these are some pretty big things that you can now solve for yourself and family in just minutes!

Part III

How to Match Your Investments to Your Needs

Chapter 7
Managing Your
Financial Buckets

I n this chapter, I will provide you with an amazing framework in which you can begin to make and manage your investments in coordination with your personal goals, preference, risk tolerance, and time horizon, consistent with some of the magic shortcuts that you just learned. This will tie your roadmap from Chapter 6 to your assets and take you from the "hope everything works out" method to strategically making investment decisions based on your desired outcome—just as the professionals do. Once you can master the bucketing approach, it will become a game changer in upgrading your financial literacy and bring everything into a perspective that is most relative to your own financial needs.

You now know that your financial dashboard from Chapters 4 and 5 will be your control panel for your overall financial life. You understand how important it is to constantly manage all the levels on your dashboard and continually maintain the appropriate balance between debt and income as well as the necessity of growing your cash flow ahead of your lifestyle. You never want to run too hot or too cold on any of your "odometers."

Now that you know how to build and maintain your dashboard, I am going to teach you how your "buckets" are going to be the levers within that dashboard that will allow you to control all your investments in conjunction with your personal goals and objectives. This is what ties your plan to your assets. Building your dashboard was the first step, and now understanding how to navigate and manage your financial buckets is the second core component of your financial literacy lesson. Your financial buckets are how you will save for your future and how you will manage your cash flow once it's time to quit working and replace the income you were receiving from your paycheck with passive income from your investment portfolio.

I want to stress here the importance of understanding and managing these buckets correctly. Your buckets are what will get you to work optional as fast as possible and what will allow you stay there once you arrive. So, make sure you get this down and reread the chapter until it all sinks in.

People have a different spin on how to use a bucketing approach. I cannot speak to any of those systems, but the one that my team and I created is based on something called a *liability driven investment* (LDI) approach. This is a strategy that historically has been used by endowments and institutions to manage their money. I have used this strategy for several years very successfully for clients who are worth several millions of dollars, and it has been a game changer. This is not a system you can outgrow, so it is all you will ever need to manage your finances properly.

You do not need all the science behind this approach, but what is important for you to know is that there is a lot of research behind the strategy that I believe makes it a superior way for most individuals to manage their money. My team and I adjusted the strategy to make it more appropriate for individuals, and we simplified it into a "bucketing approach" for you to be able to execute it on your own without the need for a PhD in finance. Once you get the hang of it, you won't look back. It's also so simple that if you have children, you can even educate them early on to set them up for success.

Your Portfolio, Bucketized

You have probably heard the term *investment portfolio*. Our definition for *investment portfolio* is a group of assets that are strategically acquired, managed, and sold, in conjunction with a desired goal, timeline, and objective for each of those assets.

This means your investments should be bought and sold with very specific purposes. The money that you need from your portfolio to buy a home within a year should be managed completely differently from money that is earmarked for retirement. Those assets for those specific goals should be segmented and managed completely differently from one another.

In contrast, what I have seen during my 25 years of meeting with prospective clients and investors is that most people truthfully do not have an investment portfolio at all. What they have is a bunch of assets that they acquired with the sole hope that they eventually will increase in price by the time they need those assets to fulfill a purpose. There was no buy discipline, sell discipline, or mandate tied to anything that they purchased. That, my friends, unfortunately is not a portfolio. That is a bunch of things you acquired normally because somebody told you it was a good idea, it "felt right," your kid was using the product, or because you saw some celebrity endorse it. Choose one of those or any other combination of emotional reasons, and it probably resonates with something you did or saw your friends or family do at some point that didn't play out too well.

Going forward, every investment you make will need to have a strategic role that it plays in your financial life. If it doesn't fit a need, it's not the right investment for you. There will be no more guessing or hoping for the best. Every financial decision you make from this point forward will have purpose and intent and will fall within one of your financial buckets tied to your specific goals and objectives.

So, let's dive into the buckets. We are going to break all your investments down and manage them within four buckets. Each bucket is going to represent three things. Number 1, the profile of the asset you can purchase in that bucket. Number 2, a specific objective for that investment. Finally, number 3, a timeframe that is associated with that investment. All your financial goals should be tied to one or more of these buckets depending on when you need them and the overall objective.

I will also give you a simple buy-and-sell discipline to attach to each of your buckets. The bucket strategy will eventually transition from helping you accumulate assets for your work optional date to distributing those assets once you stop working. The sooner your buckets are filled up, the sooner you can make work optional. Let's go!

Bucket 1: Conservative Assets

Bucket 1 is going to be your most conservative bucket. Before you can invest in *anything* else, you must first fill up your bucket 1.

I cannot stress this enough. If your bucket 1 is not at the right levels you simply cannot begin to invest elsewhere. This bucket will contain investments that are guaranteed to be there for you no matter what types of headwinds the economy faces. Stock market crash, inflation, deflation—none of these events are going to impact this bucket very much if at all. These are your most stable assets that must be there when you need them, so you cannot afford to take any risk here. These are the assets that you will have set aside for emergencies and the assets that you must count on to pay your bills when they are due. This is a very important role that this bucket plays, so I reiterate that you cannot mess around here.

Depending on your age, ability to earn, and risk level, you will have a different percentage of your assets allocated in bucket 1.

- **10+ years out:** Let's start with younger people with 10 years or more before reaching their work optional date. Most of you will use bucket 1 as your emergency fund. Your emergency fund should be a minimum of 90 days of your monthly expenses up to one year of your monthly expenses. You want this to be very liquid, so mostly invested in money market and high yield savings accounts.

I normally recommend that, depending on how secure your job or earnings ability is, you adjust your reserves up or down between the three months and one year mark. For people with very steady earnings such as doctors, police officers, and so forth, you are probably okay with having closer to 90 days. If you feel more comfortable by having more cash on your balance sheet, then you can adjust that number up to six months' worth of expenses, but I wouldn't have much more than that. For those of you with more cyclical or less predictable earnings careers such as realtors or entrepreneurs, I would recommend having between six months and one year of expenses that you always set aside in your bucket 1. The purpose of this is bucket for you is that if you become unemployed, have a dry spell, or an emergency pops up, you have enough dry powder to get you through the storm.

Bucket 1 will also be your bucket to which you allocate short-term goals that are outside of your normal budget and cash flow such as buying a new car or buying a home. If the needs to fund that goal are four years or less, this is where you can invest that money.

- **10 years out:** For those within about 10 years of reaching your work optional date, I like to bring this bucket up to about 24 months of reserves. Your emergency fund percentage of that 24 months, which should be between 3 months to 1 year, should be in high-yield savings and money market, and the rest can be invested in bonds or CDs with maturities less than 2 years to give you a little higher yield inside the bucket.
- **A few years out:** As you get within a couple years of your work optional date, you are going to start preparing to have between 4 to 6 years' worth of living expenses isolated inside your bucket 1. As you get closer to that date, you need to start making sure you are progressing toward filling this bucket up to that amount. This means most new money being deposited in your buckets should first be going to this bucket.

That leaves your work optional date in which you would need to have the bucket fully filled with four to six years of expenses in this bucket. I usually tie this number to your core expenses, which excludes your discretionary spending and is listed on your dashboard. Core expenses are the expenses that will always be there, and you need to have secured because there is little to no flexibility. For those in work optional status, you can also deduct your guaranteed income from that number. Guaranteed income streams are payments you receive such as social security, annuities, or pensions. That helps bring this number down. For example, if your annual core expenses are $50,000 and you have an annuity that pays $8,000 per year and social security at $22,000 per year, you would need to have $50,000 of core expenses minus the guaranteed income amount of $30,000, which is $20,000. Multiply that number times either four or six years, so that would be between $80,000 and $120,000 at all times sitting in bucket 1. I usually adjust this number up about 3% each year to keep up with inflation.

What you need to understand about bucket 1 is that it will always be your lowest earning bucket over the long run, so you want to minimize the amount in here but also not take on too much risk by having it underfunded. A general rule is that the safer and more liquid an asset is, the lower the return. When interest rates are high, you probably will not feel too bad having money in this bucket when you are earning a good yield on this money. When rates are low though, like we experienced between 2001 and 2021, it is very hard watching your money sit there earning so little especially when other assets like stocks and real estate are rising.

No matter what the yield is, though, and no matter what other opportunities look attractive, you must remain disciplined and stick to always securing these numbers. This is the behavioral part of investing that is so hard to follow for many, but you know that this rule is a non-negotiable and you will always stick to this calculation.

Another general rule about bucket 1, as you get into the distribution phase when you begin taking money out, is that when interest rates are higher, you should have the higher end of the four-to-six-year range invested in bucket 1. For example, if bond yields are north of 5%, or money market rates are over 3%, having six years of expenses instead of four makes sense. When they are lower, you may want to stick closer to four years.

This also depends on how risky you are. More risk = lower end of the reserves. Lower risk = higher end of the reserves. Any time you add another year of expenses to bucket 1, you are becoming more conservative, and the corollary is when you subtract a year you automatically become more aggressive. That is because bucket 1 contains the lowest risk assets, so if you add, your overall portfolio becomes safer; when you subtract, it becomes riskier. Conversely, the lower your bucket 1 allocation, the higher the expected return is over time.

That is precisely why when you are in your 20s, you typically have three to six months plus short-term goals in the bucket 1 and in work optional status, when your other income stops, you have four to six years plus short-term goals.

Bucket 1 Quick Guide

- **Timeframe:** 3 months to 6 years
- **Objective:** Stability and income
- **Types of assets:** Cash, CD, money market, municipal bonds, government bonds
- **Quantity:** 3 months to 6 years of core living expenses
- **Buy discipline:** Buy to match emergency fund or cash flow needs
- **Sell discipline:** Usually self-liquidating depending on maturity or fully liquid. Sell or mature to meet cash flow needs.

Bucket 2: Consistent Income

The primary objective for bucket 2 assets is to deliver consistent income. If the asset does not pay rent, a dividend, interest, royalty, or any type of *predictable* income stream, then it has no place in this bucket. This bucket will play a large role in your ability to continue to pay your bills and eventually make work optional.

We saw that in bucket 1 we will need to have a certain number of months or years' worth of expenses always isolated inside of that bucket. The best way to understand the power of the role that bucket 2 plays in conjunction with bucket 1 is to focus on your work-optional date. This is the date you will be looking for your buckets to start paying your bills when your regular paycheck goes away.

So, if we think back to bucket 1, you are essentially "laddering" your annual expenses inside that bucket. A ladder has rungs on it usually between four and six. In this case, each rung on the ladder equals one years' worth of your expenses. If you have a four-year bucket there are four rungs and if you have a six-year bucket, you have six rungs. Meaning, in the first year that you turn your buckets into a distribution system (taking money out) instead of an accumulation system (putting money in), you are going to start depleting one rung on your ladder each year to pay your bills.

So, how will you replace that rung on the ladder once it's taken away and spent? Bucket 2 will play a large role in accomplishing that mission. In an ideal world, you will be able to fill your bucket 2 up to an amount where the assets are enough to deliver the amount of income needed to replace that rung each year.

For example, let's say each rung represented $40,000 in expenses. If your bucket 2 assets were kicking off of $40,000 in payments over the year, by the time the year ended, you would have had enough income to replace that rung. The income being collected in bucket 2 can be in the form of dividends, interest, rental income, and so forth. The key is that you need those payments to be very secure. The price of the asset that distributes the income can fluctuate such as in assets like stocks or real estate, but the income must be stable.

Bucket 2 is the first bucket we start to introduce assets that are different from fixed income types of investments like CDs, bonds, and money market accounts that we discussed in bucket 1. Whenever we do that, we expect more risk and more price fluctuation. We won't be too worried about normal price fluctuations, but the consistency of the income derived from each investment will be an important focus for this bucket.

When you choose investments to place here you will be looking at how much, how secure, and how often the income is paid as your primary objective. You will then be managing the investment with the objective of monitoring the safety and consistency of that continued income at all times.

Dividend Growth Stocks

For a portion of my bucket 2 and the bucket 2 that I have managed for clients over the years, I have managed a portfolio of dividend growth stocks that have paid and increased their income every year since 2008 as part of that bucket.

In selecting dividend stocks, I use very strict criteria that weeds out weak companies and only includes strong companies within that list. These companies have done a remarkable job over the years of not only maintaining my income but giving me a raise every year that I owned them. Getting into the details of how to analyze stocks is a bit too much for this book, but don't fear, I will give you a couple of easy options to consider where the work is done for you when we get to the action plans and sample portfolios.

To give you an example of how dividends play a large part in the success of your bucket 2, and in investing in stocks in general, I am going to share with you a chart of P&G (Procter & Gamble). P&G has been around since 1837 and paid a dividend for 132 consecutive years. If you open your kitchen or bathroom cabinets I would bet you a decent sum of money that you own at least one P&G brand in your home. The stock has done very well over the past 20 years returning 9.48 percent annual total return,[1] but there were several years where the stock price, like all stocks, was down significantly.

The remarkable thing about P&G and many other high-quality dividend growth companies is that even though the asset price fluctuates year to year, it has always appreciated over time. More importantly for this bucket, if we use P&G as an example, the income that it pays has risen steadily every year for 66 *straight* years! That is the power of dividends. It is extremely difficult if not impossible to count on price appreciation to pay your bills each year. Dividends are a much different story when you select the right companies.

Figure 7.1 shows that stock prices can fluctuate a lot, but good dividends are consistent.

When people are looking to find stocks to add to the income part of their portfolio, stock, or other investments for their portfolio,

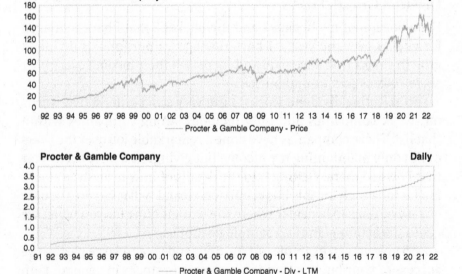

Figure 7.1   Dividends are consistent.

[1] FactSet: Total Return December 31, 2002, through December 28, 2022.

many times people make the mistake of picking only the stocks with the highest yields. They figure the higher the dividend, the more income they will receive. It sounds like it makes logical sense, but it's not the case. There are a few problems with that and why I would strongly advise against that strategy.

First, many times companies with high yields are paying such high yields because their price dropped. For example, if a stock is at $50 paying a 5% yield or $2.50 annually and the stock is cut in half to $25, the dividend of $2.50 stays the same initially, but the yield is now 10%. The same $2.50 dividend now divided by the new stock price of 25 is now a 10% yield.

You must ask yourself, why did the stock drop? Many times, stocks drop because their earnings decline, they have problems with suppliers, lawsuits, or any other number of reasons. Many times, the issues are temporary, but sometimes they are not. When these things happen, the company may no longer have the ability to continue paying the same dividends to shareholders. They may cut that dividend or even worse eliminate the dividend entirely. When they do that, the stock usually drops even further leaving shareholders with a much lower stock price and, now, zero income.

In this bucket, you must stick to companies like P&G that have great balance sheets and a long history that supports a healthy dividend that you can count on. When it comes to stocks like P&G, paper towels and toothpaste are boring, but they provide great and consistent income when you own them! Boring is sexy when it comes to your bucket 2 investing.

Real Estate Assets

Dividend stocks are not the only type of asset that pays income and can be included in your bucket 2. If you are so inclined to own and manage real estate assets like multifamily housing (apartments), self-storage, warehouses, and other commercial real estate investments, they all have proven to pay good and consistent income over time and work great in bucket 2. Just remember that, when investing in real estate, you need to make sure, after all expenses, you are getting more than you can receive from just investing in something liquid and safe like a bond with less risk. You also need to have experience in managing these types of assets or be able to afford to hire somebody who does.

If you do not feel comfortable managing real estate, you can also buy real estate investment trusts (REITs). REITs can be bought right inside your regular brokerage account just like a stock. Unlike a stock or exchange-traded fund (ETF) that we discussed previously, these REITs own a basket of real estate that is professionally managed for you and typically pays you quarterly income. You can invest in REITs that own apartments, healthcare facilities, self-storage, or various other types of real estate that you may prefer. REIT income is usually tax advantaged and consistent with high-quality REITs. We will have some REIT options for you to consider in the action plans later.

Corporate Bonds

Outside of stocks and real estate, bonds such as corporate bonds, which are issued by business, usually pay a higher rate. This would be a good bucket to add those in. Corporate bonds are riskier than government, and because of the extra risk they usually pay you more income.

Master Limited Partnerships and Business Development Companies

On the alternative side of assets, there are master limited partnerships (MLPs) and business development companies (BDCs) that are good options and two favorites of mine that you can also consider exploring. MLPs are typically oil and gas pipelines that act as toll roads in transporting oil and gas. They have a history of paying high income but also having higher risk, so you should diversify and limit exposure to this sector and MLPs in general.

BDC are companies that loan to small and midsized companies. Many times, these are floating-rate loans, meaning that when rates rise, so does the interest pay and therefore your income. Again, these have higher risk and should have limited exposure.

Two things to also know about BDCs and MLPs is that they may issue K1s, which are documents that must be included on your tax return. The K1s normally complicate and/or increase the costs associated with filing your return so you must be comfortable with that. These probably make most sense as your portfolio gets larger if they are issuing K1s. Double-check that fact before making the investment or buy them inside an ETF to avoid K1 reporting.

Summary of Bucket 2

To recap, there are many types of investments that you can place into your bucket 2. The one common denominator though is that they must pay a consistent income that you can count on to pay your expenses throughout all economic environments. We need to

Bucket 2 Quick Guide

- **Timeframe:** 5 years plus
- **Objective:** Consistent and growing income
- **Types of assets:** Dividend stocks, bonds, real estate MLPs, BDCs
- **Quantity:** Long-term goal of generating enough income to replace bucket 1 spending each year and keep pace with inflation
- **Buy discipline:** Income security and consistency is primary analysis
- **Sell discipline:** If income appears to be declining or eliminated it is probably time to sell the position

use this bucket to help replace each year's worth of expenses that we take out of bucket 1. Ideally in bucket 2, we can buy enough assets to get you very close to generating the amount of income needed to replace the income that is being depleted from your bucket 1 each year to pay your bills. You become almost bullet-proof in your plan if you are able to achieve that.

Bucket 3: Long-Term Growth

The primary objective here is long-term growth. Specifically, we are looking for assets that we believe can achieve roughly a 10% or higher annual compounded rate of return over a longer period, typically 7–10 years.

These assets may also pay some income, but unlike your bucket 2 where income was your primary objective, growth is what it is all about in bucket 3. Growth assets in general are more volatile than the income-producing assets that we have in bucket 2. Since this bucket is solely for growth, these will be the most aggressive assets that we have discussed thus far, and therefore we attach the longest timeframe with them.

If a stock like Procter & Gamble is a bucket 2 asset, then a stock like Tesla or Amazon is your bucket 3 asset. These are higher and faster growth opportunities but also no income paid and less predictable. These are stocks that have a lot of octane but will probably provide a pretty bumpier ride as they rise.

If fully occupied apartments paying monthly rent are bucket 2 assets, raw land with no income in a future path of progress is a bucket 3 asset. Just like bucket 3 stocks, bucket 3 real estate provides you the potential for more growth. The trade-off is no predictability of income. This is fully about the growth story of buying low and at some point selling high.

When you invest in growth assets, you are basically deferring current income for future appreciation. So why even buy growth assets? Well, think about if you purchased oceanfront property 30 years ago. How do you think that investment worked out for you? How about if you purchased $10,000 worth of Amazon stock at the start of 2002? Not too bad: 20 years later you had $3,081,645.29.[2] Who said that you can't make money in the stock market?

To keep pace with inflation and preserve your buying power over time, most everyone should have some money in this bucket providing that fuel. This is also the bucket where you give yourself the opportunity to not only maintain your lifestyle but also give yourself the chance to exponentially exceed it. It also gives you the opportunity to start investing for kids or grandkids if that is important to you. They call that *legacy planning*. Legacy planning is what I call a high-class problem. This means that you accumulate more money than you can spend! High-class problems are the only types of problems I want you to have more of in your life!

Figure 7.2 shows the growth of Amazon stock since 2002.

Growth investing is more speculative but typically more rewarding than conservative assets. In this bucket we discussed investing in stocks like Tesla and Amazon, but you could also look at stocks like Restoration Hardware and Crowd Strike. You may or may not have heard of these two companies, and that is the idea. They are leaders in their categories but newer businesses with the potential for big growth ahead. If you can find smaller companies before they are owned by everyone, that usually represents some of the best opportunities in investing. Investors Like Peter Lynch and even Warren Buffett made some of their early fortunes finding small, undiscovered names.

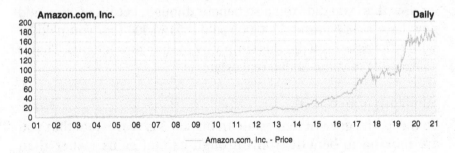

Figure 7.2 The growth of Amazon stock.

---

[2] FactSet: January 1, 2002, through December 31, 2021.

Real Estate Growth Assets

When you think of real estate in bucket 3, look at the types of real estate where you can either add value to the asset or buy in undiscovered areas that have potential. When I say value added, let's use multi-family real estate as an example. Commercial real estate is typically bought and sold off something called a *cap rate*. To simplify, a cap rate it is essentially the income that is paid from the property after expenses divided by the price paid for the real estate.

The higher the ratio of net operating income to purchase price, the higher the cap rate is. For illustration purposes, let's say that you buy a duplex property for $150,000 and the rent is $800 per month per unit and expenses associated with the property are $200 per month per unit. Let us assume that the occupancy rate was only 50%, that means the cap rate for this property is 4.8%. However, if you were able to find tenants and get to full occupancy, you would also increase the income.

The property would now be a 9.6-cap instead of a 4.8-cap and that would also increase the property valuation. Somebody would be willing to pay more for this property because the income is higher.

If you sold the property at $200,000 to a new purchaser with $14,400 in net operating income, they would actually be buying A 7.2-cap. That means they are getting more income dollar for dollar now than you did. You also benefit, though, because you would now have a 33% profit: $200,000 sold – $150,000 that you paid by selling the asset. You did this simply by finding new tenants. That is an example of value-added real estate.

Summary of Bucket 3

To recap, the growth real estate in bucket 3 is real estate that you are looking to benefit from through capital gains rather than collecting income. Remember, capital gains mean buying low and selling high. Remember taxes. When you take short-term capital gains (under one year), you pay ordinary income levels, which can be high. When you wait a year, you take capital gains, and you benefit from favorable rates, which have a max rate of 20%.

Bucket 3 Quick Guide

- **Timeframe:** 10 years+
- **Objective:** Growth
- **Types of assets:** Growth and small-cap stocks, opportunistic real estate
- **Quantity:** Based on how far from work optional. Larger allocation earlier and less later
- **Buy discipline:** Assets with realistic expectation to exceed 10% with reasonable valuations
- **Sell discipline:** When valuations exceed fair value or when your original buy thesis is nullified.

Bucket 4: Risky but High-Reward Assets

Bucket 4 is going to be your highest reward but also your most speculative and riskiest assets. The goal here will be to generate at least a 20% higher return than your bucket 3.

If you expect a 10% return in bucket 3, you should expect at least a 12% return in your bucket 4. To clarify, those extra 2 percentage points is a 20% higher expected return than a 10% return. There are a few reasons for this, but the primary thing to know about bucket 4 is that these assets are usually illiquid, meaning you cannot easily cash out if you needed the money. Whenever there is illiquidity, you should always expect what is called an "illiquidity premium." An illiquidity premium is a higher return for not having immediate access to your money.

Whenever you tie up your money without having easy access to it, you should expect something called an *illiquidity premium*. This is a rate of return that is higher than investing in something liquid, like a publicly traded stock where you can always access the money. Therefore, our rule will be that you should always expect at minimum of a 20% higher return in bucket 4 than from your bucket 3.

Private Business

Over the years I have worked with a lot of entrepreneurs. For most entrepreneurs, their biggest risk at building wealth is the same as their greatest opportunity to build wealth. That is their very own business. I have personally made some very good stock and real estate investments in my life, but nothing compares to the return I have received on businesses that I have built and sold.

If you are an entrepreneur building a business, your business is going to be considered a bucket 4 asset. It should be treated as such because if you are building your business the right way, someday you will be able to sell all or part of that business. The money you receive from the sale can then be invested in a bucket 2 asset to replace your business income with income from your passive investments. That is the holy grail of generating enough passive income to replace your work income (work optional).

Private Equity

Sticking with the theme of private business, another typical bucket 4 asset class is private equity. Private equity is typically associated with big private equity (PE) firms like KKR, Blackstone, and Apollo. They offer interest in companies typically to high-net-worth investors who do not trade on a public exchange. The goal is typically to invest at an early stage at a discount, and then receive a premium in the form of a capital gain at the exit. Exit strategies are typically events such as listing on a public exchange or selling to another private equity firm or strategic acquirer.

Real Estate

In real estate, raw land is typically what I consider a bucket 4 asset. Raw land provides no immediate income, so there will need to be improvements made to the land to generate income. Those improvements will typically require a certain expertise, require permitting, and require investing additional capital.

If you are not a developer, you are typically doing something we call *land banking*. Land banking means that you are simply holding onto the land until a time when there may be some event, such as population growth in the area, that will make the land imminently more attractive to another buyer.

Alternative Assets

Most other alternative asset classes will also be considered bucket 4 assets. These include but are not limited to classic automobiles, collectibles, wine futures, jewelry, precious metals, and fine art.

Summary of Bucket 4

One thing to note about bucket 4 is that it is not entirely necessary to have any allocation here. I have worked with many wealthy investors who preferred not to invest in alternative or illiquid assets entirely.

Bucket 4 Quick Guide

- **Timeframe:** 10 years+
- **Objective:** Growth and speculation
- **Types of assets:** Private equity alternatives, speculative real estate
- **Quantity:** Optional but typically 5% or less of your overall portfolio
- **Buy discipline:** Assets with realistic expectation to exceed 12% ROI
- **Sell discipline:** Usually upon liquidity event or when target rate of return has been reached

Bucket 4 investing is primarily done as a small allocation when you are younger in your investing career and looking for the potential to have an outside return while recognizing the risk or after you have already secured your core income needs through bucket 2 and you have excess capital left to invest. The only exception here would be investing in your own business.

The Art and Science of Managing Your Buckets

As someone who has managed money professionally and personally over a decade implementing this bucketing approach, I can tell you that it is a very simple and intuitive system even for novice investors, but there is also a bit of an art to it that creates a slight learning curve for some because, just like the life your managing the money for, its not always black and white.

Buckets 1 and 2 Tips

I could of course give you a black-and-white strategy that doesn't adapt or evolve, but you would become like Blockbuster video (bankrupt). If you want to be the Netflix of your specific industry (meaning a fast-growing $145 billion company), you need to be able to shift the strategy as things change, and they always change. This strategy is typically easiest to understand for almost everyone while you are within buckets 1 and 2. Those are the most straightforward for most people to understand and manage.

Buckets 1 and 2 are heavily numbers driven with simple rules, so most of it can be solved through simple math. For example, if you want four years' worth of reserves and your spending tallies $50,000 per year, then you would want to have $200,000 inside your bucket 1 to cover those expenses each year. You would then simply withdraw one-fourth of that bucket each year to pay your annual expenses.

If you are like many people who I have worked with over the years, you would like to have each year's worth of expenses that you withdraw from bucket 1 fully covered from the income that your bucket 2 is producing, and that number is also relatively simple to arrive at.

Let's say that you need $50,000 of income that you withdraw from bucket 1 each year. You will need to figure what yield or interest and how much money you would need to equal the $50,000 annually. For simple math if your portfolio yielded 5%, you would then need $1 million in bucket 2 if you wanted it to replenish 100% of what you spent each year. One million dollars multiplied by 5% is $50,000 in income without touching principal. If you have heard "I want to live off the interest," this is exactly the strategy that it is referring to. If your income from bucket 2 was half of that, say 2.5%, then you would need twice the size portfolio to generate that income or $2 million. So the relationship you need to understand is that the higher the yield of your portfolio, the lower the portfolio size is that you need to generate the income.

Therefore, when interest rates are low, it hurts people the most who are relying on living off the income generated from their portfolio. When interest rates rise, without taking on more risk, those same people can generate greater income. A rule of thumb here is that lower rates usually help people trying to grow their portfolio and higher rates typically help people who are withdrawing from their portfolio. There are a lot of metrics behind that rule, but in most cases it will apply.

> Ideally you will be in a low-interest-rate environment while you are working and borrowing and then a high-interest-rate environment when you are retired and withdrawing.

Buckets 3 and 4 Tips

How about bucket 3 and bucket 4 for those who decide to use that bucket? These are the hardest buckets for me to give you a hard and fast rule to live by because they are not black and white and can't be. I'll talk primarily about bucket 3 since everyone will use that bucket. For those implementing bucket 4, it is essentially the same concept as 3 with greater liquidity constraints.

As humans, we like to see patterns, have rules to live by, and simple how-to instructions associated with everything that we do: the seven biggest mistakes, a three-step process, five foods to avoid, and so forth. This is how we like to learn. We all adore simple processes. The truth is that not everything can be put into black and white, though. Some things live in the gray but for good reason. Bucket 3 is the bucket where there is gray, because you must be able use the most discretion here.

In this bucket you will need to be more opportunistic, and I need you to be flexible with how you manage this bucket on a year-to-year basis. If the rules that I give you here are too rigid, your ability to pivot and adapt based on the changing real-world opportunity and your changing lifestyle needs will be too restrictive for you. As Einstein said, "Everything should be made as simple as possible but not simpler." That is what I will attempt to do here for bucket 3.

Let me start by tackling bucket 3 with what I believe is the easiest approach for most people to understand. When we discussed buckets 1 and 2, we said that if you spent $50,000 per year and you wanted to have four years' worth of reserves in your bucket 1, you would then simply allocate your first $200,000 to bucket 1. We then said that, if we're trying to solve for 100% of our income that we distribute from bucket 1 being replenished from the income generated from your bucket 2, we would then need to figure out the amount of money and yield that you would need from your bucket 2.

We said that if your bucket 2 could generate 5% in average income, then you would need to allocate $1 million to your bucket 2 to generate that $50,000 in income each year. In this scenario, that would require $1.2 million between your bucket 1 and your bucket 2—that is, $200,000 in your bucket 1 for the four years with expenses and $1 million in your bucket 2 that is generating the $50,000 in income each year to replace what you spend.

Let's suppose that you had accumulated $1.5 million by the time you reached your work optional or retirement date. What you could then do is take $1.2 million of that $1.5 million and allocate that as we just described among the first two buckets. The $300,000 that is left over would then be the amount that you can then allocate to your bucket 3 for the growth types of investments that we discussed, which belong in this bucket.

This is what is what we will call the "use the change method," which means that after securing your lifestyle in safer investments, investing what is left over into risker assets. Most importantly, it is the one that I have seen most people stick with and have the most success with. That itself is the essence of what the art of financial planning is all about. What I described might not mathematically give you the highest ending balance, but the strategy most likely to do that might not be one that you will understand, have trust in, or can manage your lifestyle from. Therefore, that would not be the best strategy for you, even though academically it may be the soundest. The strategy that you will stick to will always be the superior strategy for you to follow.

With this strategy, your bucket 3 gives you the greatest flexibility to move the money within this bucket to where the biggest opportunity might be. Sometimes it will be in different parts of the stock market, sometimes it might be in different types of real estate. The point is that not every year will be the same risk and reward scenario. Some years things will be overvalued and some things will be undervalued. Therefore, you want to give yourself the most flexibility to be able to go where the greatest opportunity is.

Once you have secured your buckets 1 and 2, that means you secured your lifestyle. That is the most important objective in investing. When you do this, you are not heavily reliant on bucket 3 for your lifestyle and have greater flexibility within your plan. This is the optimal position to put yourself in as an investor because you're never forced to sell at an inopportune time. You can afford to do what Warren buffet says: "Be greedy when others are fearful and fearful when others are greedy," which equates to buying low and selling high—a simple but effective formula for making money!

The greatest opportunity in investing normally comes at the time of greatest risk and when things seem like they can't fail. At that time, you are usually facing maximum risk in whatever investment you are looking at. When people put themselves in a position where they are reliant on asset prices in their bucket 3 increasing in price every year just to pay their bills, it never ends well. They are forced to sell low and put themselves in jeopardy of running out of money. That in financial planning is considered a failing scenario. You want your money to outlive you, or at least end up bouncing your last check to the funeral home!

What are some other ways that you can be a bit more creative with your bucket 3? One way is the way that you manage the bucket on a year-to-year basis. Let's say you have a great year. Using your scenario where you had $300,000 invested in bucket 3, there are going to be years when you will surely see gains of 20% or more as an investor. So what you will do with those gains?

This is where it comes down to art, your own comfort level as an investor, and, once again, what the opportunity set looks like that year. It may be a year where the market did well but still seems undervalued and as though it has a long way to go. In this case you may want to let that $60,000 ride in your bucket 3. Conversely, assets may seem a bit frothy and you may want to take that $60,000 profit and book it into your bucket 2. Let's think about that. If you do that, at 5% percent yield in your bucket 2, you just added another $3,000 per year income to what you can spend each year. Every time you take some out of bucket 3 and pour it into bucket 2, you are theoretically able to upgrade your lifestyle and spend more, this is very attractive to a lot of people.

Let's also remember that I normally recommend that people only look to cover their core living expenses that they must pay each year from their buckets 1 and 2, not their discretionary expenses.

Your discretionary expenses would be things like vacations, an extra car, giving money away to family and friends, or anything that is not considered essential to running your day-to-day lifestyle. Things that you would like but are not obligated to do.

With this in mind, there are a couple of ways to look at the $3,000 that we just discussed. One way is that you would now be able to count on having $3,000 per year as a minimum vacation budget because there is the consistent income there now to pay for it. Alternatively, vacations and other discretionary expenses could be decided on a year-to-year basis. If there was an extra $60,000 in profits as we discussed, which you didn't count on, this might be a great year to take that dream vacation for $60,000. If it's a bad year in your bucket 3, then obviously you wouldn't want to make that splurge.

Looking at your budget and lifestyle from this perspective in which your nonessential expenses could be determined each year based on how well or badly your investments do is probably the most real-world application of using this strategy.

I believe that the best approach is a modified version, where you spend maybe $30,000 on a very nice vacation and take the other $30,000 and put it into bucket 2. This is the best of both worlds where you upgrade your forward income, but you also enjoy life. That is what investing is all about, creating the income that you need to live a life you love.

Once you are able get your arms around the fact that bucket 3 might not be as clear-cut as buckets 1 and 2, it becomes a bit easier to understand the whole strategy. Essentially you're securing your lifestyle with buckets 1 and 2, and then you're using bucket 3, and in the same way bucket 4 to give yourself the potential to increase that lifestyle each year by increasing the income generated through bucket 2 by investing those gains. The alternative is taking lump sums in gains each year from buckets 3 and 4 to do some of those things that you've always wanted to do. Or, as I recommended for most people that I advise, you will be splitting the difference each year by rewarding yourself with some of those capital gains, but simultaneously giving yourself the improved consistent income to enjoy things on a more regular basis by investing some of the gains back into bucket 2.

As you can see, this is a framework that allows you to make decisions that can be adapted to the current environment but are also always focused on aligning your investments with your personal goals. It seems like magic when you get the hang of it, and it is. Not only will you find yourself becoming a better investor, you will just have a lot more clarity and peace of mind when your finances are managed strategically within a framework like this. We all know that financial stress is one of the leading causes of divorce and the worst thing that you can do to your health. Next we will talk about how you can manage risk once you have secured your assets within the various buckets.

10 Rules to Reduce Risk in Your Buckets

Now that you understand how to manage your buckets, I want to give you a few simple strategies and rules for managing your risk. As I mentioned, this book is not about learning the 10% of what you need to know to become a financial analyst. This book is about mastering the 90% of what you need to understand to have financial freedom. Risk is multidimensional and ever changing, but I am going to give you my top-10 rules that will cover you and have stood the test of time and some really bad economic crisis.

With all the information that you have learned so far, you can always continue adapting and evolving from this information, and I encourage you to do so, but only after you have mastered what you have learned so far. So many times I see people diving into complex investment strategies, looking to day trade, or focusing on very speculative investments when they don't even have a net worth statement. They don't even know what their work optional numbers is, and they have no idea how to get there. If they did, I am sure they would be more intentional with their investments.

Once you understand the basics, you start to become more strategic in your investments, and you start to make investments that are consistent with your life goals, which gives you better outcomes. By having your investments strategically aligned with your personal goals and cash flow needs, you are already reducing your risk. Having a strategic plan is the first step in managing risk. When you assign purpose to your investments, you tend to be more strategic. You will ask yourself, what bucket does this fit in? Does this investment get me closer or further to my work optional number? All these things will soon become second nature.

Here are 10 well-tested rules to master from the knowledge that you have already acquired:

Rule 1: Always keep your bucket 1 full. 6–12 months of expenses when you are preretirement and 3–5 years of expenses when you stop working. You may be tempted at times to reduce this to take more risk, but that is always a bad idea. The best investors always practice risk and avoid emotional decisions.

Rule 2: Don't invest more than 5% in any one stock. When you invest more, you start to minimize the benefits of diversification and your financial future becomes much less predictable.

Rule 3: Don't allocate too much to one sector or industry. The largest part of an individual stock's performance is dependent on its industry. When tech stocks go down, more than likely companies like Google and Apple will follow. Instead, diversify your money across several sectors to maximize your portfolio.

Rule 4: Use ETFs to minimize the risk of investing in single stocks. For most people the core of the portfolio should be invested in low-cost ETFs that provide maximum diversification easily and affordably. You can buy entire indexes like the S&P 500 or a single sector like Technology or Utilities. There are thousands of ETFs today however you are looking to invest. Vanguard and iShares are two companies to consider with great options. When you get to the age-based recommendations part of the book we will provide you with some sample portfolios to help you get started.

Rule 5: Cost matters. Investing in expensive mutual funds and paying high asset-management fees to money managers who profess to be able to beat the market is usually a fool's errand. Instead look to keep all costs of your portfolio under 50 basis points (BPS). That is very easy to do today as long as you're not paying a manager 1%. High fees are one of the biggest risks to not meeting your goals.

Rule 6: Check your emotions at the door. Never make emotional investments. Stick to long-term investing fundamentals like filling your buckets with high-quality assets and avoid chasing speculative junk like obscure crypto currency plays and penny stocks. Those things usually end miserably. Once your buckets 1–3 are full and you have extra money, then its okay to put a small amount in those types of trades. This way, if they go to zero, your lifestyle is not going to be impacted. Also avoid panic selling. Bear markets occur every few years where stocks drop 20% or more. The thing you need to remember is that 100% of all previous bear markets have been buying, not selling, opportunities, so make sure you stay the course especially when it seems the darkest.

Rule 7: Rebalance your portfolio at least annually. This will force you to sell high and buy low. For example, if you started the year with 5% in Apple stock and 5% in Chevron stock, it is common for one sector to perform well while one does poorly. This is why you diversify. So if tech did well and Apple stock went up 20%, it would now become 6% of the portfolio. If energy performed poorly and Chevron went down 20%, then that would drop to 4% of your portfolio. In this example you would sell the excess Apple shares to bring it back down to 5% and use that money to buy more Chevron shares and bring that position back up to 5%. This way you are not only managing risk, but also taking profits from what ran up to buy the stock that dropped in price.

Rule 8: Never use leverage like margin and never invest money that you cannot afford to stay invested in long term. Only use money that you can keep invested consistent with the timeframes we have associated to each bucket. The whole idea of the bucketing approach is to wisely allocate assets so that you have enough liquidity to get you through rough patches that will certainly appear from time to time. When you use leverage or invest your short-term money to buys stocks, you will more than likely be forced to takes losses just to pay your bills.

Rule 9: Tune out the noise. The abundance of information today is both a blessing and a curse. Everybody has an opinion and most of them are not worth listening to unless they have the qualifications and completely understand your personal situation. Everything on social media and the Internet seems attractive because people are presenting the information they want you to see and believe. Most of these things end poorly. Promises of 10% monthly returns or a double-your-money plan in 90 days are unrealistic. Remember the old saying, if it sounds too good to be true, it more than likely is. This is a very good rule to adhere to when it comes to investing. I have seen some major scams over my years that a lot of smart people fell for. One thing to remember, whether its stocks or real estate: good high-quality investments average about 8–10% over time. Even most "experts" cannot beat those returns, so be very wary of anyone or anything that promises returns that are exponentially higher.

Rule 10: Diversify. Do not put all your eggs in one basket. Putting too much in one company's stock, buying that one stock you were sure would be the next big thing, and ultimately going all in on any one idea is a fast way to go broke. Singles and doubles will lead to home runs when you are not expecting it. When you start swinging for the fences and abandoning your discipline, those bad habits will lead to a lot of strikeouts. If you have too many of these early on, it will be hard for you to catch up. Its okay to take some moonshots, but only when you are taking care of your basics first.

Chapter 8
Minimizing Taxes

The dreaded five-letter word *taxes* plays a huge role in how much money you can accumulate and how fast you can get to your work optional. The less that you give to Uncle Sam, the more you keep for investing and in turn the more income you can spend on the things that you enjoy.

Minimizing Taxes Based on Asset Location

Asset location simply refers to the account type that you should place your different assets within to be as tax efficient as possible. There are several different account types. We are going to focus on the primary ones that you must know and can begin using now. It really all comes down to three primary types of accounts:

1. Fully taxable
2. Tax deferred
3. Tax free

A general rule of thumb is that while you are working and still in the highest tax bracket, you will want to defer as much of your income as possible. When you retire and stop having earned income, theoretically, you'll be in a lower tax rate. At that point, you could start withdrawing those funds at a lower rate than you would've paid while you were working. The holy grail of retirement income is to have the correct balance between these types of accounts to keep as much of your income in the lowest tax rates possible.

Let's look at an example of the three types of accounts in more detail.

Fully Taxable

The most basic type of a fully taxable account is the individual account. In this type of account there is only one owner. Any dividends or interest that is paid throughout the year will be reported on Form 1099 that is automatically provided to you by your custodian. The income reported on that form will be fully taxable. The same applies for any capital gains you've made throughout the year which will also be automatically reported, and it will be taxable.

It is not all bad news for a fully taxable account, because there is a benefit. In a fully taxable account, you are able to use capital losses to offset current or future capital gains. For example, say that you purchased $20,000 of Microsoft stock and 13 months later you sell your investment for $15,000. You essentially realized a capital loss of $5,000. You can use that loss to offset gains in your other investments. If you had a capital gain of $5,000 in Chevron stock, you would normally pay taxes on that gain; however, since you also have a capital loss of $5,000, you can offset the gain from Chevron with the loss from Microsoft and avoid paying taxes.

Tax Deferred

The best example of this type of account is a Traditional IRA or a Traditional 401(k) account. When you have this type of account, you do not have to report any dividends, interest, or capital gains every year. This avoids paying taxes as you go, which allows your account to grow faster. However, once you take money out of these accounts, the full amount will be taxable at your marginal tax rate.

Another benefit of a 401(k) account and to a degree, most Traditional IRAs, is that you can take a tax deduction for contributing to the account. Let's say you make $60,000 annually and you contributed 10% of your salary to the 401(k) account, when you get your W-2 statement, it will only show you made $54,000 in wages for federal tax purposes. That $6,000 decrease in wages is a benefit you get for contributing to the 401(k) plan. That's several hundred dollars in tax savings!

A final benefit to a 401(k) plan is a possible employer match. There are a few different employer match formulas, and I will show you one. To encourage you to put money away for retirement, the employer may match your contributions up to a maximum amount. Typically, you would see an employer match 100 percent of your contributions up to 5% of your annual compensation. Let's go back to the individual who makes $60,000 annually and is contributing 10%. In this case the company would match 5% or $3,000 per year in addition to what this person is already saving. In total, this individual would be investing $9,000 into their 401(k) account, which is 15% of their gross salary. The catch is that your employer may not contribute to your account unless you first put money in.

If you decided to not contribute anything to your 401(k) account and you have a contributory employer match, you will be leaving free money on the table. Check with your employer to understand their matching formula and at minimum contribute enough to get the employer's full match.

Tax Free

The Roth IRA is a tax-free account if certain basic criteria are met. Similar to a tax-deferred account, you will not have to report any dividends, interest, or capital gains on a yearly basis. The great thing about a Roth IRA is that any funds you pull out of the account are tax free (assuming you have held the Roth IRA for a minimum of five years and you are older than the age of 59½). This is a powerful feature of the Roth IRA because you avoid paying taxes legally.

The government has allowed these accounts to encourage people to save for their retirement. Another positive benefit to a Roth IRA is that you can withdraw your contributions at any time and avoid paying taxes or a penalty if you are under the age of 59½. Say you contributed $30,000 into your Roth IRA and a few years later the value of the account is $50,000; well, you can withdraw the whole $30,000 anytime without an adverse consequence. The reason Roth IRAs have this tax-free benefit is because the contributions have already been taxed.

The Roth IRA is an excellent way to begin investing for your retirement. As a general rule, young people should open a Roth IRA and capitalize on the lazy person's rule to becoming a tax-free millionaire. If you are no longer in your 20s, don't worry, you can still benefit from a Roth IRA.

To determine if you should contribute to a Roth IRA or Traditional IRA, you should compare your current federal marginal tax rate to what you think your federal marginal tax rate will be in the future. You should consider opening a Roth IRA if you either expect tax rates in the future will be higher because your income will be higher when you retire, or because a change in tax law will increase tax rates.

One thing to note is that there is an annual contribution limit to a Roth IRA (the same applies to a Traditional IRA). For 2023 that limit is $6,500 and for anyone age 50 and older that limit is $7,500. There is also a Roth IRA income limit, which means if you file as a single and make more than $153,000 in 2023, you cannot make a Roth contribution in that year. If you file jointly, that limit for 2023 is $228,000. One final note is that now most employers allow for Roth 401(k) accounts! Anyone can contribute to a Roth 401(k) regardless of whether they make more than the income limit for a Roth IRA.

Another popular tax-free account is the college savings 529 Plan. These are state-sponsored accounts for education savings that can be used for a child, another family member, or even for yourself. You can use the money for qualified K–12 private school tuition, higher education tuition as well as room and board, fees, books, supplies, equipment, computer hardware and software, and Internet access and related services.

The college savings 529 Plan is very similar to a Roth IRA, because you put after-tax contributions into the account, and if you use the money for qualified expenses, then your earnings will grow tax deferred, and you can pull everything out tax free!

The 529 Plans have been made it very easy to open and invest the money. A popular way to invest in these accounts is by using age-based target-date funds or target-enrollment funds. All you have to do is select the fund with the expected enrollment date of the student and then you are set. The fund will be managed in a way that begins more aggressive and automatically becomes more conservative as the enrollment date approaches.

Remember, the importance of getting started early so you may want to consider opening a 529 Plan soon after the birth of a child. Note that anyone can contribute to a child's 529 Plan, including grandparents and friends. For a child's birthday, some parents are encouraging a contribution into an already established 529 Plan rather than having a toy gifted to the child.

Even if you don't think your child might go to college, contributions into a 529 Plan might still make sense because a new law was passed that would allow some of the 529 Plan funds to be converted into a Roth IRA if certain criteria is met. This could turbo-charge your child's retirement if they don't use all the 529 Plan funds or decide not to go to college.

Investing Strategies to Minimize Taxes

A general rule of thumb is that while you are working and still in the highest tax bracket, you will want to defer as much of your income as possible to avoid paying unnecessary taxes. When you retire and no longer have earned income and just passive investment income, theoretically, you'll be in a lower tax rate due to the more favorable tax rates on investment income and ability to withdraw funds in a tax-efficient manner. At that point, you could start withdrawing those funds at a lower rate than you would have paid while you were working. The holy grail of retirement income is to have the correct balance between these types of accounts to keep as much of your income in the lowest tax rates possible.

In investing we must focus on the things that we can control. There is plenty that is in your hands as an investor such as market returns and the overall trajectory of the economy. Our duty as investors is to make sure that we don't miss or ignore the things that we can control. Asset location done right will add significantly to your overall investment return and boost your net worth. Don't forget to ask what this investment is for and what type of account provides the best tax advantages for your needs next time you acquire any new asset.

The same thing goes for when you begin to withdraw funds. Make sure you are aware of the tax brackets at that time in order maximize the lowest brackets possible. Tax free is always the best, so try to get as much money into that Roth as possible while you are young!

The following sections highlight some other investing strategies to minimize taxes.

Go for Long-Term Capital Gains

One of the most effective yet simple ways to minimize taxes is to avoid short-term gains. The length of time you hold your investment will dictate the tax rate applied to stock investment gains. If you hold an investment for less than a year, you will be taxed on those gains at your short-term-capital-gains tax rate. For high-income earners, that can be as high as 37% plus your state tax rate.

If you hold your investment for over a year, that gain qualifies for the long-term capital-gains tax bracket with the highest rate of 20%.[1] Of course, you don't want to make the mistake of holding on to an investment just for the sake of trying to minimize taxes.

---

[1] Assuming you do not fall into the net investment income tax (NIIT), which adds an additional 3.8%.

I have seen many cases in which someone has a substantial short-term gain and loses it all waiting for the long-term rate to kick in. All things considered, it's best to try to hold your investments for one year and a day to qualify for the lower rate.

Invest in Qualified Dividends

The holding period matters here as well. Normally, when a company pays a dividend, it is taxed like short-term gains, which means you can end up paying as high as 37%. However, if you hold that stock for a minimum period, that dividend can qualify for the long-term-capital-gains tax bracket, which is much lower.

> For common stock, here is the rule: You must have held those shares of stock unhedged for at least 61 days out of the 121-day period that began 60 days before the ex-dividend date. I said a lot, so let's break it down. An ex-dividend date is the date that the stock begins to trade without the dividend payment.

For example, if a company pays a dividend of 50 cents and has an ex-date of 10/23/2023, you must buy the stock at least the day before you will be entitled to the dividend. If you buy it on the ex-date, you will no longer get the dividend. Now before you go thinking you just found a "free lunch" and go buy stocks right before the ex-date to collect the dividend, remember this.

The stock price of the company should theoretically drop by the amount of the dividend on the ex-date. That happens because the company will pay the dividend from cash on the pay date, so that means the company now has less cash and is worth less by the amount of the dividend. In my example, the ex-date is 10/23/2023 so the period begins 60 days prior and goes on for 121 days after.

Don't worry about counting days, because your custodian who holds your account will automatically do this for you. You will get a

1099 from the custodian for the prior year, and it will break out your qualified dividends.

Max Out Your 401(k)

A 401(k) plan is a powerful way to not only save for retirement, but this account also has a couple of great benefits. A 401(k) is an employer-sponsored retirement account that allows you to contribute up to $22,500 in 2023, and if you are age 50 and older, you can contribute an additional $7,500. Here is how it works. Suppose you make $100,000 and you contribute $15,000 into the plan, that means for federal tax purposes, you would not report $100,000 as your income, but rather $85,000. If your marginal tax rate is 22%, then that would mean a $3,300 tax savings.

If the maximum was contributed to the plan, then the tax savings would be $4,950! Also, most companies will do some type of match or contribution. For example, an employer may say that they match the first 5% of what you contribute to the plan. So, if you earned $100,000 per year and elected to invest 5% of your salary or $5,000 into your plan, your employer would also contribute $5,000 to your plan. This means you are automatically doubling everything you invest!

This is free money. Never turn down free money.

What I tell everyone even if your plan is not the best is that it is a no-brainer to make sure that you are contributing at least what your employer will match. If the match is 3% percent, then do the 3%. If it is 10%, I would recommend doing the full 10%.

What is also nice about the 401(k) is that it is what I called *forced savings*. The investment is taken automatically from your pay each pay period. You know yourself and your own strengths and weaknesses better than anyone, but I am sure that you will agree that if the money just comes out of your check and does not hit your hands, it is much more likely to get invested than if it was sent to your bank account first. It's just human nature— out of sight out of mind. If you don't see the money, I promise you won't miss it. Before you know it, you will have amassed a small fortune by regularly investing, and you won't even have missed it.

If you are self-employed with no employees, you could be eligible to open a self-employed 401(k). These plans were designed to help self-employed individuals save for retirement and avoid the cost and time it takes to administer a full-blown 401(k) plan. If you are under the age of 50, the salary deferral contribution limit is $22,500 in 2023 and employer may contribute up to 25% of compensation up to the annual maximum of $66,000 for 2023. Let's say you are 45 years old, and your business type is single-owner corporation, and your wage is $200,000 annually. You would be able to contribute $22,500 as a salary deferral plus the employer portion of $43,500 for a total annual contribution of $66,000. Assuming a 24% federal marginal tax rate, that would mean $15,840 in federal tax savings!

Harvest Investment Losses

A great way to make good use of a taxable account is to harvest investment losses. As much as we would like every single investment to make us a lot of money, the reality is that some investments won't work out the way we had planned, and we will lose money. However, it is not all bad because we are able to use those losses to offset other investment gains, which ultimately leads to tax savings.

For example, if you had a loss of $5,000 in a stock investment you held in your individual account and you also had a stock gain of $5,000, well you can use the losses to offset the gains and, in this example, that would mean paying zero in taxes on the $5,000 gain.

Harvesting loses is a great tool to use, but you have to be careful not to trigger the wash sale rule or you will be disallowed to claim the loss. Technically when you trigger this rule, the loss will be added to the cost basis of the replacement security so you will be able to benefit from the loss eventually. However, being able to benefit from the loss today is more beneficial than claiming the loss in the future, so let's understand the wash sale rule so you don't trigger it.

If you sell a security at a loss and buy the same or a substantially identical security within 30 calendar days before or after the date of the sale, you will have triggered the wash sale rule.

Here is an example. Say you bought Coinbase stock at $100 and 15 days later the stock is down to $75, and you sell it. You would be able to claim a $25 per share loss on your taxes. What if Coinbase starts rapidly increasing in price and you decide to buy the stock back, but the purchase is within 30 days of the sale, you will have triggered the wash sale rule and you won't be able to claim the $25 per share loss. Some might think, well I'll just wait the 30 days and then buy Coinbase back. At first that sounds like a sound strategy, but a stock like Coinbase can move very quickly in a short period of time, and if you don't own the stock, you could miss out on a potential large gain. The goal is to harvest losses, but not give up possible gains.

So what can you do? Remember, the wash sale rule is triggered if you buy back Coinbase or a similar stock within 30 calendar days before or after the date of the sale. However, if you bought an ETF that owns a good amount of Coinbase, but also owns other stocks, then you could argue that the ETF is not similar, and you did not trigger the wash sale rule.

For example, the ARK Innovation ETF owns about 5% of Coinbase, but it also owns other growth stocks; nevertheless, the ETF is highly correlated to Coinbase. In our example, if you sold Coinbase at a $25 per share loss and then you bought ARKK ETF, you could argue that you should be allowed to claim the loss because the ETF is not similar to the stock. And by purchasing the ETF, which is highly correlated to Coinbase, you have put yourself in a position to benefit if the stock bounces back up in a short period of time.

The one thing that you never want to do is try to time the market, in this case selling Coinbase, letting the money sit in cash, and then buying it back in 31 days. Why? Because a stock can move significantly in those 31 days. It could easily move 20% or more, especially after it has experienced large recent declines. If that occurs, your tax savings may not offset how much money you missed out on by not staying invested. By buying a similar stock, you will benefit from that decision if the market moves higher.

Another thing to note is that whether an individual stock moves either up or down is largely dependent on the sector that it is in. That means if tech stocks go up or down, Apple and Google stock will largely follow the entire sector in that same direction. This is precisely why exchanging Coinbase for a tech ETF or another tech stock normally works well. Just don't exchange Apple for Procter & Gamble. That probably will not work as well. That is because those stocks are in entirely different sectors—technology and consumer staples— that normally do not move in the same direction at the same time.

Use Appreciated Assets for Charitable Contributions

For those who are charitably inclined, you can contribute long-term appreciated assets to a charity and save on taxes.

Here is an example of how this works. Suppose you purchased $20,000 worth of stock in a company five years ago. Today those shares are worth $70,000, meaning a $50,000 taxable long-term capital gain. You can do one of two things to make the donation, you can sell the stock, pay the taxes, and contribute the net proceeds or you can donate the appreciated stock directly to the charity. Both strategies will save you taxes, but here is why the latter approach is better. If you sell the stock and your marginal long-term-capital-gains tax rate is 15%, you will pay $7,500 in taxes, which would net you $62,500 that you can contribute to the charity.

If your federal marginal tax rate is 32%, then that charitable contribution would provide a $20,000 tax savings. Not bad. However, if you donate the appreciated stock directly to the charity you would not pay any long-term-capital-gains taxes, so the donation would be the full $70,000. In this instance, the tax savings would be $22,400. Therefore, by donating stock directly to the charity, it receives an additional benefit of $7,500 and you get an additional tax savings of $2,400.

Use an HSA Health Savings Account

If you have a high-deductible medical plan, you may be eligible for a health savings account. This type of account allows you to pay for current and future medical expenses.

The best part of it all is that you get a triple tax savings benefit on your federal taxes! Not only do you get an up-front tax deduction for contributions, like a Traditional IRA, but the money also grows tax deferred, and it's tax free when you pull it out, just like a Roth. So you get the federal tax benefits of a Traditional and Roth IRA.

For 2023, the maximum contribution amount for an individual is $3,850, and for a family it is $7,750. There is also a catch-up contribution of $1,000 for anyone age 55 and older.

Use the Gift Tax Annual Exclusion

For those individuals who have accumulated a substantial amount of wealth, using the annual gift tax exclusion is a good way to reduce estate taxes, also called the "death tax."

If someone dies in 2023, they have a lifetime estate exemption of $12,920,000, and anything over that amount will predominately be taxed at 40%. A good way to reduce a person's estate is by making gifts to family members that do not exceed $17,000 annually per person. If you file a joint tax return, that amount increases to $34,000 annually per beneficiary.

Consider Tax-Free Municipal Bonds

When public entities, like a local government, need to raise money to pay for a project like the construction of a school, a highway, or a hospital, they issue municipal bonds. Normally speaking, there are two types of municipal bonds, general obligation and revenue bonds. General obligation bonds are backed by the faith and full credit of the local issuing government, while revenue bonds are secured by the revenues generated by the specific project.

Municipal bonds are attractive because they are generally exempt from federal income tax, as well as state and local income tax if you are a resident of the state that issued the bond. Municipal bonds typically have a lower yield because of their favorable tax treatment. A simple way to compare the yield of a municipal bond to another bond that does not have the same favorable tax treatment is to use the tax-equivalent yield calculation. For this calculation you will take the yield of the municipal bond and divide it by 1 minus the sum of your federal and state marginal tax rate.

Here is how it works: suppose you live in California and your federal and state marginal tax rate is 24% and 9.3%, respectively, and you found a municipal bond with a yield of 5% and a corporate bond with a yield of 7%. Which bond would you choose? By using the tax-equivalent yield, we will find out.

Here is the formula:

$$0.05 / 1 - (0.24 + 0.093) = 0.075, \text{ or } 7.5\%$$

Therefore, even though the municipal bond has a yield of 5%, it is still more attractive than a corporate bond with a yield of 7%. The higher your federal and state marginal tax rate, the more attractive you will find municipal bonds.

Maximize Business Expenses

Make sure that you run all expenses related to your business through your corporate entity. An S Corp or LLC are common pass-through entities that many entrepreneurs use for their business.

Having a pass-through entity means that all net profits and loses flow through to your individual taxes, which makes it very easy to manage for small businesses. Cell phone bills, home office expenses, travel, education, subscriptions, and whatever legitimate expenses that are tied to your business should always be run through the business accounts and separate from your personal accounts.

The lower your net income from your business is, the lower your overall tax payment is. This is why I always encourage people to start a business. I will give you an example. I have a client that was a former attorney who wanted to retire. He and his wife are both foodies. They wanted to spend the early years of retirement traveling the world tasting different cuisines. I asked them, "How would you like to do all of that in a very tax-friendly way where you can write off large part of trips?"

I think you know the answer. We set up a blog and subscription/ advertising model where they were able to turn this passion into a business by sharing their journey with the world. Their new cameras, computers, and a large part of their trips became legitimate business expenses and saved them a ton in taxes. You must think outside the box a little, but there are several viable businesses you can start even part-time to help reduce your tax bill.

Hire Family Members

This can be a great way to involve family members in the business while also potentially saving in taxes and giving them a head start on investing. There are several moving parts depending on whether you are hiring your spouse, children, or parents. The rules also depend on business structure, sole proprietorship, partnership, LLC, and so forth, and if you hire your family member as an employee or independent contractor. The details are beyond the scope of this book, but I will suggest speaking with a qualified CPA to help you determine if it makes sense to hire a family member.

As I mentioned, another nice thing about hiring your kids is allowing them to get a head start on establishing an account like a Roth IRA. They can do this by allocating some or all of their earnings into their Roth. We discussed in length why getting started early makes a lot of sense. We also talked about the Roth IRA being the holy grail of investing. Tax-free! It doesn't get any better than that. Here is your chance to help your kids do both and be way ahead of the curve. Don't you wish someone opened a Roth IRA for you when you were 10 years old?

Use Real Estate Tax Advantages

Real estate is one of the most tax-advantaged investments out there. Depreciation is one major advantages of real estate investing, but there are a couple major tax benefits such as 1031 exchanges and qualified opportunity zones.

1031 Exchanges

Whenever you sell investment property and you have a gain, you generally must pay tax on the gain at the time of sale. However, if you use IRC Section 1031, you are allowed to postpone paying tax on the gain if you reinvest the proceeds in similar property as part of a qualifying like-kind exchange.

This can be a great way to defer taxes and use the full sale proceeds to purchase another qualifying property. There are two time limits that you must meet. The first limit is that you have 45 days from the date you sell the relinquished property to identify a potential replacement property. The second limit is that the replacement property must be received and the exchange completed no later than 180 days after the sale of the exchanged property or the due date (with extensions) of the income tax return for the tax year in which the relinquished property was sold, whichever is earlier.

Opportunity Zones

Opportunity zones are an economic development tool that allows people to invest in distressed areas. Investors in these programs are given an opportunity to defer and potentially reduce tax on recognized capital gains.

For example, say you are facing a significant tax liability because of capital gains. Investing in a qualified opportunity fund might make sense, provided you invest within a prescribed amount of time. Make sure to check with a qualified professional who can walk you through all the details to determine if this strategy is right for you.

Chapter 9
Buying or Avoiding Life Insurance and Annuities

Now, I couldn't write a book about managing your financial life without at least a small mention of life insurance and annuities. Life insurance and annuities by far have the most inaccurate and misleading information of any asset class that I can think of. I could write a whole book about this topic, but what I want to do in this chapter is give you a quick education and a practical guide of how to understand, use, and/or avoid life insurance and annuities in your own financial plan.

Life Insurance as an Investment?

An important thing to understand about life insurance is that it is not really meant to be an investment even though it is sold that way many times. Specifically, life insurance is a contract between the insured (you) and the insurer (the insurance company). This is a contract that will pay your beneficiary, which is usually your family (or in some cases employer or creditor), a *death benefit*, which is a certain dollar amount when you die.

To purchase life insurance coverage there needs to be what is called an *insurable need*. Let's discuss what an insurable need is. The most common insurable need for individuals is the replacement of income. For example, when you are just starting out as a young couple, most of the time you are dependent on two incomes to pay your bills. You usually take on debt together such as an auto loan, mortgage, or other financial obligations that require a certain amount of income to meet those obligations. If there were a situation in which you had a $400,000 mortgage and $40,000 auto loan that required monthly payments that could only be met if you both were working, how would you continue to meet those obligations if one of you passed away? What you could do for a small monthly payment is buy a $500,000 life insurance policy so that if one of you were to die the policy would provide the surviving partner income to either continue paying the monthly payments or pay off those debts entirely.

Why would employers buy life insurance? For many reasons, but there are two very common uses. One reason is for what we call *buy-sell agreements* in which there is a life policy in place on both partners of a business to buy out the other partner if one were to pass away. The business is usually valued at some amount, let's say $1 million. If your partner were to pass away, you probably wouldn't want their spouse running the business with you. The life insurance policy would allow you to buy out your partner's business interest and use that money to find a suitable replacement. Instead of having to pay $500,000 if they were a 50% owner out of your own pocket, you could fund the buyout with the proceeds you would receive from the life insurance you had on your partner. This death benefit in most cases is paid directly to the beneficiary such as a spouse who would automatically inherit their business interests. This would solve the problem of you having a new and unintended business partner.

The other business case is what is called a *key man policy*. If there is a key employee that the business is heavily dependent on, you could buy a life insurance policy that would provide funding to help buffer losing that specific employee. The death benefit that is received could help provide the funds necessary to replace that employee if they were to pass away. This is especially important for small businesses that many times are very vulnerable to losing an employee early on who may have a lot of intellectual knowledge that may have not yet been disseminated to other team members.

Another use for life insurance is when a lender wants to reduce their risk by requiring you to obtain a life insurance policy. This policy would be put in place to pay off a loan if you were to pass away and be unable to continue making the payments. This would typically be set up only during the period the loan is still under the repayment process.

Life insurance for the most part is a specified dollar amount and a tax-free benefit to the beneficiary, which makes it a great asset to meet the needs we just mentioned. The question is, should you have life insurance, and with all the different types of insurance out there, which is the right one for your situation?

Several types of life insurance exist, but they all really come down to two types you should know about: permanent and term life coverage. *Permanent coverage* is meant to be active until the day you die. *Term coverage* is meant to be active over a certain time, called the *term period*. The term period is typically anywhere between 10 and 30 years.

Permanent Life Insurance

Permanent insurance is called *whole life, universal life, indexed universal life,* and *variable universal life.*

Put simply, there are usually two components of your permanent life premium payment. The first is the insurance component, and the second is a subaccount that helps keep the policy in place "permanently." The subaccount either will be a fixed interest rate or it could be tied to some calculation around a financial index like the S&P 500 in the case of an indexed universal policy, or it could even be tied to specific stocks in the case of a variable life policy.

What is important to know is that these types of policies are usually much more expensive than term policies because they are set to cover you into your older ages when you would probably not be insurable and also because they are building cash value that you can later access. This means that if at some point you wanted to cancel the policy or access it for a loan, you could have some value inside the policy. It is because of this feature and big commissions that many insurance salesmen oversell permanent life insurance.

As a rule of thumb, I am going to tell you that unless you have already secured your financial future and have already maxed out your accounts like your Roth, IRA, 401(k), and so forth, 99% of the time permanent insurance does not make any sense for you. If you are already wealthy, then there are credible uses like estate tax planning, or looking at leveraging your transferable estate for your beneficiaries that are credible use cases for which I would endorse permanent insurance.

Most people reading this book are just not there yet, so I don't want to see you making the common mistake of buying permanent insurance at this stage. You are much better off buying term insurance and investing the savings in real investments and tax-favorable accounts like a Roth.

Term Life Insurance

Let's talk next about the only type of life insurance that I personally own, which is term life insurance. Term is going to give you the most bang for your buck and is going to do specifically what you need it to do for you in your financial life. Insurance in general is there to eliminate or minimize a risk that you cannot financially afford.

What I want you to do right now is think of a pair of nice shoes that you own. How much did you pay for them? Maybe it's some Manolo Blahniks or some designer sneakers? Whatever they are. How much did you pay? Let's say they are $1,000. Would you pay a monthly bill to insure them? No. Why not? The reason is that the dollar amount, while large, would not financially ruin you if they were damaged or stolen. What about if your car got stolen or your house burned down? Would that be worth insuring? Of course, because those types of losses could be catastrophic. I want you to insure the risks that you cannot afford to lose to insure yourself as cheaply as possible.

Term life insurance is the best way to do that. At my company Real Talk Insurance solutions, we run life quotes all the time for customers. It is significant how much you can save when you look at a term versus permanent policies. There are several sources online to run a quote, but for under $100 monthly I have seen young families secure their future with $1 million term polices compared to the thousands they would have spent on permanent policies.

Too many times I see young families buy permanent life policies with $100,000 or $200,000 death benefits, but the monthly cost is too high. They end up underinsuring themselves so that an insurance salesperson makes a nice commission. I have a big problem with that. For young healthy people, buy as big of a term policy to cover all their liabilities while it is cheap. For most term policies you can also convert this later to permanent coverage at the same rate you achieved when you were originally insured. This is important because if you become unhealthy and find you need to extend coverage, you will be able to qualify at that great rate you originally received. This is also called *insuring your insurability*.

The thing to understand about your insurable need is that as you get older, it will decrease. For example, if you take out a 30-year mortgage, in 30 years it's paid off. No need to insure it any longer than that. It's the same thing for the rest of your finances. As you age, not only do your bills decrease as you pay off the debt, but your asset will increase because you have been saving for all those years. When your house is paid off and kids are gone to college, there is really no need for the insurance any longer. Buying term insurance when you are young is smart because it helps protect you during the vulnerable time when a death could financially cripple your family. That in essence is what insurance is for.

When all else fails, remember this: buy term and invest the savings. Don't let yourself get "sold" on a permanent policy.

The Misinformation of Annuities

Like life insurance, there is a tremendous amount of misinformation floating around out there about annuities. I am not going to be able to provide you an in-depth education on annuities in this section, but I will hit on the minimum stuff you should know, giving you enough information to know what further research to do before purchasing an annuity.

What Is an Annuity?

First, what is an annuity? An *annuity* is an insurance contract between you and the insurance company in which you exchange a premium payment either as a lump-sum amount or series of payments in exchange for guaranteed income from the insurer at some point. The annuity can be a deferred annuity or an immediate annuity.

- A deferred annuity is where you will collect a payment at a future date. Usually, the longer you wait to collect, the higher the payment will be. For example, if you invest $100,000 today, the amount the insurance company will pay you until the day you die will be $550 monthly. If you were to wait 10 years to start collecting, that could be closer to $1,200 monthly.
- An immediate annuity is where after you make the premium payment, you begin receiving payments right away. An immediate annuity is established where the payment schedule can be made based on one person's life, or if you're married, it can also be set up to pay over two lives. When you choose one life, the payment is going to be a higher amount than when you choose two lives. This is because the insurance will guarantee that they pay out that amount until you die. If the payment is based on two lives, then those payments would have to be made for a longer period than on a single life. For example, if you put in $100,000 on a single life, you may receive $900 monthly for the rest of your life. If it that payment was based on two lives, it could be $650. The amount will be dependent on the life expectancy of each individual. The shorter the period of time the insurer has

to pay, then the higher the payment would be. Two lives would be longer than one life. Two young people would have a lower payment than two older people. This is because the amount of time the insurer needs to pay the younger people until they die is longer than older people based on average life expectancy.

Even the lottery system uses annuities. When you hear of people winning the lottery, there are always two options to collect your prize. One option is a lump sum, which is usually about half the amount of the prize money advertised, or the annuity in which you get the full amount, but it's paid out over a long period of time in installments. The lottery officials will do this by taking the amount of money, typically half of the advertised amount, and purchasing an annuity for the full prize amount. They are using an annuity to obtain that leverage to use a smaller amount now to pay more, which is the advertised amount over time.

If you ever win the lottery, I always recommend now that you are educated to collect the lump sum. For one reason, you can always buy your own annuity with a better payout, but the more important is that you will almost certainly get a higher payout by investing it properly.

The sad truth for most people who are not financially literate, though, is that the annuity is probably their best bet. You have probably heard the horror stories of the lottery winners going broke. If you are not prepared to receive that type of wealth, it will most likely end very poorly. The guaranteed payments associated with an annuity that you cannot outlive are a smart choice for people who cannot be trusted with that much money at once.

Types of Annuities

We said that there are both deferred and immediate annuities, but what other flavors are there, and what are the different features? There are various features and types of annuities. The most common are fixed annuities, indexed annuities, and variable annuities. For this book we will cover those three and talk about the most common features that I have seen used with the different annuities.

Fixed Annuities

A *fixed annuity* is the simplest of the three. It will usually pay you a guaranteed rate for a fixed period of time, just as a bond would, which we already learned about in Chapter 5.

For example, it may pay you 5% interest for four years. The interest is usually compounded. The difference and a nice feature with an annuity is that *all* annuities are tax deferred, meaning there is no tax paid until you take the money out. This is a good feature if you have already maxed out your other tax favorable accounts like IRAs and 401(k)s and don't need the money until you're 59½. If you take the money out prior to that, just like a retirement account; there will be a penalty. Unlike a bond, with an annuity there is typically a surrender charge imposed by the insurance company if you take the money out prior to the term period ending, which in our example would be four years. You will want to make sure you are prepared to hold the annuity the full term to avoid those charges.

So when and why would you use a fixed annuity? As mentioned, a fixed annuity should be used only if you have already maxed out your other retirement accounts and you can afford to have the money invested until you are of retirement age. If the answer is no to those two questions, then it's best to pass on a fixed annuity. If the answer is yes, then compare rates with A-rated or better carriers to find the most compelling offer and compare it against other investment options that are taxable to see what the better after-tax investment would be for you.

In general, the best time to look at fixed annuities are when interest rates are high and to avoid them when they are low.

Indexed Annuities

Indexed annuities are one of the most common annuities I have seen used incorrectly in personal financial planning. They can be a great tool but are most often oversold by insurance salesman disguised as "financial advisors" who think that indexed annuities can cure cancer. You know what they say, when the only tool you have in your tool belt is a hammer, everything looks like a nail!

So what is an indexed annuity? An *indexed annuity* is a fixed annuity that has a minimum guarantee to maintain its value. It cannot lose money. The way that you earn money is through some calculation based on a financial index like the S&P 500, which is the one most commonly used. It's important to note that you are *not* investing in the S&P 500; rather, you are receiving a fixed rate of interest based on what the index does.

The most common method and easiest one to understand is what is called a *point-to-point crediting method* with a cap. It works like this. If the S&P does 12%, you will receive a fixed interest rate base on that return until, let's say, 5% when it gets capped. You don't get anything after that. Conversely, if the S&P 500 drops 12%, you just get zero that year; you don't lose. Each year it does this and either credits zero or the rate you earned up to the cap.

The crediting is done once a year over the surrender period, which is usually 10 years. Now, I am going to hurt a lot of people's feelings. I believe that this is a horrible investment. If you have 10 years to wait, you are almost always better off investing directly in the index itself without the fees or surrender period associated with an indexed annuity. I won't debate the point here as I have done that with 100% success over my career, but I will also asterisk my statement by saying that for some, it could be a great investment with one caveat.

Indexed annuities these days have something called *income riders*. These income riders would normally provide you a much higher crediting amount, say 7% fixed annually, if that amount is used toward taking income at some future time. When you decide to take that income, it is a guaranteed stream of monthly income that you cannot outlive.

From someone who has worked for over two decades with people in retirement, I can tell you this with 100% confidence: people with guaranteed income in retirement have better retirements and actually have better financial performance in their other assets. Why? Spending your retirement worrying about the ups and downs of the economy and the stock market is a horrible fate. The stress isn't necessary, and it negatively impacts your health and most often causes you to make poor emotional investment decisions like selling at market lows. When your core expenses are paid every month by guaranteed sources that are not impacted by the economy or stock market, you feel better and make better investment decisions.

I suggest that for most people, especially if you find yourself a bit behind, having your core expenses guaranteed is a great way to retire. I would say that only if you are purchasing an indexed annuity with an income rider should you consider index annuities. Otherwise, I say avoid them.

Here is my rule if you consider an indexed annuity: look at your core expenses only (not vacations, etc.). Subtract your Social Security (a guaranteed payment) and any pensions (another guaranteed income amount) and only purchase an annuity in an amount that will provide income, not to exceed the deficit of what those provide in income against your expenses.

Example of an Indexed Annuity

Here is an example of Randy and Lucille.

Annual Core Expenses

- $85,000

Guaranteed Income Sources

- Randy and Lucille's combined Social Security is $41,000 annually.
- Lucille's teachers' pension is $31,000 annually.
- Total $41,000 + $31,000 = **$72,000 annually.**

Deficit

Total expenses $85,000
   minus
Total income $72,000
$13,000 in an annuity (max income that should be purchased)

The **$13,000** is what needs to be solved for. Annuity rates change, but they could get a quote to see, based on how long they can wait and what the income rider is paying, how much they would need to invest in an annuity to guarantee that amount. Say it was $150,000. Then that is the maximum amount I would recommend someone invest in an annuity. The rest of the expenses can be paid by other assets. Do not become overallocated to annuities. You will need your other assets to help keep up with inflation and provide liquidity.

We have an annuity calculator on our website (www .closeyourwealthgaptools.com) to see what the max amount of income you should consider covering with an annuity is.

Variable Annuities

Much of what I said about indexed annuities will apply to variable annuities with a couple exceptions. First, let's talk about the crediting method of variable annuities. Variable annuities are technically a security, so you are investing in securities created by the insurance company. Because of this, you also have the risk of losing principal because the investments are tied to stocks. Just like an index annuity, many people attach an income rider to these, and if those riders are more compelling than what is offered by an index annuity, I believe you should compare the two.

Variable annuities also have a tax-deferred feature, which means if you have maxed out all of your retirement options and still have money that you will not need until retirement, then they may be appropriate to consider. Variable annuities have evolved over the years. Many have several investment options like ETFs, low expenses, and no surrender fees. If you are considering a variable annuity, these are the three things to demand:

1. No surrender charges
2. Low fees
3. Multiple investment choices

And remember, *only* if you have maxed out all of your retirement options should these be considered.

Chapter 10
Developing a Wealth-Maximizing Mindset

Throughout the book, I provided you with a framework to understand your cash flow and determine whether you have a surplus or a deficit. I gave you some ideas to make your expenses leaner and quickly enhance your income. I showed you how to maximize your balance sheet and, when you do that, increase your net worth. We reviewed the assets you need in your portfolio and how you should apply them in your personal financial roadmap. We looked at ways to minimize risk, and we showed you ways that you can reduce your tax bill so that you keep more of your hard-earned money in your own pocket.

Now that we have taken care of those initial steps, in this final chapter of Part III we'll look at the bigger picture and, some would say, more qualitative things you need to do to exponentially grow cash flow and grow your wealth. What are some of the things that are not taught in economics courses or outlined in most books? These are the things that we are going to dive into now.

If you are trying to build wealth, the first thing you must do is transform your way of thinking into a wealth-maximizing mindset. My definition of a wealth-maximizing mindset is a way of thinking that maximizes every economic decision that you make in a manner the helps you achieve your goals in the fastest possible timeframe. This mindset asks, is there a better, smarter, or faster way to do things with every financial decision that you make going forward?

Developing this new wealth-maximizing mindset and retiring your current mindset is an essential component in the transformation that you must make to upgrade your life. Unless I can get you to upgrade your mindset, the rest of this information is just that, information. I need you to get to a point where this information is second nature and actionable and not just informative.

Part of acting is the inherent belief that your action will result in a positive outcome. Would you spend an hour on the treadmill in the morning if you believed it would have no positive impact on your health or appearance? I don't think you would really put yourself through that. Would you spend time and money learning how to invest and improve your finances if you thought the information would do nothing to improve your quality of life? These questions are obviously rhetorical.

To become wealthy, you must believe that becoming more financially literate and changing your mindset are two key components in achieving wealth. The great part is that I am living proof that it will do just that if you apply yourself. I have also helped and seen hundreds of others do the same thing as myself, so I know that it really works for normal people like us. The ultimate test though is whether you will believe it yourself.

Can you convince yourself that this new information will change your life? Are you willing to change what you have been doing and apply it to your daily life? Are you willing to go against the status quo that believes mediocrity is in your future?

To make it a little easier, I want to share with you some of the most common traits that people with a wealth-maximizing mindset share. During my 25 years of experience, I have created a list of some of the main factors that I have identified as being essential to building a wealth-maximizing mindset.

These are things that I have seen time and again that will lead to an increase in your net worth if you practice them consistently. We need to get you to making the wealth-maximizing decisions in life intuitively without having to think too hard about it.

What I am sharing with you are things that I have been able to do, things I have helped clients do, and things I have learned from several years of working with some of the world's most successful and wealthy people that truly work. If you can master these things, you will have the mindset you need to take the information you have already learned and the rest of the information that I will give you and execute so that you can change your life for the better.

- Believe and invest in yourself.
- Ditch the safety of a paycheck.
- Stop looking for that one investment to make you rich.
- Build relationships.
- Fall in love with passive income.
- Have extreme focus and clarity.
- Be accountable to someone or something.

Believe and Invest in Yourself

For most people, it is easier to sell products or services to other people than it is for them to sell themselves. Most people find it easier to sell the benefits of something or someone else whom they have greater faith in than themselves. I too had this same problem as a young wealth advisor. I always sold other people's research, our firm's capabilities, or I used news articles as third-party validation of a point that I was trying to make because I didn't believe I had the credibility to influence people with my just own opinion.

The problem is, by doing this, you will never be able to build your own credibility with yourself or in the eyes of others. Without credibility you will never achieve your highest income potential no matter what you do or sell. You must invest in yourself. I am an alumnus of four different universities, earned several designations, spoke on numerous stages, and appeared in over a thousand television broadcasts. Each time I did one of those things, it was to convince my toughest critic that I was worthy—myself.

Once I was able to believe in myself, believe that I had become the expert, and watched how the information I provided changed people's lives, my earnings skyrocketed to a new level. When you invest in yourself, that is the benefit. Investing in yourself eventually leads to believing in yourself and when you believe in yourself you have much greater outcomes. People want to do business with confident experts. Investing and believing in yourself is the first step in achieving the wealth-maximizing mindset.

Unless you can sell you to yourself, nobody else is going to buy you either. Self-deprecation is not a winning strategy. One of the best marketing and sales tools you can ever master is the confidence that you exude when you talk about the value you can deliver as an employee, consultant, or business owner. People want to invest in, employ, follow, and do business with people who believe they are the best. People who second guess themselves and don't believe they deserve to be in the room will always get left behind. This is an important economic lesson, because all throughout your life if you need to earn, you need to be able to sell yourself. You have probably heard that you need to believe in what you are doing or selling. This is why. If you don't believe, nobody else will either.

The hardest person to sell is yourself. That is because you cannot hide whether you believe in yourself or your product. It's very hard for us to lie to ourselves and that shows through to others. It's time to get excited about you and what you have to offer. When you can do that, you are making a serious wealth maximizing decision. Remember, in your quest for financial freedom, the number-one area we should be focusing on is exponential growth of our income. We cannot cost cut our way to wealth. So, we must start investing in and believing in ourselves.

Ditch the Safety of a Steady Paycheck

To upgrade your life, we need to first work on upgrading your income. Unfortunately, I have never seen anyone 9-to-5 their way to wealth, so you must ditch the idea of the status quo and the comfort of an hourly wage. For most of my career working with very wealthy people, I have seen them build their wealth in one of three ways.

- They were senior executives who worked for companies that they received stock options in (ownership).
- They were entrepreneurs who sold their business or generated extreme cash flow that they continually invested.
- They were professional athletes that signed major contracts.

Well, for most people the professional-athlete path is out of the question, so that really leaves us with two legitimate choices. Either obtain equity in another company (intrapreneurs) or build equity in your own company (entrepreneurs). The sooner you choose one of these paths the better.

I have never seen anybody whose income was squarely within the national average achieve financial freedom. Hourly employees live hourly lives. This is the day and age of the entrepreneur and the intrapreneur. Websites like Fiverr and Upwork allow you to freelance jobs anywhere across the world now. Most companies are now also looking to hire people who are comfortable being uncomfortable, can problem solve, and can quickly adapt to the ever-changing needs of their consumers. This is exactly what being an entrepreneur is all about: organized chaos and loving it.

You are probably already familiar with the types of entrepreneurs who start, develop, and run their own businesses from scratch. Intrapreneurs are bit different but have a lot of the same characteristics and opportunities. Intrapreneurs are people with an entrepreneurial mindset and work ethic that use their skillset to help build something within a larger organization earning equity along the way. They are compensated by ways such as commissions, bonuses, and equity, which means they are paid for performance. This differs from a salary capped position. High performers always prefer this arrangement over a salary cap because they are willing to bet on themselves.

The sooner you can start building equity in a company you are part of or one that you have built yourself, the sooner you will begin building wealth. Truthfully, there is no right or wrong answer on whether entrepreneur or intrapreneur is the right choice. It depends on you. If you have the experience, education, and willingness to lead and build a team toward a scalable business, then go for it. Many people find that they can better leverage their talents by plugging themselves into an already well-oiled machine, though. I have seen both paths work equally well.

You just need to do a good self-assessment to determine which path is right for you and then don't look back. A lot also comes down to timing. Do you have an original idea for which the timing is right and there is no viable alternative? Are you being approached by the next Amazon to become an early employee? All of this must be considered. What I am sure of though is that plugging into an assembly line type of position with no future for advancement is not what is going to get you where you want to be. Leveraging your ability to earn equity, uncapped compensation, incentives, and so forth are all the types of things you must identify to maximize your income potential.

Stop Looking for That One Investment to Make You Rich

Have you ever lost more money than you care to mention on a bad investment? Did you ever overleverage yourself on something that you thought would change your life but ended in failure? Wealthy people didn't get to where they are there from buying one piece of real estate or from one hot stock tip they received.

Wealth comes from the power of compounding over time. Wealth does not come from making one great investment but from making multiple solid investments over a lifetime. Wealth comes from time in the market, not timing the market, meaning that you are never going to pick the best time to buy or sell but being invested over long periods of time works out well.

Timing is just about impossible to do. The good news is that you don't have to. By being in the market and consistently making investments over long periods of time, you will capture both the highs and lows, which all average out allowing you to buy right in the middle over time.

This strategy is called *dollar cost averaging*, and it works great if you follow it. Nobody, I repeat *nobody,* is smart enough to time things perfectly over time. I would give up trying to learn how to time things yourself or the notion that there is somebody out there who can do it for you. Both quests usually lead to lost time and lost money, not to wealth building.

After all these years of financial education and experience at the highest levels of wealth management, I have learned that the adage "if it sounds too good to be true than it probably is" still works well. Greed blinds people to the amount of risk they are taking sometimes. Promises of high returns should be carefully evaluated and not salivated over.

There are of course exceptions to every rule, but my rule to my clients has been that anything over 10% a year should raise a red flag for you to at least dive a little deeper into how these returns are being achieved. I cannot tell you how many people I have saved from various types of scams over the years by staying true to that rule.

Follow your instincts, and don't be blinded by fast-talking salespeople by promises of grandeur. Instead of looking for than one perfect investment, start making several good investments consistently over time. Singles and doubles consistently give you a much better average than occasionally hitting a home run.

Build Mutually Rewarding Relationships

Most investment books will never talk about the value of relationships because it is not an easy mathematical equation to quantify in your earnings trajectory. I can personally tell you, though, that everything good and bad that has happened in my life is because of a relationship.

I work with a lot of entrepreneurs who start new businesses. A lot of these businesses are based on great ideas that come with great solutions, great processes, and what appears to be the ability to execute on scale. After all, these principles are what most good businesses are usually based on. The old inexperienced me made a lot of early investments in businesses that sounded good on paper, but never were able to execute in the real world. I spent countless hours trying to figure out what went wrong.

As I grew older and looked at my own businesses, and what had transpired, I realized that unless you have the right relationships to open doors, do favors for you, and put you in the right company, it may be very hard to succeed. I think this is a fact that unfortunately most people never understand. We have heard it's not what you know but who you know. I say it's both what and who that create wealth. You simply can't have one without the other.

I told you everything good that's happened in my life has come from relationships. That's the truth. Unless there were people who were able to put me in front of other people to buy my product or service, help me cut costs, find the right employee, or arrange meetings that took us to the next level, I wouldn't have had a quarter of the success I had in my life.

A friend of mine, Josh Altman, is on a popular show called *Million Dollar Listing*. Josh has been one of the most successful realtors in the world for the past several years. Although Josh is an intelligent guy, he himself will tell you that his single greatest value is the relationships that he has. Josh has invested more time, money, effort, and energy in building relationships than just about anybody else I've ever known. I've personally spoken to some of Josh's biggest clients. They jokingly say he might not be the most analytical person out there, but they know that they can always count on him. Whenever they pick up the phone or whatever they

need, they know that Josh will get it taken care of. This type
of investment that Josh has made in his clients has earned
him a tremendous amount of loyalty, and it plays the largest
role in his financial success today.

So please understand that the right relationships will make or
break you. Most people will tell you that you are the average of
your five closest relationships. Look around you. If you average
out the five closest relationships that you currently have, does the
average point to somewhere that you want to be in life? Are those
people there now or at least on a trajectory to get to where you want
to be? If not, you have some work to do about exchanging those
relationships.

It may seem harsh, but if you are around people with a broken mindset who come from a position of scarcity and excuses, it
will be very difficult for you to continue to grow. People who are
constantly doubting you or discouraging your growth but have not
grown themselves are detrimental to your future. If you find yourself surrounded by people who don't support where you are going
and are more about your past, it might be time to politely exit stage
left and upgrade your circle so that you can upgrade your life. If you
continue to keep yourself inside of a crowd that is not growing and
improving, it is going to make your journey to the top much harder.

There is a saying that it's hard to soar like an eagle when you are
flying with turkeys. Ditch the turkeys and start looking for a flock
that you can soar with.

Maximize Your Passive Income

Wealthy people love passive income. I love passive income, and once
you get started creating it, you too will become obsessed with passive
income. Passive income means money hitting your bank account
each month without you having to work for it. Passive income can
come from many sources: royalties, licensing agreements, stocks,

dividends, bond yields, passive business ownership, real estate income, and so forth. Whatever it is, passive income is the best type of income there is.

Passive income is really what we're all aspiring to have. Imagine the day where the amount of passive income that hits your account each month is more than enough to pay all your bills. Yes, meaning that you no longer must work for the money you earn. When you reach the point where you have more money coming in from your investments than you need, it's a glorious thing. The wealthy realize that every dollar that they invest in their income-generating bucket 2 gives them more income that continues to come in.

When you understand what passive income does for you, you start to look at the world a little differently. You start to look at frivolous expenses as taking away from having more income hitting your bank account. When you opt to spend on something that is not wealth generating and you realize that is putting you further from your goals, that purchase takes on greater meaning. You start to ask is it really worth it? Am I going to receive more joy or utility from this purchase than I would from taking that same money and putting it into an investment that generates income?

I would say that the single greatest thing that comes from passive income, and really the primary reason that we're all investing, is the financial freedom that we are able to achieve from it. I have been asked many times what the greatest thing about wealth accumulation is, and my response is always the same: choice. When you no longer do things because you must earn a dollar and you do them simply because you want to do them, that's a big paradigm shift for most people in their lives and it becomes very addictive. I bet you are probably in a situation today where you do work, meet with people, say yes to things, and so forth that you really don't want to do. You know that if you don't do those things however, that in some shape or form it will probably impact your ability to earn and care for yourself and for your family. That is the feeling that I am trying to eliminate with this book. It's a horrible feeling that I would like to remove for the world.

The more passive income I can help you generate, the faster we will get to removing that burden from your life. Passive income and all this information you are digesting to increase your financial literacy and build a wealth-maximizing mindset really takes on a much bigger fight. Remember when I told you this information just isn't about what stock bond or what piece of real estate to buy? It's not just numbers and symbols you need to learn but also how you need to look and live your life in order to maximize your choice in life.

Have Extreme Focus and Clarity

Unless they won the lottery, wealthy people did not become wealthy by chance. More than likely from a very early time in their life, they realized the power of focus and clarity in achieving their goals. They realized and respected the value of their time, and they understood that chasing the shiny ball or losing sight of what they were trying to accomplish would only take them further away from what they were working to accomplish.

Building wealth is not a single event; it's a process that one must start as early as possible. This is why financial literacy is important to closing your wealth gap. The longer it takes for someone to become informed, the harder it will be for them to break out of their current situation. You must achieve extreme focus and clarity immediately.

Some people confuse focus for clarity and vice versa. They are different though. First, you need a strong focus on what activity you are going to build wealth from. The question that you need to ask yourself is at this point today, what value do you possess or could you obtain that will allow you to deliver a product or service to a marketplace that will provide greater value and have a more positive impact on people than a viable current alternative? This is your personal wealth value proposition. We have said time and again that growing your income is going to be the number-one key in your ability to build wealth.

We said that there are many ways that you can increase your income. We talked about being an intrapreneur or an entrepreneur. We talked about working for a larger organization where you're able to obtain equity. There are lots of ways to do this, but it starts with your personal value proposition. It truly can be anything. I've seen people make huge amounts of money in just about every occupation, service, or product that you can imagine. What it is really is not extremely important.

The important part is the level of excellence that you deliver. What are you going to be able to deliver that impacts people's lives in a more positive way than a current alternative? You could think of this as an employee within an organization. This could be a product that you're creating or a service that you're developing. Whatever it is, it must dominate. Unless you're able to do that you're going to have a very hard time reaching success.

So the first thing you need to do is have a clear focus. That focus right now might be going into the medical field for example. Maybe you're 18 years old and you're thinking what's the best way to spend my time in college. Having a focus to leave in eight years with a medical degree is a very good focus. The clarity needs to be what specifically am I doing on a day-to-day basis to make sure I achieve this degree within a given timeframe.

Now once you leave, there are going to be several alternatives for you that might develop greater clarity. You might want to start a private practice in which you take your eight years of education, experience, and so forth and start to parlay this into a scalable business. Perhaps your focus might be in construction as a luxury contractor. The clarity might be to focus on homes $5 million and above within a certain zip code. Whatever it is, you need to have a serious focus and clarity on being the best in your space. You want to be dominant and go into it with that mindset to win. Nothing less.

Whenever somebody thinks about whatever it is you decide to do, you want yourself, and/or your company to be the number-one name that pops to mind. When you think about sneakers, you probably think Nike. When you think fast food, I am sure McDonald's comes to mind. Shipping something? FedEx. New cell phone? Apple. This is the type of dominance that you need to strive for.

The wealthy look to dominate market share and the dominant mind share, and ultimately they end up dominating wallet share. They have extreme clarity and focus on winning at what they do. They are specialists and experts. They are not generalists who accept mediocrity.

Achieving perfection and expertise takes serious time for most occupations. I would say it's usually at least 8 to 10 years in most fields. I always say never hire an investment advisor with less than 10 years' experience. They have not made enough mistakes yet. Let them make those mistakes with their own and other people's money before your trust them with yours. The time it takes to achieve expertise is real. This is why it's so important to pick one thing as soon as possible. It doesn't matter so much as what it is, but it's about dialing into that one thing and taking all your efforts, time, and energy to become the best at it. People who pop in and out from career to career, job to job, very rarely achieve wealth. Just pick that one thing and become a rockstar at it.

Greatness Comes from Accountability and Execution

The closer you get to rockstar status, the more you are going to appreciate this rule, but I caution you not to wait that long. The sooner you begin to implement this into your life, the better off you will be.

Tim Grover, who wrote the best-selling books *Relentless and Winning*, is somebody I admire and respect. Every time I have met with Tim, I have been impressed by his passion, his commitment, and his no nonsense way of telling people exactly where they stand and what it will take for them to become the best versions of themselves.

For most, Tim will probably tell you that greatness is not in the cards, not because they don't have the opportunity but because most people will not push themselves, make the necessary sacrifices, or develop the mindset it takes to achieve greatness. For the greats, though, they realize that this rule is what takes you from great to legendary. The difference in the two I believe is that legends become legends due to their prolonged and consistent periods of greatness. There are a lot of greats out there. There are people, deceased or living, who are or who were great at what they did but didn't become legends either. I have not achieved enough in my own life yet to single those people out but I am sure you can think of a few.

You can also think of people who are and will be legends. Tom Brady, LeBron James, and Floyd Mayweather immediately come to mind. Steve Jobs was a business legend. John McCain was a political and war hero legend. Tim knows about legends. He worked with both Michael Jordan and Kobe Bryant. Both legends.

If Kobe and Jordan were so great, then why did they hire Tim? My belief is because they were focused on becoming legends. They had each reached the pinnacle of their respective careers and metaphorically became the smartest people in the room. When you're the smartest person in the room, it's very hard to find people to tell you the things that you need to hear. Most will tell you what you want to hear. They will reassure you of your greatness and validate the work you have already done. They will not tell you your weaknesses and where you can improve. They will validate what you have already accomplished but not discuss all the work that still lies ahead. They will not hold you accountable to become the absolute best version of yourself.

Accountability is what creates legends. Accountability is what will bring out the best version of you. Accountability is exactly why Kobe and MJ hired Tim. Without accountability, goals and plans are nothing more than dreams. For your goals and plans, for your vison and mission to become reality, you must execute. No matter how motivated you think you are, you will never be able to hold yourself to your highest level of accountability.

I am somebody who has been working out regularly since I was 12 years old. I have competed at the highest levels in various sports. I have had 7% body fat, six-pack abs, and everything else we all seek. However, as most of you who train regularly know, the abs come and go. Consistency is the hardest part. Anyone can train and diet to a six-pack, but can you maintain it for years?

From time to time, I hire a personal trainer to get me back on track. When I have the right trainer, it's life-changing. The truth is, I usually know as much or more than most trainers when it comes to diet and nutrition, but their pushing me and holding me accountable to the mirror and the scale each week makes a huge difference in my progress. Why? Because without their accountability I may do one less rep, 10 minutes less of cardio, and in general not push myself to my limits. When I pay for advice and must answer to somebody else for my own goals, I never fail.

My advice is find a mentor, coach, consultant, or someone who you know has executed at the highest levels that will create a consistent level accountability for you. It's the same reason I have had some smart multimillionaires and billionaires hire me for financial guidance. I have even had trained economists and other financial experts as clients. Not because they were incompetent or unable to manage their own investments but because they knew when it came to their own finances and portfolio, they would not implement the same level of rigor and discipline they would for somebody else. They would typically take shortcuts and abandon most risk principles that they use for others.

I promise you, paying for high-quality accountability will be one of the best investments you make, hands down.

Part IV

A Financial Case Study

Chapter 11
Building Your Own Action Plan

In managing money for more 25 years, I have realized that although we all think of ourselves as having unique needs, most of us just want to accomplish the same things, which are making work optional, supporting our families and charities that we care about, protecting ourselves from unforeseen events, keeping more of what we earn, and leaving a financial legacy for the next generations to continue to improve on.

We want our money to work hard for us, and nobody I have ever met wants to go backward financially. All those things can be accomplished by making the right financial decisions early and consistently. I hope, by this point in the book, you have begun to build the confidence and skillset to begin to make the wealth-maximizing decisions on your own.

If you still have questions or are feeling a bit unsure, though, that is normal; you are not alone. This is a lot of information to learn. Managing your financial future is not like trying to learn to assemble a nightstand from Ikea. The rewards for putting the pieces of your financial life together are far greater, though. Mastering this information is going to put you so much further ahead of an average person and help you for a lifetime, so continue to use this book and the resources I am providing you to get your financial house in order and progressing.

As you identify what you are improving your finances for, remember to keep things in perspective. We said that everyone's idea of financial success or what is "enough" money is going to be largely dependent on their individual preferences and lifestyle. What may be luxurious for you may be just standard fare for someone else's lifestyle. I have learned from two decades of working with very wealthy people that no two scenarios are the same. I am characterizing these people as being "wealthy" solely based on their net worth. It has nothing to do with the cars they drive, the homes they own, vacations that they take, or the clothes that they wear. For each one of them, it is all very different. Some drove Ferraris, and some had Ford pickup trucks. Those types of personal choices can be said across the board for everything that they did or owned. "Wealth" is very individual.

You must decide for yourself what is important to you and what your own definition of wealth is. I would caution this, though. In today's day of social media influencers where everyone looks like they are a billionaire, it is easy to get caught up in chasing what it looks like you must have to be successful. That is a dangerous game that is almost certain to keep you broke. There will always be someone richer, faster, smarter, better looking, stronger, and so on. The most important competition that you should maintain is the competition against your optimal self. What is important is that you continually compete against yourself to maximize your highest potential. Do not settle for anything less.

Meet Jackson and Maria

To illustrate for you how this information all works together in an action plan that you can implement, I created a case study of a fictitious couple: Jackson and Maria. We first are introduced to Jackson and learn what he begins doing correctly early in his financial life. He then marries Maria; they have children, and together as a family, they consistently implement all the information that you have learned in this book.

In this book I talk a lot about beating mediocrity and shooting for the stars. That is because I learned a long time ago that your greatest barrier to achieving more is your mindset and knowledge. I know that armed with the right mindset and this information, the number of zeros that can be attached to your net worth is honestly unlimited. I truly believe that. Entrepreneurship, creating or earning equity, and bigger-picture thinking is what I have seen really create "generational wealth."

What I also wanted to show you, though, is just how very powerful the financial information you have learned in this book really is, even if you do nothing super extraordinary.

I created Jackson and Maria to show you a real-world example of how it all comes together. You will see that, in our case study, both Jackson and Maria make good but not amazing salaries. What they do is start young and consistently make what we have been referring to as the "wealth-maximizing decisions" every step of the way. By doing this alone, I think you will be very surprised, as you go through their lives, the amount of wealth they are able to create by just being consistent and having a plan they execute.

Although this is a fictitious case, I built this study based on real-life situations of ordinary people who I have worked with over the years to implement these lessons and achieve real wealth. If Jackson and Maria can do it, there is no reason you cannot. I want this to be the minimum bar for you, especially if you are young.

If you want to see the power of what we said about what being an entrepreneur or earning equity as an entrepreneur can do, I also have created a couple of case studies you can access on our website (www.closeyourwealthgaptools.com) to see what those financial journeys look like. Talk about wealth!

You will have to decide the right path for you, but staying stagnant is not one of the options. We have calculators on the site that will help you specially determine where you are at today and a path to get to where you want to be. Make sure you are using these tools to dial in your own path after learning about Jackson and Maria.

A Qualified Second Opinion

The truth is that I cannot fully supplement a personalized financial plan here in the book, and this is not an attempt to do that with our case study, but it is information that has been consistent with what I have advised for various clients in these situations and information that I have seen work well in the real world. I tried to keep it simple and to the basics that I believe you should be able to do on your own. I am not going to get into individual stock picking, sophisticated strategies, or obscure investments that you could of course pursue on your own if you desire.

I want to just give you the meat and potatoes that I think will serve you well even if it's all you ever do financially. I want this information to be reliable and keep you from guessing or listening to bad financial advice when it comes to managing your personal financial life. This is all very well crafted, vetted, and time-tested information I am confident will get you started off on the right foot.

In our case study of Jackson and Maria, I used a variety of exchange-traded funds (ETFs) that I have used in the past simply to illustrate how you can invest in an easy and inexpensive way that accomplishes your goals.

This is not a specific recommendation to implement yourself; it's simply an example what a portfolio could look like. In reality, I use multiple asset classes as the portfolio grows, and I recommend as your portfolio grows that you seek some professional guidance if you do not have experience in selecting investments on your own.

I would at minimum advise that, after you craft your plan and before you begin to execute on it for the first time, you get a second opinion from a certified financial planner that you could pay for an hour or two of time just to make sure you are on the right track. If you don't have a financial planner, you can go to letsmakeaplan .org, which is the certified financial planner's (CFP's) free tool for investors to locate a qualified advisor in your area. At my firm Real Talk Capital (www.realtalkcapital.com), you can also get advice from a CFP for as little as $500 per year. Don't shortcut it. You will already have saved a lot of time and money by putting it together yourself. Pay a little extra for the personal advice.

Selecting a Custodian

When you begin to invest, you are also going to need a custodian to start making your investments. The custodian is where all your accounts will be set up and your assets will be located. You will make your buys and sells here and collect all your income inside these accounts. You will be provided with online access and receive all your regular tax reporting here. Most of the custodians will provide you now with a decent level of free information on investing, reports on different stocks, and real-time quotes for no cost. Many will even provide you with tools to help manage your accounts and employ strategies to help with taxes such as tax loss harvesting that we discussed in the book.

Your custodian will be able to establish both your qualified accounts like a Roth IRA and your regular taxable accounts. There are many options out there to set up your accounts. I am going to be honest and say that I am not a fan of investing at the big banks for a multitude of reasons that I won't cover here, even though it may seem convenient. "Convenience" is not always the wealth-maximizing decision, though. I am going to provide a list of custodians that I feel could all be a good place to go for self-directed investors. If you are already working with or plan to work with a financial planner, they will also have options of custodians that they work with who are more than likely good but just might not be available to retail investors.

I would love to provide you with more choices, but unfortunately, there is a lot of consolidation in the custodial space, so there are becoming fewer options of where you can open your accounts. For example, TD Ameritrade used to be a great option and one of the largest independent custodians out there, but they were recently acquired by Charles Schwab, so that was one of the larger custodians that I had to remove from my list. I am sure this trend of consolidation will continue, but for now, the following are a few well established names that I feel comfortable recommending:

- Charles Schwab (www.charlesschwab.com)
- Fidelity (www.fidelity.com)
- Interactive Brokers (www.interactivebrokers.com)

> When you open your account, I strongly recommend that you do one thing. We talked about dollar cost averaging and all the benefits associated. Whatever account you set up, make sure that you are setting it up to be funded automatically each month. This is something easy to do and makes it much more likely that you stay on your financial roadmap. I don't care if it's only $25 a month. You should start with whatever you can afford and increase it as your income grows.

Your Plan for Success

It's almost time to meet our power couple. In the following chapters, you will see what they are doing right and the steps you can take if you find yourself behind. At the end of our case study, in Chapter 19, I will also provide you with a quick-reference executive summary that you can quickly check against where you stand today and actions that you need to take to get on track.

Before we begin our case study, I am going to teach you one final secret that you can add to the 20X work-optional rule, which you learned earlier in Chapter 6. This time, instead of determining what you need to live today's lifestyle, let's stop for a second and understand what your "ideal" lifestyle will cost you. You can go back to your expense worksheet and, instead of logging in what you are spending today, look at those same categories and price in what you will be spending with your ideal lifestyle. For example, maybe your mortgage today is $2,200 a month on a $300,000 home. If you want a $1 million home, that would jump to about $7,000 a month. If your vacation budget is $1,500 a year, but in reality you would want it to be $10,000 per year, then price that in. I think you get the point.

Just update those new expenses and then multiply that number by 20. That will give you the exact dollar amount that you need to reach. If you are already living your dream lifestyle, then no problem, you are already there with the standard 20X calculation that you have completed. Alternatively, if you believe that your expenses may actually be less once you stop working because maybe you are downsizing a house, the kids are coming off of your payroll, or you plan to move to a less expensive state or country, then you can do the exact same thing, but you will simply reduce those expenses. Take those reduced expenses and multiply those by 20, and you'll get your number for your plan to success.

Chapter 12
Start Young: What to Do Ages 0–18

I started this book illustrating the challenge our nation faces because of the expanding wealth gap between the ultra-wealthy and everyone else. I attribute a large part of the wealth gap to the lack of understanding of basic financial planning principles. The best way I see to fix the wealth gap is to learn what the wealthy are doing and follow along when appropriate. Some of you reading this book might think "it's too late for me." I disagree. Getting started now is better than dwelling on being behind.

I firmly believe that aside from bettering our own individual lives, the best way to address the wealth gap is by increasing the financial literacy of our children. Just like it's never too late to get started, it is never too early to begin.

We must educate our children about money. My philosophy is that people don't accumulate money for the sake of having a lot of it, but rather people want money because of what it will allow them to do for them and their family. You may disagree with my philosophy, but one thing certain is that money is important in our society. So let's teach our children the basic financial principles you learned in this book.

Children need to know that money does not grow on trees and that parents work hard to earn a wage or salary. I would encourage you to speak to your kids about what you do for a living and how you make money. You should also include them on basic decisions that involve money. For example, if you are planning a family trip, look at a few alternatives and then have your kids help you calculate how many hours you will have to work in order to earn enough money to pay for the vacation. Having kids set up a lemonade stand, sell Girl Scout cookies, or even setting up an online store is a great way to teach children about money and entrepreneurship.

Don't forget to talk to your kids about debt, especially credit cards. Let them know that using a credit card is not free money and that it will have to be repaid with interest. Get them to understand when you buy something using debt, you are essentially pulling forward future earnings because you will have to take future dollars to pay for today's purchase.

Opening a custodial account for the benefit of the child is also a great way to help kids get ahead financially and also to educate them on how the stock market works. Purchase a few shares of stock that they would recognize like Disney or Roblox and take the time to teach them that they are owners of the company. Connect the dots for them and explain that, as people visit Disneyland or spend money on Roblox, this increases the revenue of the company, and it benefits them as part owners.

A 529 College Savings Plan is a great way to save for a child's education. I talked about the benefits in Chapter 8, so I won't get into the details here. One idea to increase the value of these accounts is to tell family and friends that your child has a 529 Plan and for their birthday, rather than get a lot of toys, you would appreciate a contribution to their account. If you have young children, then only have a few people donate to this account or it won't sit well with the child!

Another great way to generate funds for this account is to take old toys and break them into two piles. One pile is to donate, and the other is to sell on an online store. This will teach the child to give to others while also learning about business. Plus, now you have money to deposit into their education account.

If you own a business and your child is old enough, you could put them on payroll and use the earned income to fund a Roth IRA. This technique is more complicated than the others, so make sure you speak with your CPA to guide you through the process.

The goal is to get kids to feel comfortable with money and understand how it works. Don't be afraid to speak to your child about money. You will be surprised how quickly they pick things up.

Chapter 13

Welcome to Adulthood: What to Do Ages 18–24

Welcome to adulthood! Meet Jackson. Jackson is an 18-year-old man who just graduated from Kennedy High and is getting ready to start college this fall at UCLA. He is not sure what his major will be, but he enjoys learning about businesses, so he is leaning toward a bachelor's degree in business administration.

The summer before starting college, Jackson signed up for an online course and learned the basic principles of financial planning. He went through a calculator that was provided to him and it showed him that if he wanted to accumulate $1,000,000 at age 60, he would need to invest $1,859.99 annually, assuming a 10% return per year. Therefore, Jackson opened a Roth IRA and decided he would work part-time in order to be able to invest $1,859.99 per year. His living expenses, tuition, and room and board will be paid by taking on student loans. Jackson was given an estimate that he would have to take on $60,000 in loans over the four years. Figure 13.1 summarizes Jackson's financial situation.

Balance Sheet	
Assets	**Amount**
Liquid	
Checking Account	$ 1,000.00
Savings Account	$ 800.00
Emergency Account	$ –
Investment Accounts	$ –
Retirement Accounts (i.e. 401(k), Roth)	$ –
Illiquid	$ –
Home	$ –
Private Business	$ –
Automobiles	$ –
Total Assets	**$ 1,800.00**
Liabilities	**Amount**
Mortgage Balance	$ –
Credit Card Debt	$ –
Automobile Loan	$ –
Student Loans	$ (15,000.00)
Total Liabilities	**$(15,000.00)**

Net Worth Statement	
Total Assets	**$ 1,800.00**
Total Liabilities	**$ (15,000.00)**
Net Worth	**$ (13,200.00)**

Cashflow Statement	
Inflow	**Amount**
Annual Salary	$ 15,000.00
Student Loan	$ 15,000.00
Total Inflow	**$ 30,000.00**
Outflow	**Amount**
Savings	$ (1,859.99)
Living Expenses—Needs*	$ (28,140.01)
Living Expenses—Wants	$ –
Total Outflow	**$(30,000.00)**
Surplus/Deficit	**$ (0.00)**

*Includes taxes and cost of college

Figure 13.1 Jackson's current investment dashboard.

What He Is Doing Right

Here are the areas in which Jackson is staying on track:

Emergency Account: Jackson is focused on getting through college, so he has not begun to think about establishing an emergency account.

Life Insurance: Jackson does not have a life insurance policy. At the moment, nobody relies on his income and therefore he does not have an insurable need. As I've mentioned in this book, I believe life insurance is important when someone has an insurable need. However, if nobody's lifestyle will be adversely affected if Jackson were to pass away, then he does not need life insurance.

Proper Saving/Investment Rate: Jackson just opened his Roth IRA and will be depositing the $1,859.99 by year's end.

Roth IRA			
Age	Starting Value	Savings Amount	Ending Value
18	$ –	$1,859.99	$ 1,859.99

Debt Management: Jackson does not have any debt except for the $15,000 student loan that was provided to him for his freshman year.

Where He Should Be Investing

Jackson is a young man and has the capacity to allocate his portfolio in an aggressive manner. He won't need to touch the money in the accounts for 30-plus years, so he should be investing more heavily in stocks. In his Roth IRA, Jackson has the flexibility to invest in individual stocks, bonds, ETFs, and mutual funds. ETFs are a great way to get asset class exposure at a very inexpensive cost.

Jackson will be investing in our aggressive bucket asset allocation. Here is the breakdown of how he will be investing:

Aggressive	
Stocks	100.00%
Bonds	0.00%
Category	**Weight**
Bucket | 1	**0.00%**
IGSB	0.00%
IGIB	0.00%
SCHO	0.00%
VTIP	0.00%
BND	0.00%
Bucket | 2	**30.00%**
AMLP	2.10%
PFF	2.10%
HYG	2.10%
VNQ	2.10%
NOBL	16.50%
VIGI	5.10%
Bucket | 3	**70.00%**
VONE	35.00%
VO	14.00%
VIOO	7.00%
MTUM	7.00%
VWO	7.00%
Total	**100.00%**

Bucket 1: Jackson does not have exposure to this bucket because he plans to hold his emergency funds in an outside account. I display bucket 1 so that you can see the type of bond ETFs we would use if someone required this bucket.

Bucket 2: This bucket has a mandate to produce income and we have included several ETFs to diversify our income source. Here is a breakdown of the asset exposure in this bucket:

- Alerian MLP (Ticker AMLP) provides exposure to master limited partnerships which focus on natural resource-related activities, including oil, gas, coal, timber, and certain ways of transporting commodities.
- iShares Preferred & Income Securities (Ticker PFF) gives us access to preferred stock of mostly financial institutions like

Bank of America, Citigroup, JPMorgan Chase, and many other big commercial banks.

- iBoxx $ High Yield Corporate Bond (Ticker HYG) offers coverage to high-yield bonds of major corporations. This asset class provides higher yields than purchasing investment grade corporate bonds.
- Vanguard Real Estate (Ticker VNQ) provides broad-based real estate exposure including residential, industrial and health care properties.
- ProShares S&P 500 Dividend Aristocrats (Ticker NOBL) gives us access to the biggest corporations in America that have consistently paid and increased their dividend for a minimum of 25 years.
- Vanguard International Dividend Appreciation (Ticker VIGI) offers coverage to large companies outside of the United States that have a strong record of growing dividends year over year.

Bucket 3: The objective for this bucket is long term growth and we have provided access to several asset classes that meet this criterion.

- Vanguard Russell 1000 (Ticker VONE) gives exposure to the largest 1,000 corporations in the U.S.
- Vanguard Mid-Cap (Ticker VO) offers coverage to midsize companies in the United States.
- Vanguard S&P Small-Cap 600 (Ticker VIOO) gives access to the smallest 2% size corporations in the United States.
- iShares MSCI USA Momentum Factor (Ticker MTUM) invest in large and midsize companies that have trending stocks that are outperforming their peers.
- Vanguard FTSE Emerging Markets (Ticker VWO) invest in large, midsize, and small companies located in emerging markets around the world.

What You Should Do If You Are Behind

Jackson is just getting started, so you really should not be too far behind. If you don't have a source of income to save $1,859.99 annually, then you should start to think about what you can do to earn a minimum $35.77 per week. That will allow you to save the annual target of $1,859.99.

Chapter 14

The Ramp-Up Years: What to Do Ages 24–30

Jackson is now 24 years old and has been in the workforce for two years. He started out as a business administration major, but after his sophomore year, he decided he wanted to become an engineer and switched majors. Jackson was able to work part time while in college and he was able to hit his annual investment goal of $1,859.99.

Jackson underestimated his living needs in college and ended up taking $70,000 of student loans; he also signed up for a credit card his junior year and accumulated a balance of $10,000 by the time he graduated, but now he only owes $7,000. When he started as an engineer his annual salary was $40,000, and today he gets paid $44,100. Jackson's employer offered a 401(k) and he began to contribute 5% of his salary and his employer contributes an additional 4% of his annual pay.

Jackson now has a checking account with $2,000, a savings account with $3,000 and an emergency account with $15,000. He took out a car loan with a current balance of $20,000. His current monthly expenses are $2,830.11, which includes his student loan payment of $805 and his car payment of $375. Jackson is now thinking about purchasing a home and has calculated that he needs

$24,000 for the down payment and closing cost. His new goal is to save that amount in the next four years. Figure 14.1 summarizes Jackson's financial situation.

Balance Sheet	
Assets	**Amount**
Liquid	
Checking Account	$ 2,000.00
Savings Account	$ 3,000.00
Emergency Account	$ 15,000.00
Investment Accounts	$ –
Retirement Accounts (i.e. 401(k), Roth)	$ 22,090.97
Illiquid	$ –
Home	$ –
Private Business	$ –
Automobiles	$ 20,000.00
Total Assets	**$ 62,090.97**
Liabilities	**Amount**
Mortgage Balance	$ –
Credit Card Debt	$ (7,000.00)
Automobile Loan	$ (20,000.00)
Student Loans	$ (59,519.61)
Total Liabilities	**$ (86,519.61)**

Net Worth Statement	
Total Assets	**$ 62,090.97**
Total Liabilities	**$ (86,519.61)**
Net Worth	**$ (24,428.64)**

Cashflow Statement	
Inflow	**Amount**
Annual Salary	$ 44,100.00
Other	$ –
Total Inflow	**$ 44,100.00**
Outflow	**Amount**
Savings	$ (4,064.99)
Living Expenses—Needs*	$ (40,035.01)
Living Expenses—Wants	$ –
Total Outflow	**$ (44,100.00)**
Surplus/Deficit	**$ –**
*Includes taxes	

Figure 14.1   Current investment dashboard.

The Ramp-Up Years: What to Do Ages 24–30   171

What He Is Doing Right

Here are the areas where Jackson is staying on track:

Emergency Account: Jackson's monthly expenses are $2,830.11, which means he should have a minimum of three times that amount in his emergency account for a total of $8,490.33. If he wanted to maintain six months of living expenses in this account, he would need a total of $16,980.66. Right now, he has $15,000 in the emergency account, which is just under six months of living expense. Jackson has the right amount in his emergency account.

Life Insurance: Jackson still does not have an insurable need, so he should not own a life insurance policy.

Proper Saving/Investment Rate: Jackson has now been investing $1,859.99 per year into his Roth IRA and he has averaged a rate of return of 10%. Here is how he currently stands:

Roth IRA Age	Starting Value	Savings Amount	Ending Value
18	$ –	$1,859.99	$ 1,859.99
19	$ 1,859.99	$1,859.99	$ 3,905.98
20	$ 3,905.98	$1,859.99	$ 6,156.57
21	$ 6,156.57	$1,859.99	$ 8,632.22
22	$ 8,632.22	$1,859.99	$ 11,355.43
23	$ 11,355.43	$1,859.99	$ 14,350.97

Jackson has also been investing in his company 401(k) account and saving 5% of his salary while his employer matches an additional 4%. He has also been able to accumulate a 10% rate of return. Here is how things are going in this account:

401(k) Age	Salary	Starting Value	Savings Amount	Ending Value
18	$ –	$ –	$ –	$ –
19	$ –	$ –	$ –	$ –
20	$ –	$ –	$ –	$ –
21	$ –	$ –	$ –	$ –
22	$ 40,000	$ –	$ 3,600.00	$ 3,600.00
23	$ 42,000	$ 3,600.00	$ 3,780.00	$ 7,740.00

Debt Management: When Jackson graduated from college, he took on more loans than he had anticipated, and he also accumulated some credit card debt. Jackson has been paying a little over $805 per month to his student loans, which has him on a path to pay it off 10 years after graduating. He has been making payments for two years and has brought the balance down from $70,000 to $59,519.61. Jackson still has credit card debt of $7,000 and he needs to focus on paying that down soon. Credit cards carry very high interest rates and therefore the balance should be paid down as quickly as possible.

Home Purchase Goal: Jackson said he wanted to save $24,000 for a home down payment and closing cost. Here is how Jackson determined that amount. He figures that he can buy a home with a value of $400,000 and put down 5.0%. That means he needs $20,000 for the down payment. He estimates closing cost would be about $4,000. Jackson would have to save $5,651.76 for the next four years at an annual interest rate of 4.0% to accumulate $24,000 in four years. Below is the path to accomplish his goal:

Current Home Savings	$ –		
Rate of Return	4.0%		
Current Age	24		
Target Age	28		
Account Value Goal at Target Age	$ 24,000		
Annual Savings Needed	($5,651.76)		

Home Savings Account			
Age	Starting Value	Savings Amount	Ending Value
24	$ –	$5,651.76	$ 5,651.76
25	$ 5,651.76	$5,651.76	$ 11,529.59
26	$ 11,529.59	$5,651.76	$ 17,642.54
27	$ 17,642.54	$5,651.76	$ 24,000.00
28	$ 24,000.00		

Where He Should Be Investing

In his Roth IRA Jackson continues with his original aggressive bucket allocation of 100% stocks and 0% bonds. Jackson is still very young, and his aggressive allocation is fine.

Aggressive	
Stocks	100.00%
Bonds	0.00%
Category	**Weight**
Bucket | 1	**0.00%**
IGSB	0.00%
IGIB	0.00%
SCHO	0.00%
VTIP	0.00%
BND	0.00%
Bucket | 2	**30.00%**
AMLP	2.10%
PFF	2.10%
HYG	2.10%
VNQ	2.10%
NOBL	16.50%
VIGI	5.10%
Bucket | 3	**70.00%**
VONE	35.00%
VO	14.00%
VIOO	7.00%
MTUM	7.00%
VWO	7.00%
Total	**100.00%**

In his 401(k) he could make his asset allocation choice simple by electing to invest in a target date fund that aligns with a date when he will turn 60 years old. These funds will have roughly 95–100% invested in stocks and 5–0% invested in bonds. As his retirement date approaches, the fund will automatically move away from stocks and invest more in bonds.

What You Should Do If You Are Behind

Jackson is on a path to accumulate $1,000,000 in his Roth IRA and now is even doing better by contributing to his employer 401(k) plan. If you did not get started at age 18 like Jackson, and you are 24 today, you are not that far behind. I would encourage you to open a Roth IRA today and begin investing. Time is of the essence to benefit from the power of compounding.

I've created the following roadmap for you to follow to get to $1,000,000 by the time you are 60. What you will notice is that you will have to save $3,343.06 annually instead of $1,859.99. That is because you got started six years after Jackson. If you wait another year to get started, the annual amount you will have to invest would be $3,689.71! So get started now.

Current Account Value	$ –		
Rate of Return	10.0%		
Current Age	24		
Target Age	60		
Account Value Goal at Target Age	$ 1,000,000		
Annual Savings Needed	($3,343.06)		

| | Roth IRA | | |
Age	Starting Value	Savings Amount	Ending Value
24	$ –	$3,343.06	$ 3,343.06
25	$ 3,343.06	$3,343.06	$ 7,020.43
26	$ 7,020.43	$3,343.06	$ 11,065.54
27	$ 11,065.54	$3,343.06	$ 15,515.16
28	$ 15,515.16	$3,343.06	$ 20,409.74
29	$ 20,409.74	$3,343.06	$ 25,793.78
30	$ 25,793.78	$3,343.06	$ 31,716.22
31	$ 31,716.22	$3,343.06	$ 38,230.90
32	$ 38,230.90	$3,343.06	$ 45,397.06
33	$ 45,397.06	$3,343.06	$ 53,279.83
34	$ 53,279.83	$3,343.06	$ 61,950.87
35	$ 61,950.87	$3,343.06	$ 71,489.03
36	$ 71,489.03	$3,343.06	$ 81,980.99
37	$ 81,980.99	$3,343.06	$ 93,522.15
38	$ 93,522.15	$3,343.06	$ 106,217.43
39	$ 106,217.43	$3,343.06	$ 120,182.24
40	$ 120,182.24	$3,343.06	$ 135,543.53
41	$ 135,543.53	$3,343.06	$ 152,440.95
42	$ 152,440.95	$3,343.06	$ 171,028.10
43	$ 171,028.10	$3,343.06	$ 191,473.98
44	$ 191,473.98	$3,343.06	$ 213,964.44
45	$ 213,964.44	$3,343.06	$ 238,703.95
46	$ 238,703.95	$3,343.06	$ 265,917.41
47	$ 265,917.41	$3,343.06	$ 295,852.21
48	$ 295,852.21	$3,343.06	$ 328,780.50
49	$ 328,780.50	$3,343.06	$ 365,001.61
50	$ 365,001.61	$3,343.06	$ 404,844.83
51	$ 404,844.83	$3,343.06	$ 448,672.38
52	$ 448,672.38	$3,343.06	$ 496,882.68
53	$ 496,882.68	$3,343.06	$ 549,914.02
54	$ 549,914.02	$3,343.06	$ 608,248.48
55	$ 608,248.48	$3,343.06	$ 672,416.39
56	$ 672,416.39	$3,343.06	$ 743,001.10
57	$ 743,001.10	$3,343.06	$ 820,644.27
58	$ 820,644.27	$3,343.06	$ 906,051.76
59	$ 906,051.76	$3,343.06	$ 1,000,000.00

Chapter 15
Learn and Earn: What to Do Ages 30–40

Jackson is now 34 years old and a lot has changed in the past decade. Jackson is doing really well in his career and continues to get annual pay increases of 5%. Jackson continues to make 401(k) contribution of 5% of his annual pay. His company continued to match 4% of his total income. Jackson continued to fund his Roth IRA with $1,859.99 per year. Jackson was able to save the $24,000 for the home down payment and closing cost. When he bought the house, it was worth $400,000 and now it has a value of $536,038.

A few years ago, a woman by the name of Maria started working at the same company as Jackson. They both worked very closely and developed a relationship. Three years ago, they married and now have two children: Andrew, who is two years old, and Pedro, who is six months old.

Maria stayed at home a few months after childbirth and then returned to work. Maria is 38 years old, and her annual salary is $74,218. Maria is contributing 5% of her total take-home pay to her 401(k) account and the employer matches 4%. When Maria was 20 years old, she opened a Roth IRA and contributed $1,000 year.

Balance Sheet	
Assets	**Amount**
Liquid	
Checking Account	$ 8,000.00
Savings Account	$ 15,000.00
Emergency Account	$ 56,000.00
Investment Accounts	$ –
Retirement Accounts (i.e. 401(k), Roth)	$ 356,750.96
Illiquid	$ –
Home	$ 536,038.00
Private Business	$ –
Automobiles	$ –
Total Assets	**$ 971,788.96**
Liabilities	**Amount**
Mortgage Balance	$ (347,312.22)
Credit Card Debt	$ –
Automobile Loan	$ –
Student Loans	$ (5,000.00)
Total Liabilities	**$ (352,312.22)**

Net Worth Statement	
Total Assets	**$ 971,788.96**
Total Liabilities	**$ (352,312.22)**
Net Worth	**$ 619,476.74**

Cashflow Statement	
Inflow	**Amount**
Annual Salary—Jackson	$ 71,834.25
Annual Salary—Maria	$ 74,217.74
Total Inflow	**$ 146,051.99**
Outflow	**Amount**
Savings	$ (10,162.59)
Living Expenses—Needs*	$ (135,889.40)
Living Expenses—Wants	$ –
Total Outflow	**$ (146,051.99)**
Surplus/Deficit	**$ –**
*Includes taxes	

Figure 15.1 Current investment dashboard.

Jackson and Maria have $8,000 in their checking account, $15,000 in their savings account and $56,000 in their emergency account. Their monthly expenses are $9,259.70, which includes their car-lease payments of $800 and the mortgage.

Jackson paid off his student loans and Maria has $5,000 of student debt, but they plan to pay it off this year. When each child was born, they opened a 529 College Plan with the intention of funding 50% of the expected cost. Figure 15.1 summarizes Jackson and Maria's financial situation.

What They Are Doing Right

Here are the areas where they are staying on track:

Emergency Account: Jackson and Maria have monthly expenses of $9,259.70. Right now, they have $56,000 in the emergency account, which is six months of living expenses. Jackson and Maria have an adequate emergency account balance.

Life Insurance: Jackson and Maria have two children, and they don't have life insurance. They both have an insurable need because they have minor children. As I've mentioned, term insurance is suitable to protect their children financially should either Jackson or Maria pass away prematurely. In this case, we will assume that both Jackson and Maria want to protect their after-tax income until age 60 for Jackson and age 64 for Maria, which is when they expect to retire. Jackson would need to purchase a $1.1 million term life insurance policy. If he were to pass away today, Maria would invest the proceeds and begin to distribute what Jackson would have made in income after tax.

Here is an illustration of how this would work:

Inputs		
Annual Income for Jackson		$ 71,834.25
Marginal Federal & State Tax Rate		20%
Years Until Retirement		26
Net Portfolio Return		8.0%
Life Insurance Needs		
Simple Rule of Thumb Method 10x Current Income		$ 718,342.53
Income Replacement Method		$1,101,899.36

Year	After-Tax Income	Start Portfolio Value	End Portfolio Value
0	$ 57,467.40	$ 1,101,899.36	$ 1,127,986.51
1	$ 60,340.77	$ 1,127,986.51	$ 1,153,057.40
2	$ 63,357.81	$ 1,153,057.40	$ 1,176,875.56
3	$ 66,525.70	$ 1,176,875.56	$ 1,199,177.84
4	$ 69,851.99	$ 1,199,177.84	$ 1,219,671.93
5	$ 73,344.59	$ 1,219,671.93	$ 1,238,033.53
6	$ 77,011.82	$ 1,238,033.53	$ 1,253,903.45
7	$ 80,862.41	$ 1,253,903.45	$ 1,266,884.33
8	$ 84,905.53	$ 1,266,884.33	$ 1,276,537.10
9	$ 89,150.80	$ 1,276,537.10	$ 1,282,377.20
10	$ 93,608.34	$ 1,282,377.20	$ 1,283,870.37
11	$ 98,288.76	$ 1,283,870.37	$ 1,280,428.14
12	$ 103,203.20	$ 1,280,428.14	$ 1,271,402.93
13	$ 108,363.36	$ 1,271,402.93	$ 1,256,082.74
14	$ 113,781.53	$ 1,256,082.74	$ 1,233,685.31
15	$ 119,470.60	$ 1,233,685.31	$ 1,203,351.89
16	$ 125,444.13	$ 1,203,351.89	$ 1,164,140.38
17	$ 131,716.34	$ 1,164,140.38	$ 1,115,017.96
18	$ 138,302.16	$ 1,115,017.96	$ 1,054,853.07
19	$ 145,217.26	$ 1,054,853.07	$ 982,406.67
20	$ 152,478.13	$ 982,406.67	$ 896,322.83
21	$ 160,102.03	$ 896,322.83	$ 795,118.46
22	$ 168,107.14	$ 795,118.46	$ 677,172.23
23	$ 176,512.49	$ 677,172.23	$ 540,712.51
24	$ 185,338.12	$ 540,712.51	$ 383,804.35
25	$ 194,605.02	$ 383,804.35	$ 204,335.27
26	$ 204,335.27	$ 204,335.27	$ (0.00)

Maria would need to be insured for about $1.1 million. If Maria were to pass away today, Jackson would take the life insurance proceeds, invest them, and begin to take distributions in the amount of Maria's after-tax income.

Here is an illustration of how this would happen:

Inputs		
Annual Income for Maria		$ 74,217.74
Marginal Federal & State Tax Rate		20%
Years Until Retirement		26
Net Portfolio Return		8.0%
Life Insurance Needs		
Simple Rule of Thumb Method 10x Current Income		$ 742,177.36
Income Replacement Method		$1,067,450.47
Year	After Tax Income	Start Portfolio Value	End Portfolio Value
0	$ 59,374.19	$ 1,067,450.47	$ 1,088,722.38
1	$ 62,342.90	$ 1,088,722.38	$ 1,108,489.84
2	$ 65,460.04	$ 1,108,489.84	$ 1,126,472.18
3	$ 68,733.05	$ 1,126,472.18	$ 1,142,358.27
4	$ 72,169.70	$ 1,142,358.27	$ 1,155,803.65
5	$ 75,778.18	$ 1,155,803.65	$ 1,166,427.51
6	$ 79,567.09	$ 1,166,427.51	$ 1,173,809.25
7	$ 83,545.45	$ 1,173,809.25	$ 1,177,484.91
8	$ 87,722.72	$ 1,177,484.91	$ 1,176,943.17
9	$ 92,108.85	$ 1,176,943.17	$ 1,171,621.06
10	$ 96,714.30	$ 1,171,621.06	$ 1,160,899.30
11	$ 101,550.01	$ 1,160,899.30	$ 1,144,097.23
12	$ 106,627.51	$ 1,144,097.23	$ 1,120,467.30
13	$ 111,958.89	$ 1,120,467.30	$ 1,089,189.08
14	$ 117,556.83	$ 1,089,189.08	$ 1,049,362.83
15	$ 123,434.67	$ 1,049,362.83	$ 1,000,002.41
16	$ 129,606.41	$ 1,000,002.41	$ 940,027.68
17	$ 136,086.73	$ 940,027.68	$ 868,256.22
18	$ 142,891.06	$ 868,256.22	$ 783,394.37
19	$ 150,035.62	$ 783,394.37	$ 684,027.46
20	$ 157,537.40	$ 684,027.46	$ 568,609.26
21	$ 165,414.27	$ 568,609.26	$ 435,450.59
22	$ 96,870.30	$ 435,450.59	$ 365,666.71
23	$ 99,049.88	$ 365,666.71	$ 287,946.17
24	$ 101,278.51	$ 287,946.17	$ 201,601.08
25	$ 103,557.27	$ 201,601.08	$ 105,887.31
26	$ 105,887.31	$ 105,887.31	$ 0.00

Proper Saving/Investment Rate: Jackson has continued to invest $1,859.99 per year into his Roth IRA and his annualized rate of return is 10%. The following illustration shows you how his Roth IRA has grown over the years.

Roth IRA			
Age	Starting Value	Savings Amount	Ending Value
18	$ –	$1,859.99	$ 1,859.99
19	$ 1,859.99	$1,859.99	$ 3,905.98
20	$ 3,905.98	$1,859.99	$ 6,156.57
21	$ 6,156.57	$1,859.99	$ 8,632.22
22	$ 8,632.22	$1,859.99	$ 11,355.43
23	$ 11,355.43	$1,859.99	$ 14,350.97
24	$ 14,350.97	$1,859.99	$ 17,646.05
25	$ 17,646.05	$1,859.99	$ 21,270.65
26	$ 21,270.65	$1,859.99	$ 25,257.71
27	$ 25,257.71	$1,859.99	$ 29,643.47
28	$ 29,643.47	$1,859.99	$ 34,467.81
29	$ 34,467.81	$1,859.99	$ 39,774.58
30	$ 39,774.58	$1,859.99	$ 45,612.03
31	$ 45,612.03	$1,859.99	$ 52,033.22
32	$ 52,033.22	$1,859.99	$ 59,096.53
33	$ 59,096.53	$1,859.99	$ 66,866.18

His 401(k) account is growing quickly because he is contributing 5% of his income and his employer has continued to match 4% annually. The following is an illustration of how his 401(k) account has grown.

401(k)				
Age	Salary	Starting Value	Savings Amount	Ending Value
18	$ –	$ –	$ –	$ –
19	$ –	$ –	$ –	$ –
20	$ –	$ –	$ –	$ –
21	$ –	$ –	$ –	$ –
22	$ 40,000	$ –	$ 3,600.00	$ 3,600.00
23	$ 42,000	$ 3,600.00	$ 3,780.00	$ 7,740.00
24	$ 44,100	$ 7,740.00	$ 3,969.00	$ 12,483.00
25	$ 46,305	$ 12,483.00	$ 4,167.45	$ 17,898.75
26	$ 48,620	$ 17,898.75	$ 4,375.82	$ 24,064.45
27	$ 51,051	$ 24,064.45	$ 4,594.61	$ 31,065.51
28	$ 53,604	$ 31,065.51	$ 4,824.34	$ 38,996.40
29	$ 56,284	$ 38,996.40	$ 5,065.56	$ 47,961.60
30	$ 59,098	$ 47,961.60	$ 5,318.84	$ 58,076.60
31	$ 62,053	$ 58,076.60	$ 5,584.78	$ 69,469.04
32	$ 65,156	$ 69,469.04	$ 5,864.02	$ 82,279.97
33	$ 68,414	$ 82,279.97	$ 6,157.22	$ 96,665.19

Maria has a Roth IRA and has been making $1,000 contributions since she was 20 years old. Here is how her account is growing:

Roth IRA Age	Starting Value	Savings Amount	Ending Value
20	$ –	$1,000.00	$ 1,000.00
21	$ 1,000.00	$1,000.00	$ 2,100.00
22	$ 2,100.00	$1,000.00	$ 3,310.00
23	$ 3,310.00	$1,000.00	$ 4,641.00
24	$ 4,641.00	$1,000.00	$ 6,105.10
25	$ 6,105.10	$1,000.00	$ 7,715.61
26	$ 7,715.61	$1,000.00	$ 9,487.17
27	$ 9,487.17	$1,000.00	$ 11,435.89
28	$ 11,435.89	$1,000.00	$ 13,579.48
29	$ 13,579.48	$1,000.00	$ 15,937.42
30	$ 15,937.42	$1,000.00	$ 18,531.17
31	$ 18,531.17	$1,000.00	$ 21,384.28
32	$ 21,384.28	$1,000.00	$ 24,522.71
33	$ 24,522.71	$1,000.00	$ 27,974.98
34	$ 27,974.98	$1,000.00	$ 31,772.48
35	$ 31,772.48	$1,000.00	$ 35,949.73
36	$ 35,949.73	$1,000.00	$ 40,544.70
37	$ 40,544.70	$1,000.00	$ 45,599.17

Maria's 401(k) account is growing because she consistently contributes 5% of her salary and her employer matches another 4%.

401(k) Age	Salary	Starting Value	Savings Amount	Ending Value
20	$ –	$ –	$ –	$ –
21	$ –	$ –	$ –	$ –
22	$ 34,000	$ –	$ 3,060.00	$ 3,060.00
23	$ 35,700	$ 3,060.00	$ 3,213.00	$ 6,579.00
24	$ 37,485	$ 6,579.00	$ 3,373.65	$ 10,610.55
25	$ 39,359	$ 10,610.55	$ 3,542.33	$ 15,213.94
26	$ 41,327	$ 15,213.94	$ 3,719.45	$ 20,454.78
27	$ 43,394	$ 20,454.78	$ 3,905.42	$ 26,405.68
28	$ 45,563	$ 26,405.68	$ 4,100.69	$ 33,146.94
29	$ 47,841	$ 33,146.94	$ 4,305.73	$ 40,767.36
30	$ 50,233	$ 40,767.36	$ 4,521.01	$ 49,365.11
31	$ 52,745	$ 49,365.11	$ 4,747.06	$ 59,048.69
32	$ 55,382	$ 59,048.69	$ 4,984.42	$ 69,937.97
33	$ 58,152	$ 69,937.97	$ 5,233.64	$ 82,165.41
34	$ 61,059	$ 82,165.41	$ 5,495.32	$ 95,877.27
35	$ 64,112	$ 95,877.27	$ 5,770.09	$ 111,235.08
36	$ 67,318	$ 111,235.08	$ 6,058.59	$ 128,417.18
37	$ 70,684	$ 128,417.18	$ 6,361.52	$ 147,620.42

College Savings: Maria and Jackson have been investing in their children's 529 Plan since they were born. Their goal is to pay for 50% of the total cost, which includes tuition, room and board, and books. They would like their children to attend UCLA.

As of 2023, it would cost about $129,876 to pay 100% of Andrew's college costs, and in 18 years that cost would be $286,828 assuming a 4.5% inflation rate. Since Maria and Jackson want to pay only 50% of that cost, their target account value when Andrew is 18 would be $143,414. If they invest $4,218.18 annually in the 529 Plan at a 7.0% rate of return, they will hit their target.

The following shows how this would play out.

Andrew		
529 Plan Account Value	$	–
Rate of Return	7.0%	
Current Age	0	
Target Age	18	
Full Cost of College Today	$	129,876
Inflation Rate	4.5%	
Full Cost of College in the Future	$	286,828
Parents Will Cover College Cost	50%	
Account Value Goal at Target Age	$	143,414
Annual Savings Needed	($4,218.18)	
Monthly Savings Needed	($351.52)	

College Investment Account			
Age	Starting Value	Savings Amount	Ending Value
0	$ –	$4,218.18	$ 4,218.18
1	$ 4,218.18	$4,218.18	$ 8,731.64
2	$ 8,731.64	$4,218.18	$ 13,561.04
3	$ 13,561.04	$4,218.18	$ 18,728.50
4	$ 18,728.50	$4,218.18	$ 24,257.68
5	$ 24,257.68	$4,218.18	$ 30,173.90
6	$ 30,173.90	$4,218.18	$ 36,504.26
7	$ 36,504.26	$4,218.18	$ 43,277.74
8	$ 43,277.74	$4,218.18	$ 50,525.37
9	$ 50,525.37	$4,218.18	$ 58,280.33
10	$ 58,280.33	$4,218.18	$ 66,578.14
11	$ 66,578.14	$4,218.18	$ 75,456.79
12	$ 75,456.79	$4,218.18	$ 84,956.95
13	$ 84,956.95	$4,218.18	$ 95,122.12
14	$ 95,122.12	$4,218.18	$ 105,998.85
15	$ 105,998.85	$4,218.18	$ 117,636.96
16	$ 117,636.96	$4,218.18	$ 130,089.73
17	$ 130,089.73	$4,218.18	$ 143,414.19
18	$ 143,414.19		

Where They Should Be Investing

In their Roth IRAs, both Maria and Jackson continue to invest aggressively. They both have 100% invested in stocks.

AGGRESSIVE	
Stocks	100.00%
Bonds	0.00%
CATEGORY	WEIGHT
BUCKET | 1	0.00%
Igsb	0.00%
Igib	0.00%
Scho	0.00%
Vtip	0.00%
Bnd	0.00%
BUCKET | 2	30.00%
Amlp	2.10%
Pff	2.10%
Hyg	2.10%
Vnq	2.10%
Nobl	16.50%
Vigi	5.10%
BUCKET | 3	70.00%
Vone	35.00%
Vo	14.00%
Vioo	7.00%
Mtum	7.00%
Vwo	7.00%
TOTAL	100.00%

In their 401(k) accounts, both Maria and Jackson hold a target date fund that aligns with their retirement age of 60 for Jackson and 64 for Maria. Their 401(k) plan allows them to invest in an aggressive target date fund that has a 95% allocation to stocks and 5% to bonds.

What You Should Do If You Are Behind

Jackson has put his Roth IRA on autopilot and is on track to hit his $1,000,000 target by the time he is 60 years old. Now, he is doing even better because his target of $1,000,000 does not consider his 401(k) account! When you include Maria's assets, they are both doing very well as a household. I understand that not everyone will be in the position that Jackson and Maria find themselves. That is why I'm going to show you what you can do if you are 34 years old and find yourself behind. There are thousands of different scenarios, but I'll show you two.

- The first one will assume you have not saved anything, and you intend to accumulate $1,000,000 by the time you are 60 years of age.
- In the second scenario, I will illustrate your path to the same target, but you are 50% behind from where your account value should be today.

In the first scenario in which you have not saved anything, you will need to invest $9,159.04 per year at a rate of return of 10% in order to get to $1,000,000 by the time you are 60 years old. In this scenario, you can invest $6,500 into a Roth IRA, and the remaining amount can be invested into your 401(k) account. If you don't have a 401(k) account, then open a taxable brokerage account and invest it there. You'll have to utilize some of the tax-minimization strategies I showed you in this book in order to diminish the impact of taxes.

Behind by	100%		
Current Account Value	$ –		
Rate of Return	10.0%		
Current Age	34		
Target Age	60		
Account Value Goal at Target Age	$ 1,000,000		
Annual Savings Needed	($9,159.04)		

Age	Starting Value	Savings Amount	Ending Value
34	$ –	$9,159.04	$ 9,159.04
35	$ 9,159.04	$9,159.04	$ 19,233.98
36	$ 19,233.98	$9,159.04	$ 30,316.42
37	$ 30,316.42	$9,159.04	$ 42,507.10
38	$ 42,507.10	$9,159.04	$ 55,916.85
39	$ 55,916.85	$9,159.04	$ 70,667.57
40	$ 70,667.57	$9,159.04	$ 86,893.37
41	$ 86,893.37	$9,159.04	$ 104,741.74
42	$ 104,741.74	$9,159.04	$ 124,374.95
43	$ 124,374.95	$9,159.04	$ 145,971.49
44	$ 145,971.49	$9,159.04	$ 169,727.67
45	$ 169,727.67	$9,159.04	$ 195,859.48
46	$ 195,859.48	$9,159.04	$ 224,604.47
47	$ 224,604.47	$9,159.04	$ 256,223.95
48	$ 256,223.95	$9,159.04	$ 291,005.39
49	$ 291,005.39	$9,159.04	$ 329,264.96
50	$ 329,264.96	$9,159.04	$ 371,350.50
51	$ 371,350.50	$9,159.04	$ 417,644.59
52	$ 417,644.59	$9,159.04	$ 468,568.08
53	$ 468,568.08	$9,159.04	$ 524,583.93
54	$ 524,583.93	$9,159.04	$ 586,201.36
55	$ 586,201.36	$9,159.04	$ 653,980.54
56	$ 653,980.54	$9,159.04	$ 728,537.63
57	$ 728,537.63	$9,159.04	$ 810,550.43
58	$ 810,550.43	$9,159.04	$ 900,764.51
59	$ 900,764.51	$9,159.04	$ 1,000,000.00

In scenario 2, I assumed that you have been investing, but your account value is not where it should be to be on track. In this case, your account value is 50% of where it should be, which means you need to invest $5,509.51 annually at a 10% rate of return in order to get to $1,000,000 by the time you are 60 years old.

Behind by	50%		
Current Account Value	$ 33,433.09		
Rate of Return	10.0%		
Current Age	34		
Target Age	60		
Account Value Goal at Target Age	$ 1,000,000		
Annual Savings Needed	($5,509.51)		

Age	Starting Value	Savings Amount	Ending Value
34	$ 33,433.09	$5,509.51	$ 42,285.91
35	$ 42,285.91	$5,509.51	$ 52,024.02
36	$ 52,024.02	$5,509.51	$ 62,735.93
37	$ 62,735.93	$5,509.51	$ 74,519.04
38	$ 74,519.04	$5,509.51	$ 87,480.46
39	$ 87,480.46	$5,509.51	$ 101,738.02
40	$ 101,738.02	$5,509.51	$ 117,421.34
41	$ 117,421.34	$5,509.51	$ 134,672.99
42	$ 134,672.99	$5,509.51	$ 153,649.80
43	$ 153,649.80	$5,509.51	$ 174,524.30
44	$ 174,524.30	$5,509.51	$ 197,486.24
45	$ 197,486.24	$5,509.51	$ 222,744.38
46	$ 222,744.38	$5,509.51	$ 250,528.33
47	$ 250,528.33	$5,509.51	$ 281,090.68
48	$ 281,090.68	$5,509.51	$ 314,709.26
49	$ 314,709.26	$5,509.51	$ 351,689.71
50	$ 351,689.71	$5,509.51	$ 392,368.19
51	$ 392,368.19	$5,509.51	$ 437,114.53
52	$ 437,114.53	$5,509.51	$ 486,335.49
53	$ 486,335.49	$5,509.51	$ 540,478.56
54	$ 540,478.56	$5,509.51	$ 600,035.93
55	$ 600,035.93	$5,509.51	$ 665,549.03
56	$ 665,549.03	$5,509.51	$ 737,613.45
57	$ 737,613.45	$5,509.51	$ 816,884.31
58	$ 816,884.31	$5,509.51	$ 904,082.26
59	$ 904,082.26	$5,509.51	$ 1,000,000.00

If you are behind and cannot invest what's needed to catch up, then do what you can. Remember my rule of thumb that you should be investing 10% of your gross income. The key is to get started and not to get paralyzed. You can do this!

Chapter 16
Full Speed Ahead: What to Do Ages 40–50

Adecade has gone by, and now Jackson is 44 and Maria is 48. Their son Andrew is 12 years old, and their son Pedro is 10½ years old. The family has continued in their path, and things have developed just as they had anticipated.

Jackson is now making $117,010 in total annual compensation and Maria is making $120,893 per year. Both Maria and Jackson continue to put away 5% of their income into the company 401(k) plan and their employer still matches 4%. Jackson continues to fund his Roth IRA with $1,859.99 per year and Maria is still contributing $1,000 to her Roth IRA.

Four years ago, they opened a joint brokerage account and began investing $5,000 annually. They continue to live in the home Jackson purchased and it is now worth $873,150; they thought of upgrading to another home but decided to remodel their current home instead. Both Andrew and Pedro attend public school and their parents continue to fund their 529 Plan.

In terms of assets, Maria and Jackson have $12,000 in their checking account, $30,000 in their savings account and $78,500 in their emergency account. Their monthly expenses are $13,084.35, which includes their mortgage and car payments of $900. Figure 16.1

Balance Sheet	
Assets	**Amount**
Liquid	
Checking Account	$ 12,000.00
Savings Account	$ 30,000.00
Emergency Account	$ 78,500.00
Investment Accounts	$ 23,205.00
Retirement Accounts (i.e. 401(k), Roth)	$ 1,224,553.30
Illiquid	$ –
Home	$ 873,150.00
Private Business	$ –
Automobiles	$ –
Total Assets	**$ 2,241,408.30**
Liabilities	**Amount**
Mortgage Balance	$ (258,533.72)
Credit Card Debt	$ –
Automobile Loan	$ –
Student Loans	$ –
Total Liabilities	**$ (258,533.72)**

Net Worth Statement	
Total Assets	**$ 2,241,408.30**
Total Liabilities	**$ (258,533.72)**
Net Worth	**$ 1,982,874.59**

Cashflow Statement	
Inflow	**Amount**
Annual Salary—Jackson	$ 117,010.43
Annual Salary—Maria	$ 120,892.87
Total Inflow	**$ 237,903.30**
Outflow	**Amount**
Savings	$ (28,191.52)
Living Expenses—Needs*	$ (150,000.00)
Living Expenses—Wants	$ (59,711.79)
Total Outflow	**$ (237,903.31)**
Surplus/Deficit	**$ (0.00)**
*Includes taxes	

Figure 16.1   Current investment dashboard.

summarizes the family's current financial dashboard and updated account values.

What They Are Doing Right

Here are the areas where Jackson is staying on track:

Emergency Account: Jackson and Maria have monthly expenses of $13,084.35. Right now, they have $78,500 in the emergency account, which is six months of living expenses. Jackson and Maria have an adequate emergency account balance.

Life Insurance: Both Jackson and Maria purchased life insurance with a death benefit of $1.1 million and $1.1 million, respectively. That amount continues to be adequate, given the amount of assets they have accumulated. Running the life insurance analysis again using the updated values for Jackson shows that he needs $1.2 million, which means he is short $100,000.

Inputs			
Annual Income for Jackson			$ 117,010.43
Marginal Federal & State Tax Rate			25%
Years Until Retirement			16
Net Portfolio Return			8.0%
Life Insurance Needs			
Simple Rule of Thumb Method 10x Current Income			$1,170,104.29
Income Replacement Method			$1,202,228.63
Year	After-Tax Income	Start Portfolio Value	End Portfolio Value
0	$ 87,757.82	$ 1,202,228.63	$ 1,203,628.47
1	$ 92,145.71	$ 1,203,628.47	$ 1,200,401.38
2	$ 96,753.00	$ 1,200,401.38	$ 1,191,940.25
3	$ 101,590.65	$ 1,191,940.25	$ 1,177,577.57
4	$ 106,670.18	$ 1,177,577.57	$ 1,156,579.98
5	$ 112,003.69	$ 1,156,579.98	$ 1,128,142.40
6	$ 117,603.87	$ 1,128,142.40	$ 1,091,381.60
7	$ 123,484.07	$ 1,091,381.60	$ 1,045,329.34
8	$ 129,658.27	$ 1,045,329.34	$ 988,924.75
9	$ 136,141.18	$ 988,924.75	$ 921,006.25
10	$ 142,948.24	$ 921,006.25	$ 840,302.65
11	$ 150,095.66	$ 840,302.65	$ 745,423.55
12	$ 157,600.44	$ 745,423.55	$ 634,848.96
13	$ 165,480.46	$ 634,848.96	$ 506,917.98
14	$ 173,754.48	$ 506,917.98	$ 359,816.58
15	$ 182,442.21	$ 359,816.58	$ 191,564.32
16	$ 191,564.32	$ 191,564.32	$ 0.00

However, the family has accumulated enough assets that can be used to supplement the life insurance shortfall. The same analysis can be done on Maria and the results would be the same; no additional life insurance is needed.

Proper Saving/Investment Rate: Jackson has continued to invest $1,859.99 per year into his Roth IRA and his annualized rate of return is 10%. The following illustration shows you how his Roth IRA has grown over the years.

Roth IRA Age	Starting Value	Savings Amount	Ending Value
18	$ –	$1,859.99	$ 1,859.99
19	$ 1,859.99	$1,859.99	$ 3,905.98
20	$ 3,905.98	$1,859.99	$ 6,156.57
21	$ 6,156.57	$1,859.99	$ 8,632.22
22	$ 8,632.22	$1,859.99	$ 11,355.43
23	$ 11,355.43	$1,859.99	$ 14,350.97
24	$ 14,350.97	$1,859.99	$ 17,646.05
25	$ 17,646.05	$1,859.99	$ 21,270.65
26	$ 21,270.65	$1,859.99	$ 25,257.71
27	$ 25,257.71	$1,859.99	$ 29,643.47
28	$ 29,643.47	$1,859.99	$ 34,467.81
29	$ 34,467.81	$1,859.99	$ 39,774.58
30	$ 39,774.58	$1,859.99	$ 45,612.03
31	$ 45,612.03	$1,859.99	$ 52,033.22
32	$ 52,033.22	$1,859.99	$ 59,096.53
33	$ 59,096.53	$1,859.99	$ 66,866.18
34	$ 66,866.18	$1,859.99	$ 75,412.78
35	$ 75,412.78	$1,859.99	$ 84,814.05
36	$ 84,814.05	$1,859.99	$ 95,155.45
37	$ 95,155.45	$1,859.99	$ 106,530.99
38	$ 106,530.99	$1,859.99	$ 119,044.08
39	$ 119,044.08	$1,859.99	$ 132,808.48
40	$ 132,808.48	$1,859.99	$ 147,949.31
41	$ 147,949.31	$1,859.99	$ 164,604.24
42	$ 164,604.24	$1,859.99	$ 182,924.65
43	$ 182,924.65	$1,859.99	$ 203,077.11

Jackson's 401(k) account is also growing quickly. Two things have contributed to this outcome. First, Jackson is saving a total of 9% per year, including the 4% employer match. Second, his income continues to grow at an annual rate of 5%. That means even though he is saving 9% of his annual income, the absolute amount keeps increasing because his income is increasing.

401(k) Age	Salary	Starting Value	Savings Amount	Ending Value
18	$ –	$ –	$ –	$ –
19	$ –	$ –	$ –	$ –
20	$ –	$ –	$ –	$ –
21	$ –	$ –	$ –	$ –
22	$ 40,000	$ –	$ 3,600.00	$ 3,600.00
23	$ 42,000	$ 3,600.00	$ 3,780.00	$ 7,740.00
24	$ 44,100	$ 7,740.00	$ 3,969.00	$ 12,483.00
25	$ 46,305	$ 12,483.00	$ 4,167.45	$ 17,898.75
26	$ 48,620	$ 17,898.75	$ 4,375.82	$ 24,064.45
27	$ 51,051	$ 24,064.45	$ 4,594.61	$ 31,065.51
28	$ 53,604	$ 31,065.51	$ 4,824.34	$ 38,996.40
29	$ 56,284	$ 38,996.40	$ 5,065.56	$ 47,961.60
30	$ 59,098	$ 47,961.60	$ 5,318.84	$ 58,076.60
31	$ 62,053	$ 58,076.60	$ 5,584.78	$ 69,469.04
32	$ 65,156	$ 69,469.04	$ 5,864.02	$ 82,279.97
33	$ 68,414	$ 82,279.97	$ 6,157.22	$ 96,665.19
34	$ 71,834	$ 96,665.19	$ 6,465.08	$ 112,796.79
35	$ 75,426	$ 112,796.79	$ 6,788.34	$ 130,864.81
36	$ 79,197	$ 130,864.81	$ 7,127.75	$ 151,079.04
37	$ 83,157	$ 151,079.04	$ 7,484.14	$ 173,671.08
38	$ 87,315	$ 173,671.08	$ 7,858.35	$ 198,896.54
39	$ 91,681	$ 198,896.54	$ 8,251.27	$ 227,037.46
40	$ 96,265	$ 227,037.46	$ 8,663.83	$ 258,405.04
41	$ 101,078	$ 258,405.04	$ 9,097.02	$ 293,342.56
42	$ 106,132	$ 293,342.56	$ 9,551.87	$ 332,228.69
43	$ 111,439	$ 332,228.69	$ 10,029.47	$ 375,481.02

Maria continues to make $1,000 annual contributions to her Roth IRA. The following is how her account has grown over the years:

Roth IRA			
Age	Starting Value	Savings Amount	Ending Value
20	$ –	$1,000.00	$ 1,000.00
21	$ 1,000.00	$1,000.00	$ 2,100.00
22	$ 2,100.00	$1,000.00	$ 3,310.00
23	$ 3,310.00	$1,000.00	$ 4,641.00
24	$ 4,641.00	$1,000.00	$ 6,105.10
25	$ 6,105.10	$1,000.00	$ 7,715.61
26	$ 7,715.61	$1,000.00	$ 9,487.17
27	$ 9,487.17	$1,000.00	$ 11,435.89
28	$ 11,435.89	$1,000.00	$ 13,579.48
29	$ 13,579.48	$1,000.00	$ 15,937.42
30	$ 15,937.42	$1,000.00	$ 18,531.17
31	$ 18,531.17	$1,000.00	$ 21,384.28
32	$ 21,384.28	$1,000.00	$ 24,522.71
33	$ 24,522.71	$1,000.00	$ 27,974.98
34	$ 27,974.98	$1,000.00	$ 31,772.48
35	$ 31,772.48	$1,000.00	$ 35,949.73
36	$ 35,949.73	$1,000.00	$ 40,544.70
37	$ 40,544.70	$1,000.00	$ 45,599.17
38	$ 45,599.17	$1,000.00	$ 51,159.09
39	$ 51,159.09	$1,000.00	$ 57,275.00
40	$ 57,275.00	$1,000.00	$ 64,002.50
41	$ 64,002.50	$1,000.00	$ 71,402.75
42	$ 71,402.75	$1,000.00	$ 79,543.02
43	$ 79,543.02	$1,000.00	$ 88,497.33
44	$ 88,497.33	$1,000.00	$ 98,347.06
45	$ 98,347.06	$1,000.00	$ 109,181.77
46	$ 109,181.77	$1,000.00	$ 121,099.94
47	$ 121,099.94	$1,000.00	$ 134,209.94

Maria's 401(k) is also beginning to grow quickly. Like Jackson, the growth of the account is also attributed to her healthy savings rate of 9%, including the employer match and her annual income increase of 5%.

401(k) Age	Salary	Starting Value	Savings Amount	Ending Value
20	$ –	$ –	$ –	$ –
21	$ –	$ –	$ –	$ –
22	$ 34,000	$ –	$ 3,060.00	$ 3,060.00
23	$ 35,700	$ 3,060.00	$ 3,213.00	$ 6,579.00
24	$ 37,485	$ 6,579.00	$ 3,373.65	$ 10,610.55
25	$ 39,359	$ 10,610.55	$ 3,542.33	$ 15,213.94
26	$ 41,327	$ 15,213.94	$ 3,719.45	$ 20,454.78
27	$ 43,394	$ 20,454.78	$ 3,905.42	$ 26,405.68
28	$ 45,563	$ 26,405.68	$ 4,100.69	$ 33,146.94
29	$ 47,841	$ 33,146.94	$ 4,305.73	$ 40,767.36
30	$ 50,233	$ 40,767.36	$ 4,521.01	$ 49,365.11
31	$ 52,745	$ 49,365.11	$ 4,747.06	$ 59,048.69
32	$ 55,382	$ 59,048.69	$ 4,984.42	$ 69,937.97
33	$ 58,152	$ 69,937.97	$ 5,233.64	$ 82,165.41
34	$ 61,059	$ 82,165.41	$ 5,495.32	$ 95,877.27
35	$ 64,112	$ 95,877.27	$ 5,770.09	$ 111,235.08
36	$ 67,318	$ 111,235.08	$ 6,058.59	$ 128,417.18
37	$ 70,684	$ 128,417.18	$ 6,361.52	$ 147,620.42
38	$ 74,218	$ 147,620.42	$ 6,679.60	$ 169,062.06
39	$ 77,929	$ 169,062.06	$ 7,013.58	$ 192,981.84
40	$ 81,825	$ 192,981.84	$ 7,364.25	$ 219,644.28
41	$ 85,916	$ 219,644.28	$ 7,732.47	$ 249,341.18
42	$ 90,212	$ 249,341.18	$ 8,119.09	$ 282,394.39
43	$ 94,723	$ 282,394.39	$ 8,525.05	$ 319,158.87
44	$ 99,459	$ 319,158.87	$ 8,951.30	$ 360,026.06
45	$104,432	$ 360,026.06	$ 9,398.86	$ 405,427.52
46	$109,653	$ 405,427.52	$ 9,868.81	$ 455,839.08
47	$115,136	$ 455,839.08	$ 10,362.25	$ 511,785.24

Maria and Jackson opened a joint brokerage account and began investing in the same asset allocation as their Roth IRA, and in the last four years the account has grown to $23,205.00.

Trust Account Year	Starting Value	Savings Amount	Ending Value
1	$ –	$5,000.00	$ 5,000.00
2	$ 5,000.00	$5,000.00	$ 10,500.00
3	$ 10,500.00	$5,000.00	$ 16,550.00
4	$ 16,550.00	$5,000.00	$ 23,205.00

College Savings: Maria and Jackson continue to save into Andrew and Pedro's 529 Plans. These accounts are not being invested as aggressively as their other accounts, and that is why they assumed a 7.0% annualized rate of return. The account is on track to have $143,414.19 when Andrew turns 18 years old. At the moment, the account has a value of $75,456.79. Since the 529 Plans have been earmarked for their children's college expenses, we have left them out of the balance sheet.

Andrew			
529 Plan Account Value	$ –		
Rate of Return	7.0%		
Current Age	0		
Target Age	18		
Full Cost of College Today	$ 129,876		
Inflation Rate	4.5%		
Full Cost of College in the Future	$ 286,828		
Parents Will Cover College Cost	50%		
Account Value Goal at Target Age	$ 143,414		
Annual Savings Needed	($4,218.18)		
Monthly Savings Needed	($351.52)		

College Investment Account			
Age	Starting Value	Savings Amount	Ending Value
0	$ –	$4,218.18	$ 4,218.18
1	$ 4,218.18	$4,218.18	$ 8,731.64
2	$ 8,731.64	$4,218.18	$ 13,561.04
3	$ 13,561.04	$4,218.18	$ 18,728.50
4	$ 18,728.50	$4,218.18	$ 24,257.68
5	$ 24,257.68	$4,218.18	$ 30,173.90
6	$ 30,173.90	$4,218.18	$ 36,504.26
7	$ 36,504.26	$4,218.18	$ 43,277.74
8	$ 43,277.74	$4,218.18	$ 50,525.37
9	$ 50,525.37	$4,218.18	$ 58,280.33
10	$ 58,280.33	$4,218.18	$ 66,578.14
11	$ 66,578.14	$4,218.18	$ 75,456.79

Estate Planning: Maria and Jackson have been meaning to speak with an estate attorney to discuss if setting up a trust is a good idea for them. After speaking with the attorney, it was decided that a living trust would be created in which Maria and Jackson are the grantors (the persons who set up the trust) and the trustees (the persons who manage the trust).

Both Maria and Jackson will also be the beneficiaries of the trust. Both children were set up as successor trustees and beneficiaries if both Maria and Jackson were no longer living. The attorney advised them to set up a guardianship clause that stated who would oversee their children if they were still minors when Maria and Jackson were no longer alive.

Part of the living-trust process was to set up power of attorney for financial and health purposes. The way it was set up is that if Jackson were to become incapacitated but still living, Maria would be able to handle Jackson' financial and healthcare affairs. The opposite was set up for Maria; if she were still living but incapacitated, Jackson would be the one who could make financial and medical decisions for her.

The attorney also set up a will and told them a will can be used to pass assets to beneficiaries, but it does not avoid probate, which can be a costly and time-consuming process. That is where the living trust comes into play because it avoids probate, and assets can be passed down to beneficiaries in an efficient manner. Finally, the attorney told them to "fund" the trust, meaning reregister appropriate assets in the name of the trust.

Where They Should Be Investing

In their Roth IRAs, both Maria and Jackson continue to invest aggressively. They both have 100% invested in stocks.

Aggressive	
Stocks	100.00%
Bonds	0.00%
Category	Weight
Bucket | 1	0.00%
IGSB	0.00%
IGIB	0.00%
SCHO	0.00%
VTIP	0.00%
BND	0.00%
Bucket | 2	30.00%
AMLP	2.10%
PFF	2.10%
HYG	2.10%
VNQ	2.10%
NOBL	16.50%
VIGI	5.10%
Bucket | 3	70.00%
VONE	35.00%
VO	14.00%
VIOO	7.00%
MTUM	7.00%
VWO	7.00%
Total	100.00%

In their 401(k) accounts, both Maria and Jackson hold a target date fund that aligns with their retirement age of 60 for Jackson and 64 for Maria. Their 401(k) plan allows them to invest in an aggressive target date fund that has a 95% allocation to stocks and 5% to bonds.

In their brokerage account the asset mix is the same as in their Roth IRAs.

Jackson and Maria thought about investing more conservatively in their accounts. Although after thinking about it for a while, they decided to keep their current allocation. Jackson remembered what he had learned in his online academy investment class where he was taught that the expected return of his portfolio is related to the asset allocation. That means if they invested a bit more conservatively, they could no longer expect to generate 10% from their portfolio. Maria also reminded Jackson that they won't need to take distributions from the accounts for over a decade so they should continue to invest aggressively.

What You Should Do If You Are Behind

Maria and Jackson are well on their way to becoming work optional at 60 years old. Jackson has continued to fund his Roth IRA like clockwork, and now he is seeing first hand the benefit of compounding interest. Unfortunately, not everyone will be able to get started at 18 years old, which is why I'm going to provide you with three paths you can take if you are 44 years old and have not gotten started or if you have begun but your account value is not on track to get to $1,000,000 by the time you turn 60 years old.

If you are 44 now and want $1,000,000 to be work optional, but you have not begun to save, then you will have to invest $27,816.62

for the next 16 years at a rate of 10% to achieve your goal. The following shows how this path would evolve over time:

Behind by	100%		
Current Account Value	$ –		
Rate of Return	10.0%		
Current Age	44		
Target Age	60		
Account Value Goal at Target Age	$ 1,000,000		
Annual Savings Needed	($27,816.62)		
Age	Starting Value	Savings Amount	Ending Value
44	$ –	$27,816.62	$ 27,816.62
45	$ 27,816.62	$27,816.62	$ 58,414.90
46	$ 58,414.90	$27,816.62	$ 92,073.01
47	$ 92,073.01	$27,816.62	$ 129,096.94
48	$ 129,096.94	$27,816.62	$ 169,823.25
49	$ 169,823.25	$27,816.62	$ 214,622.20
50	$ 214,622.20	$27,816.62	$ 263,901.04
51	$ 263,901.04	$27,816.62	$ 318,107.76
52	$ 318,107.76	$27,816.62	$ 377,735.16
53	$ 377,735.16	$27,816.62	$ 443,325.30
54	$ 443,325.30	$27,816.62	$ 515,474.45
55	$ 515,474.45	$27,816.62	$ 594,838.51
56	$ 594,838.51	$27,816.62	$ 682,138.98
57	$ 682,138.98	$27,816.62	$ 778,169.50
58	$ 778,169.50	$27,816.62	$ 883,803.07
59	$ 883,803.07	$27,816.62	$1,000,000.00

Since the required annual investment amount is substantially greater than what can be contributed into a Roth IRA, I assumed the investment would take place in a taxable brokerage account. For simplicity of the example, I ignore taxes and transaction cost. Remember to go back to the section in the book where I talk about tax loss harvesting because that will help minimize the impact of taxes.

The second path I'll provide is if you have gotten started but are behind. To be on track your account value would have to be

$203,077.11, but I'll assume you are 50% behind with an account value of $101,538.55. In this case you would have to invest $14,838.31 annually to achieve an account value of $1,000,000 by your 60th birthday. The following illustration shows you the path of this scenario.

Behind by	50%		
Current Account Value	$ 101,538.55		
Rate of Return	10.0%		
Current Age	44		
Target Age	60		
Account Value Goal at Target Age	$ 1,000,000		
Annual Savings Needed	($14,838.31)		
Age	Starting Value	Savings Amount	Ending Value
44	$ 101,538.55	$14,838.31	$ 126,530.72
45	$ 126,530.72	$14,838.31	$ 154,022.09
46	$ 154,022.09	$14,838.31	$ 184,262.61
47	$ 184,262.61	$14,838.31	$ 217,527.17
48	$ 217,527.17	$14,838.31	$ 254,118.20
49	$ 254,118.20	$14,838.31	$ 294,368.32
50	$ 294,368.32	$14,838.31	$ 338,643.46
51	$ 338,643.46	$14,838.31	$ 387,346.11
52	$ 387,346.11	$14,838.31	$ 440,919.03
53	$ 440,919.03	$14,838.31	$ 499,849.24
54	$ 499,849.24	$14,838.31	$ 564,672.47
55	$ 564,672.47	$14,838.31	$ 635,978.02
56	$ 635,978.02	$14,838.31	$ 714,414.13
57	$ 714,414.13	$14,838.31	$ 800,693.85
58	$ 800,693.85	$14,838.31	$ 895,601.54
59	$ 895,601.54	$14,838.31	$1,000,000.00

The final example I'll provide is if you want to reach work optional by age 60 and you are behind by 25%. In this case you will need to save $8,349.15 to hit your target.

Behind by	25%		
Current Account Value	$ 152,307.83		
Rate of Return	10.0%		
Current Age	44		
Target Age	60		
Account Value Goal at Target Age	$ 1,000,000		
Annual Savings Needed	($8,349.15)		
Age	Starting Value	Savings Amount	Ending Value
44	$ 152,307.83	$8,349.15	$ 175,887.76
45	$ 175,887.76	$8,349.15	$ 201,825.69
46	$ 201,825.69	$8,349.15	$ 230,357.40
47	$ 230,357.40	$8,349.15	$ 261,742.29
48	$ 261,742.29	$8,349.15	$ 296,265.67
49	$ 296,265.67	$8,349.15	$ 334,241.39
50	$ 334,241.39	$8,349.15	$ 376,014.67
51	$ 376,014.67	$8,349.15	$ 421,965.29
52	$ 421,965.29	$8,349.15	$ 472,510.97
53	$ 472,510.97	$8,349.15	$ 528,111.21
54	$ 528,111.21	$8,349.15	$ 589,271.48
55	$ 589,271.48	$8,349.15	$ 656,547.78
56	$ 656,547.78	$8,349.15	$ 730,551.70
57	$ 730,551.70	$8,349.15	$ 811,956.02
58	$ 811,956.02	$8,349.15	$ 901,500.77
59	$ 901,500.77	$8,349.15	$1,000,000.00

There are many scenarios that I could have shown you and still not covered all the possible cases. The important part is that you get started if you have not already, and if you are behind, continue pushing forward.

Chapter 17

Catch Up and Assess: What to Do Ages 50–60

Another decade has gone by, and Jackson is now 54 and Maria is 58. Their children are no longer boys. Andrew is 22 years old, and their son Pedro is 20½ years old.

Jackson' current salary is $190,598 and Maria is making $196,922 and they each continue to contribute 5% of their income in the 401(k) accounts and the employer also continues to match 4%. Jackson continues to fund his Roth IRA with $1,859.99 per year using the "back door" Roth contribution strategy. Maria is also contributing $1,000 into her Roth IRA using the "back door" contribution method. Two years ago, they began investing $10,000 annually into their brokerage account, and they still live in the same home.

In terms of assets, Maria and Jackson have $20,000 in their checking account, $50,000 in their savings account, and $126,000 in their emergency account. Their monthly expenses are $21,011.52, which includes their mortgage and car payments of $1,200. Figure 17.1 summarizes the family's current financial dashboard and updated account values.

Balance Sheet	
Assets	**Amount**
Liquid	
Checking Account	$ 20,000.00
Savings Account	$ 50,000.00
Emergency Account	$ 126,000.00
Investment Accounts	$ 150,374.92
Retirement Accounts (i.e. 401(k), Roth)	$ 3,634,929.66
Illiquid	$ –
Home	$ 1,422,270.00
Private Business	$ –
Automobiles	$ –
Total Assets	**$ 5,403,574.58**
Liabilities	**Amount**
Mortgage Balance	$ (97,010.40)
Credit Card Debt	$ –
Automobile Loan	$ –
Student Loans	$ –
Total Liabilities	**$ (97,010.40)**

Net Worth Statement	
Total Assets	**$ 5,403,574.58**
Total Liabilities	**$ (97,010.40)**
Net Worth	**$ 5,306,564.18**

Cashflow Statement	
Inflow	**Amount**
Annual Salary—Jackson	$ 190,597.66
Annual Salary—Maria	$ 196,921.75
Total Inflow	**$ 387,519.41**
Outflow	**Amount**
Savings	$ (32,235.96)
Living Expenses—Needs*	$ (280,000.00)
Living Expenses—Wants	$ (75,283.45)
Total Outflow	**$ (387,519.41)**
Surplus/Deficit	**$ (0.00)**
*Includes taxes	

Figure 17.1 Current investment dashboard.

What They Are Doing Right

Here are the areas where they are staying on track:

Emergency Account: Jackson and Maria have monthly expenses of $21,011.52. Right now, they have $126,000 in the emergency account, which is 6 months of living expenses. Therefore, Jackson and Maria have an adequate emergency account balance.

Life Insurance: When Jackson and Maria purchased life insurance, their life was very different. They had minor children, and they were ramping up their careers. Today, both of their children are adults and the 529 Plans are being used to pay for their college and living expenses. Originally, the goal was to protect their income should either pass away prematurely. However, they now have sufficient assets and no longer have an insurable need. Nevertheless, the monthly cost of the life insurance they have now is relatively small, so it's okay if they want to keep paying it until the policy expires in a few years.

Proper Saving/Investment Rate: Jackson has continued to invest $1,859.99 per year into his Roth IRA using the "back door" Roth contribution strategy and has averaged a 10% rate of return. Jackson is only a few years away from turning 60 years old and is on track to his goal of $1,000,000. Right now he has accumulated $556,373.18 in this account, but in just a few years the account will reach it's target! That is how compounding works.

| Roth IRA | | | |
Age	Starting Value	Savings Amount	Ending Value
18	$ –	$1,859.99	$ 1,859.99
19	$ 1,859.99	$1,859.99	$ 3,905.98
20	$ 3,905.98	$1,859.99	$ 6,156.57
21	$ 6,156.57	$1,859.99	$ 8,632.22
22	$ 8,632.22	$1,859.99	$ 11,355.43
23	$ 11,355.43	$1,859.99	$ 14,350.97
24	$ 14,350.97	$1,859.99	$ 17,646.05
25	$ 17,646.05	$1,859.99	$ 21,270.65
26	$ 21,270.65	$1,859.99	$ 25,257.71
27	$ 25,257.71	$1,859.99	$ 29,643.47
28	$ 29,643.47	$1,859.99	$ 34,467.81
29	$ 34,467.81	$1,859.99	$ 39,774.58
30	$ 39,774.58	$1,859.99	$ 45,612.03
31	$ 45,612.03	$1,859.99	$ 52,033.22
32	$ 52,033.22	$1,859.99	$ 59,096.53
33	$ 59,096.53	$1,859.99	$ 66,866.18
34	$ 66,866.18	$1,859.99	$ 75,412.78
35	$ 75,412.78	$1,859.99	$ 84,814.05
36	$ 84,814.05	$1,859.99	$ 95,155.45
37	$ 95,155.45	$1,859.99	$ 106,530.99
38	$ 106,530.99	$1,859.99	$ 119,044.08
39	$ 119,044.08	$1,859.99	$ 132,808.48
40	$ 132,808.48	$1,859.99	$ 147,949.31
41	$ 147,949.31	$1,859.99	$ 164,604.24
42	$ 164,604.24	$1,859.99	$ 182,924.65
43	$ 182,924.65	$1,859.99	$ 203,077.11
44	$ 203,077.11	$1,859.99	$ 225,244.81
45	$ 225,244.81	$1,859.99	$ 249,629.28
46	$ 249,629.28	$1,859.99	$ 276,452.20
47	$ 276,452.20	$1,859.99	$ 305,957.41
48	$ 305,957.41	$1,859.99	$ 338,413.14
49	$ 338,413.14	$1,859.99	$ 374,114.45
50	$ 374,114.45	$1,859.99	$ 413,385.89
51	$ 413,385.89	$1,859.99	$ 456,584.47
52	$ 456,584.47	$1,859.99	$ 504,102.90
53	$ 504,102.90	$1,859.99	$ 556,373.18

Jackson's 401(k) account is also doing great with a current balance of $1,177,116.14.

401(k) Age	Salary	Starting Value	Savings Amount	Ending Value
18	$ –	$ –	$ –	$ –
19	$ –	$ –	$ –	$ –
20	$ –	$ –	$ –	$ –
21	$ –	$ –	$ –	$ –
22	$ 40,000	$ –	$ 3,600.00	$ 3,600.00
23	$ 42,000	$ 3,600.00	$ 3,780.00	$ 7,740.00
24	$ 44,100	$ 7,740.00	$ 3,969.00	$ 12,483.00
25	$ 46,305	$ 12,483.00	$ 4,167.45	$ 17,898.75
26	$ 48,620	$ 17,898.75	$ 4,375.82	$ 24,064.45
27	$ 51,051	$ 24,064.45	$ 4,594.61	$ 31,065.51
28	$ 53,604	$ 31,065.51	$ 4,824.34	$ 38,996.40
29	$ 56,284	$ 38,996.40	$ 5,065.56	$ 47,961.60
30	$ 59,098	$ 47,961.60	$ 5,318.84	$ 58,076.60
31	$ 62,053	$ 58,076.60	$ 5,584.78	$ 69,469.04
32	$ 65,156	$ 69,469.04	$ 5,864.02	$ 82,279.97
33	$ 68,414	$ 82,279.97	$ 6,157.22	$ 96,665.19
34	$ 71,834	$ 96,665.19	$ 6,465.08	$ 112,796.79
35	$ 75,426	$ 112,796.79	$ 6,788.34	$ 130,864.81
36	$ 79,197	$ 130,864.81	$ 7,127.75	$ 151,079.04
37	$ 83,157	$ 151,079.04	$ 7,484.14	$ 173,671.08
38	$ 87,315	$ 173,671.08	$ 7,858.35	$ 198,896.54
39	$ 91,681	$ 198,896.54	$ 8,251.27	$ 227,037.46
40	$ 96,265	$ 227,037.46	$ 8,663.83	$ 258,405.04
41	$ 101,078	$ 258,405.04	$ 9,097.02	$ 293,342.56
42	$ 106,132	$ 293,342.56	$ 9,551.87	$ 332,228.69
43	$ 111,439	$ 332,228.69	$ 10,029.47	$ 375,481.02
44	$ 117,010	$ 375,481.02	$ 10,530.94	$ 423,560.06
45	$ 122,861	$ 423,560.06	$ 11,057.49	$ 476,973.56
46	$ 129,004	$ 476,973.56	$ 11,610.36	$ 536,281.27
47	$ 135,454	$ 536,281.27	$ 12,190.88	$ 602,100.28
48	$ 142,227	$ 602,100.28	$ 12,800.42	$ 675,110.73
49	$ 149,338	$ 675,110.73	$ 13,440.44	$ 756,062.24
50	$ 156,805	$ 756,062.24	$ 14,112.46	$ 845,780.93
51	$ 164,645	$ 845,780.93	$ 14,818.09	$ 945,177.11
52	$ 172,878	$ 945,177.11	$ 15,558.99	$ 1,055,253.82
53	$ 181,522	$1,055,253.82	$ 16,336.94	$ 1,177,116.14

Maria continues to contribute $1,000 into her Roth IRA using the "back door" Roth contribution strategy. Here is how her account had grown over the years:

Roth IRA Age	Starting Value	Savings Amount	Ending Value
20	$ –	$1,000.00	$ 1,000.00
21	$ 1,000.00	$1,000.00	$ 2,100.00
22	$ 2,100.00	$1,000.00	$ 3,310.00
23	$ 3,310.00	$1,000.00	$ 4,641.00
24	$ 4,641.00	$1,000.00	$ 6,105.10
25	$ 6,105.10	$1,000.00	$ 7,715.61
26	$ 7,715.61	$1,000.00	$ 9,487.17
27	$ 9,487.17	$1,000.00	$ 11,435.89
28	$ 11,435.89	$1,000.00	$ 13,579.48
29	$ 13,579.48	$1,000.00	$ 15,937.42
30	$ 15,937.42	$1,000.00	$ 18,531.17
31	$ 18,531.17	$1,000.00	$ 21,384.28
32	$ 21,384.28	$1,000.00	$ 24,522.71
33	$ 24,522.71	$1,000.00	$ 27,974.98
34	$ 27,974.98	$1,000.00	$ 31,772.48
35	$ 31,772.48	$1,000.00	$ 35,949.73
36	$ 35,949.73	$1,000.00	$ 40,544.70
37	$ 40,544.70	$1,000.00	$ 45,599.17
38	$ 45,599.17	$1,000.00	$ 51,159.09
39	$ 51,159.09	$1,000.00	$ 57,275.00
40	$ 57,275.00	$1,000.00	$ 64,002.50
41	$ 64,002.50	$1,000.00	$ 71,402.75
42	$ 71,402.75	$1,000.00	$ 79,543.02
43	$ 79,543.02	$1,000.00	$ 88,497.33
44	$ 88,497.33	$1,000.00	$ 98,347.06
45	$ 98,347.06	$1,000.00	$ 109,181.77
46	$ 109,181.77	$1,000.00	$ 121,099.94
47	$ 121,099.94	$1,000.00	$ 134,209.94
48	$ 134,209.94	$1,000.00	$ 148,630.93
49	$ 148,630.93	$1,000.00	$ 164,494.02
50	$ 164,494.02	$1,000.00	$ 181,943.42
51	$ 181,943.42	$1,000.00	$ 201,137.77
52	$ 201,137.77	$1,000.00	$ 222,251.54
53	$ 222,251.54	$1,000.00	$ 245,476.70
54	$ 245,476.70	$1,000.00	$ 271,024.37
55	$ 271,024.37	$1,000.00	$ 299,126.81
56	$ 299,126.81	$1,000.00	$ 330,039.49
57	$ 330,039.49	$1,000.00	$ 364,043.43

Maria's 401(k) account is also growing rather fast and beginning to benefit from the power of compounding interest.

401(k) Age	Salary	Starting Value	Savings Amount	Ending Value
20	$ –	$ –	$ –	$ –
21	$ –	$ –	$ –	$ –
22	$ 34,000	$ –	$ 3,060.00	$ 3,060.00
23	$ 35,700	$ 3,060.00	$ 3,213.00	$ 6,579.00
24	$ 37,485	$ 6,579.00	$ 3,373.65	$ 10,610.55
25	$ 39,359	$ 10,610.55	$ 3,542.33	$ 15,213.94
26	$ 41,327	$ 15,213.94	$ 3,719.45	$ 20,454.78
27	$ 43,394	$ 20,454.78	$ 3,905.42	$ 26,405.68
28	$ 45,563	$ 26,405.68	$ 4,100.69	$ 33,146.94
29	$ 47,841	$ 33,146.94	$ 4,305.73	$ 40,767.36
30	$ 50,233	$ 40,767.36	$ 4,521.01	$ 49,365.11
31	$ 52,745	$ 49,365.11	$ 4,747.06	$ 59,048.69
32	$ 55,382	$ 59,048.69	$ 4,984.42	$ 69,937.97
33	$ 58,152	$ 69,937.97	$ 5,233.64	$ 82,165.41
34	$ 61,059	$ 82,165.41	$ 5,495.32	$ 95,877.27
35	$ 64,112	$ 95,877.27	$ 5,770.09	$ 111,235.08
36	$ 67,318	$ 111,235.08	$ 6,058.59	$ 128,417.18
37	$ 70,684	$ 128,417.18	$ 6,361.52	$ 147,620.42
38	$ 74,218	$ 147,620.42	$ 6,679.60	$ 169,062.06
39	$ 77,929	$ 169,062.06	$ 7,013.58	$ 192,981.84
40	$ 81,825	$ 192,981.84	$ 7,364.25	$ 219,644.28
41	$ 85,916	$ 219,644.28	$ 7,732.47	$ 249,341.18
42	$ 90,212	$ 249,341.18	$ 8,119.09	$ 282,394.39
43	$ 94,723	$ 282,394.39	$ 8,525.05	$ 319,158.87
44	$ 99,459	$ 319,158.87	$ 8,951.30	$ 360,026.06
45	$ 104,432	$ 360,026.06	$ 9,398.86	$ 405,427.52
46	$ 109,653	$ 405,427.52	$ 9,868.81	$ 455,839.08
47	$ 115,136	$ 455,839.08	$ 10,362.25	$ 511,785.24
48	$ 120,893	$ 511,785.24	$ 10,880.36	$ 573,844.12
49	$ 126,938	$ 573,844.12	$ 11,424.38	$ 642,652.91
50	$ 133,284	$ 642,652.91	$ 11,995.60	$ 718,913.79
51	$ 139,949	$ 718,913.79	$ 12,595.37	$ 803,400.55
52	$ 146,946	$ 803,400.55	$ 13,225.14	$ 896,965.74
53	$ 154,293	$ 896,965.74	$ 13,886.40	$ 1,000,548.72
54	$ 162,008	$ 1,000,548.72	$ 14,580.72	$ 1,115,184.31
55	$ 170,108	$ 1,115,184.31	$ 15,309.76	$ 1,242,012.50
56	$ 178,614	$ 1,242,012.50	$ 16,075.24	$ 1,382,288.99
57	$ 187,545	$ 1,382,288.99	$ 16,879.01	$ 1,537,396.90

Their joint account was reregistered to their living trust. That way, if both Jackson and Maria were to pass away prematurely, their children would be able to assume the account in an efficient manner. They were investing $5,000 annually, but two years ago, they increased it to $10,000 annually, Today, the account value is $150,374.92.

Trust Account			
Year	Starting Value	Savings Amount	Ending Value
1	$ –	$5,000.00	$ 5,000.00
2	$ 5,000.00	$5,000.00	$ 10,500.00
3	$ 10,500.00	$5,000.00	$ 16,550.00
4	$ 16,550.00	$5,000.00	$ 23,205.00
5	$ 23,205.00	$5,000.00	$ 30,525.50
6	$ 30,525.50	$5,000.00	$ 38,578.05
7	$ 38,578.05	$5,000.00	$ 47,435.86
8	$ 47,435.86	$5,000.00	$ 57,179.44
9	$ 57,179.44	$5,000.00	$ 67,897.38
10	$ 67,897.38	$5,000.00	$ 79,687.12
11	$ 79,687.12	$5,000.00	$ 92,655.84
12	$ 92,655.84	$5,000.00	$ 106,921.42
13	$ 106,921.42	$10,000.00	$ 127,613.56
14	$ 127,613.56	$10,000.00	$ 150,374.92

College Savings: Andrew's 529 Plan was depleted completely and was enough to pay for 50% of the total college cost. The annual contributions of $4,218.18 invested at 7.0% grew the account to $143,414.19 when Andrew turned 18 years old. When Andrew started college $35,853.55 was distributed annually from the account to pay for 50% of the college cost. After four years of college, the account had a balance of $0.00. The following shows how this scenario played out:

Andrew				
529 Plan Account Value	$ –			
Rate of Return	7.0%			
Current Age	0			
Target Age	18			
Full Cost of College Today	$ 129,876			
Inflation Rate	4.5%			
Full Cost of College in the Future	$ 286,828			
Parents Will Cover College Cost	50%			
Account Value Goal at Target Age	$ 143,414			
Annual Savings Needed	($4,218.18)			
Monthly Savings Needed	($351.52)			

College Investment Account				
Age	Starting Value		Savings Amount	Ending Value
0	$	–	$4,218.18	$ 4,218.18
1	$	4,218.18	$4,218.18	$ 8,731.64
2	$	8,731.64	$4,218.18	$ 13,561.04
3	$	13,561.04	$4,218.18	$ 18,728.50
4	$	18,728.50	$4,218.18	$ 24,257.68
5	$	24,257.68	$4,218.18	$ 30,173.90
6	$	30,173.90	$4,218.18	$ 36,504.26
7	$	36,504.26	$4,218.18	$ 43,277.74
8	$	43,277.74	$4,218.18	$ 50,525.37
9	$	50,525.37	$4,218.18	$ 58,280.33
10	$	58,280.33	$4,218.18	$ 66,578.14
11	$	66,578.14	$4,218.18	$ 75,456.79
12	$	75,456.79	$4,218.18	$ 84,956.95
13	$	84,956.95	$4,218.18	$ 95,122.12
14	$	95,122.12	$4,218.18	$ 105,998.85
15	$	105,998.85	$4,218.18	$ 117,636.96
16	$	117,636.96	$4,218.18	$ 130,089.73
17	$	130,089.73	$4,218.18	$ 143,414.19
18	$	143,414.19	($35,853.55)	$ 107,560.65
19	$	107,560.65	($35,853.55)	$ 71,707.10
20	$	71,707.10	($35,853.55)	$ 35,853.55
21	$	35,853.55	($35,853.55)	$ –

Estate Planning: Many years have gone by since the living trust and other documents were drafted. It is time for Maria and Jackson to speak to an estate attorney to review the documents and make appropriate updates. Now that Andrew and Pedro are adults, it would be important to share with them the assets that have been accumulated by Jackson and Maria. Sharing their financial dashboard with their sons would be a good starting point. Unfortunately, wealth that is inherited is often squandered away by the first or second generation, so it is important that Andrew and Pedro understand how to manage money.

Where They Should Be Investing

Jackson and Maria have been investing for many years and have experienced many market ups and downs. They have become very comfortable with market volatility and plan to continue to invest aggressively. Normally, as individuals approach their work-optional age, the portfolio becomes more aggressive, but in the case of Jackson and Maria, they feel comfortable keeping a 100% stock allocation to continue to expect 10% annual returns over the long term.

Their Roth IRAs and brokerage accounts continue to be invested in the following:

Aggressive	
Stocks	100.00%
Bonds	0.00%
Category	**Weight**
Bucket | 1	**0.00%**
IGSB	0.00%
IGIB	0.00%
SCHO	0.00%
VTIP	0.00%
BND	0.00%
Bucket | 2	**30.00%**
AMLP	2.10%
PFF	2.10%
HYG	2.10%
VNQ	2.10%
NOBL	16.50%
VIGI	5.10%
Bucket | 3	**70.00%**
VONE	35.00%
VO	14.00%
VIOO	7.00%
MTUM	7.00%
VWO	7.00%
Total	**100.00%**

In their 401(k) accounts, they moved away from a target date fund, and after researching the plan investment lineup, they decided to invest in five all-equity funds.

What You Should Do If You Are Behind

Now we are six years from getting to the target of $1,000,000 by age 60. To be on track at age 54, you would need a current account value of $556,373.18. Hopefully, by now you have gotten started so I'm going to illustrate four scenarios if you are behind. The first scenario will be of someone behind by 25%, the second will be someone behind 50%, the third will be someone behind 75%. In the fourth scenario, I will show you some additional adjustments that can be made.

In the first scenario, the account value is $417,279.89, which puts you 25% behind target. In this case to get back on track, you will have to invest $33,796.84 annually for the next six years at a rate of 10%. This will get you to the $1,000,000 target.

Behind by	25%		
Current Account Value	$ 417,279.89		
Rate of Return	10.0%		
Current Age	54		
Target Age	60		
Account Value Goal at Target Age	$ 1,000,000		
Annual Savings Needed	($33,796.84)		
Age	Starting Value	Savings Amount	Ending Value
54	$ 417,279.89	$33,796.84	$ 492,804.72
55	$ 492,804.72	$33,796.84	$ 575,882.03
56	$ 575,882.03	$33,796.84	$ 667,267.07
57	$ 667,267.07	$33,796.84	$ 767,790.61
58	$ 767,790.61	$33,796.84	$ 878,366.51
59	$ 878,366.51	$33,796.84	$ 1,000,000.00

In the second scenario, the account value is $278,186.59 or 50% of the target. In this case to get back on track you will have to invest $65,733.69 annually for the next six years at a rate of 10%. This will get you to the $1,000,000 target.

Behind by	50%		
Current Account Value	$ 278,186.59		
Rate of Return	10.0%		
Current Age	54		
Target Age	60		
Account Value Goal at Target Age	$ 1,000,000		
Annual Savings Needed	($65,733.69)		
Age	Starting Value	Savings Amount	Ending Value
54	$ 278,186.59	$65,733.69	$ 371,738.94
55	$ 371,738.94	$65,733.69	$ 474,646.52
56	$ 474,646.52	$65,733.69	$ 587,844.85
57	$ 587,844.85	$65,733.69	$ 712,363.02
58	$ 712,363.02	$65,733.69	$ 849,333.01
59	$ 849,333.01	$65,733.69	$ 1,000,000.00

In the third scenario, the account value is $139,093.30, which is 75% behind target. In this case, to get back on track you will have to invest $97,670.53 annually for the next six years at a rate of 10%. This will get you to the $1,000,000 target.

Behind by	75%		
Current Account Value	$ 139,093.30		
Rate of Return	10.0%		
Current Age	54		
Target Age	60		
Account Value Goal at Target Age	$ 1,000,000		
Annual Savings Needed	($97,670.53)		
Age	Starting Value	Savings Amount	Ending Value
54	$ 139,093.30	$97,670.53	$ 250,673.16
55	$ 250,673.16	$97,670.53	$ 373,411.01
56	$ 373,411.01	$97,670.53	$ 508,422.64
57	$ 508,422.64	$97,670.53	$ 656,935.44
58	$ 656,935.44	$97,670.53	$ 820,299.52
59	$ 820,299.52	$97,670.53	$ 1,000,000.00

In the fourth scenario, the account value is $139,093.30 or 75% behind target. In this case the individual is okay pushing back their work-optional date by five years to age 65. They are also okay with accumulating $500,000 instead of $1,000,000. In his scenario, this person would have to invest $5,566.33 annually for the next 11 years at a rate of 10%. This will get them to the target of $500,000 at age 65.

Current Account Value	$ 139,093.30
Rate of Return	10.0%
Current Age	54
Target Age	65
Account Value Goal at Target Age	$ 500,000
Annual Savings Needed	($5,566.33)

Brokerage Account			
Age	Starting Value	Savings Amount	Ending Value
54	$ 139,093.30	$5,566.33	$ 158,568.96
55	$ 158,568.96	$5,566.33	$ 179,992.18
56	$ 179,992.18	$5,566.33	$ 203,557.73
57	$ 203,557.73	$5,566.33	$ 229,479.83
58	$ 229,479.83	$5,566.33	$ 257,994.15
59	$ 257,994.15	$5,566.33	$ 289,359.89
60	$ 289,359.89	$5,566.33	$ 323,862.21
61	$ 323,862.21	$5,566.33	$ 361,814.76
62	$ 361,814.76	$5,566.33	$ 403,562.57
63	$ 403,562.57	$5,566.33	$ 449,485.15
64	$ 449,485.15	$5,566.33	$ 500,000.00

If you are behind, don't dwell on it too much. Just get to work and try to invest as much as you can. Remember that you have levers you can pull to make things work. I showed you two levers.

- You can cut your target goal, which will mean spending less money in retirement.
- You can push your work-optional age to a later date.

You can also try to find ways to increase your income by creating a side hustle, and this will allow you more money to invest. If you find yourself in this situation, you are not alone. You will have to put your pride aside and roll up your sleeves and work harder than you have in the past. Even if you are behind, work optional at a reasonable age is still doable. Let's go!

Chapter 18

The Work-Optional Years: What to Do Ages 60+

S ix years have gone by, and today is Jackson' 60th birthday and Maria is 64. They have made it and done very well for themselves. Jackson and Maria decided to retire and enjoy the rest of their lives doing things they could not do while they were working.

Their children are now adults, and each is living in their own home. Jackson and Maria paid off their mortgage over their scheduled 30-year period. Now, Jackson and Maria have a very important task before they go enjoy their work-optional years. They must now turn their nest egg into income-generating assets in order to fund their lifestyle.

They plan to live off $300,000 each year adjusted for inflation and net of taxes. They are going to take one-third from Roth assets, one-third from the Traditional 401(k), and one-third from the trust investment account. They will be investing in the holy grail portfolio and will keep two years of projected living expenses in their bucket 1. In addition, they like to keep $25,000 in their checking account and $50,000 in their savings account. Figure 18.1 shows their current financial dashboard.

Balance Sheet

Assets		Amount
Liquid		
Checking Account	$	25,000.00
Savings Account	$	50,000.00
Emergency Account	$	–
Investment Accounts	$	343,554.44
Retirement Accounts (i.e. 401(k), Roth)	$	6,762,528.36
Illiquid	$	–
Home	$	1,906,000.00
Private Business	$	–
Automobiles	$	–
Total Assets	**$**	**9,087,082.80**

Liabilities		Amount
Mortgage Balance	$	–
Credit Card Debt	$	–
Automobile Loan	$	–
Student Loans	$	–
Total Liabilities	**$**	**–**

Net Worth Statement

Total Assets	**$ 9,087,082.80**	
Total Liabilities	**$**	**–**
Net Worth	**$ 9,087,082.80**	

Cashflow Statement

Inflow		Amount
Portfolio Distributions	$	340,909.09
Total Inflow	**$**	**340,909.09**

Outflow		Amount
Taxes*	$	(40,909.09)
Living Expenses—Needs	$	(200,000.00)
Living Expenses—Wants	$	(100,000.00)
Total Outflow	**$**	**(340,909.09)**
Surplus/Deficit	**$**	**–**

*Assumes a 12% blended tax rate

Figure 18.1   Current investment dashboard.

What They Are Doing Right

Here are the areas where they are staying on track:

Emergency Account: Since Jackson and Maria are now retired, they no longer need an emergency account to protect them from an unforeseen situation. If an unexpected expense were to occur, they would use their assets to pay for it.

Life Insurance: Jackson and Maria no longer have an insurable need. Their term life insurance policies expired and there is no need to purchase additional coverage at the moment.

Proper Saving/Investment Rate: Here is a breakdown of all their accounts:

Jackson is a perfect example of someone who set a plan early on and stayed with it. He continued to invest $1,859.99 year after year into his Roth IRA. In total, he contributed $78,119.62 and now on his 60th birthday his account is worth $1,000,000.

Roth IRA			
Age	Starting Value	Savings Amount	Ending Value
18	$ –	$1,859.99	$ 1,859.99
19	$ 1,859.99	$1,859.99	$ 3,905.98
20	$ 3,905.98	$1,859.99	$ 6,156.57
21	$ 6,156.57	$1,859.99	$ 8,632.22
22	$ 8,632.22	$1,859.99	$ 11,355.43
23	$ 11,355.43	$1,859.99	$ 14,350.97
24	$ 14,350.97	$1,859.99	$ 17,646.05
25	$ 17,646.05	$1,859.99	$ 21,270.65
26	$ 21,270.65	$1,859.99	$ 25,257.71
27	$ 25,257.71	$1,859.99	$ 29,643.47
28	$ 29,643.47	$1,859.99	$ 34,467.81
29	$ 34,467.81	$1,859.99	$ 39,774.58
30	$ 39,774.58	$1,859.99	$ 45,612.03
31	$ 45,612.03	$1,859.99	$ 52,033.22
32	$ 52,033.22	$1,859.99	$ 59,096.53
33	$ 59,096.53	$1,859.99	$ 66,866.18
34	$ 66,866.18	$1,859.99	$ 75,412.78
35	$ 75,412.78	$1,859.99	$ 84,814.05
36	$ 84,814.05	$1,859.99	$ 95,155.45
37	$ 95,155.45	$1,859.99	$ 106,530.99
38	$ 106,530.99	$1,859.99	$ 119,044.08
39	$ 119,044.08	$1,859.99	$ 132,808.48
40	$ 132,808.48	$1,859.99	$ 147,949.31
41	$ 147,949.31	$1,859.99	$ 164,604.24
42	$ 164,604.24	$1,859.99	$ 182,924.65
43	$ 182,924.65	$1,859.99	$ 203,077.11
44	$ 203,077.11	$1,859.99	$ 225,244.81
45	$ 225,244.81	$1,859.99	$ 249,629.28
46	$ 249,629.28	$1,859.99	$ 276,452.20
47	$ 276,452.20	$1,859.99	$ 305,957.41
48	$ 305,957.41	$1,859.99	$ 338,413.14
49	$ 338,413.14	$1,859.99	$ 374,114.45
50	$ 374,114.45	$1,859.99	$ 413,385.89
51	$ 413,385.89	$1,859.99	$ 456,584.47
52	$ 456,584.47	$1,859.99	$ 504,102.90
53	$ 504,102.90	$1,859.99	$ 556,373.18
54	$ 556,373.18	$1,859.99	$ 613,870.49
55	$ 613,870.49	$1,859.99	$ 677,117.53
56	$ 677,117.53	$1,859.99	$ 746,689.28
57	$ 746,689.28	$1,859.99	$ 823,218.20
58	$ 823,218.20	$1,859.99	$ 907,400.01
59	$ 907,400.01	$1,859.99	$ 1,000,000.00

Jackson's 401(k) account has grown very quickly the past few years. That is the power of compounding at work. On his 60th birthday his account value was $2,233,358.36.

401(k) Age	Salary	Starting Value	Savings Amount	Ending Value
18	$ –	$ –	$ –	$ –
19	$ –	$ –	$ –	$ –
20	$ –	$ –	$ –	$ –
21	$ –	$ –	$ –	$ –
22	$ 40,000	$ –	$ 3,600.00	$ 3,600.00
23	$ 42,000	$ 3,600.00	$ 3,780.00	$ 7,740.00
24	$ 44,100	$ 7,740.00	$ 3,969.00	$ 12,483.00
25	$ 46,305	$ 12,483.00	$ 4,167.45	$ 17,898.75
26	$ 48,620	$ 17,898.75	$ 4,375.82	$ 24,064.45
27	$ 51,051	$ 24,064.45	$ 4,594.61	$ 31,065.51
28	$ 53,604	$ 31,065.51	$ 4,824.34	$ 38,996.40
29	$ 56,284	$ 38,996.40	$ 5,065.56	$ 47,961.60
30	$ 59,098	$ 47,961.60	$ 5,318.84	$ 58,076.60
31	$ 62,053	$ 58,076.60	$ 5,584.78	$ 69,469.04
32	$ 65,156	$ 69,469.04	$ 5,864.02	$ 82,279.97
33	$ 68,414	$ 82,279.97	$ 6,157.22	$ 96,665.19
34	$ 71,834	$ 96,665.19	$ 6,465.08	$ 112,796.79
35	$ 75,426	$ 112,796.79	$ 6,788.34	$ 130,864.81
36	$ 79,197	$ 130,864.81	$ 7,127.75	$ 151,079.04
37	$ 83,157	$ 151,079.04	$ 7,484.14	$ 173,671.08
38	$ 87,315	$ 173,671.08	$ 7,858.35	$ 198,896.54
39	$ 91,681	$ 198,896.54	$ 8,251.27	$ 227,037.46
40	$ 96,265	$ 227,037.46	$ 8,663.83	$ 258,405.04
41	$ 101,078	$ 258,405.04	$ 9,097.02	$ 293,342.56
42	$ 106,132	$ 293,342.56	$ 9,551.87	$ 332,228.69
43	$ 111,439	$ 332,228.69	$ 10,029.47	$ 375,481.02
44	$ 117,010	$ 375,481.02	$ 10,530.94	$ 423,560.06
45	$ 122,861	$ 423,560.06	$ 11,057.49	$ 476,973.56
46	$ 129,004	$ 476,973.56	$ 11,610.36	$ 536,281.27
47	$ 135,454	$ 536,281.27	$ 12,190.88	$ 602,100.28
48	$ 142,227	$ 602,100.28	$ 12,800.42	$ 675,110.73
49	$ 149,338	$ 675,110.73	$ 13,440.44	$ 756,062.24
50	$ 156,805	$ 756,062.24	$ 14,112.46	$ 845,780.93
51	$ 164,645	$ 845,780.93	$ 14,818.09	$ 945,177.11
52	$ 172,878	$ 945,177.11	$ 15,558.99	$ 1,055,253.82
53	$ 181,522	$ 1,055,253.82	$ 16,336.94	$ 1,177,116.14
54	$ 190,598	$ 1,177,116.14	$ 17,153.79	$ 1,311,981.54
55	$ 200,128	$ 1,311,981.54	$ 18,011.48	$ 1,461,191.18
56	$ 210,134	$ 1,461,191.18	$ 18,912.05	$ 1,626,222.35
57	$ 220,641	$ 1,626,222.35	$ 19,857.66	$ 1,808,702.24
58	$ 231,673	$ 1,808,702.24	$ 20,850.54	$ 2,010,423.00
59	$ 243,256	$ 2,010,423.00	$ 21,893.06	$ 2,233,358.36

Maria's Roth IRA has grown to $652,640.76. The following shows how the account grew to that value.

Roth IRA Age	Starting Value	Savings Amount	Ending Value
20	$ –	$1,000.00	$ 1,000.00
21	$ 1,000.00	$1,000.00	$ 2,100.00
22	$ 2,100.00	$1,000.00	$ 3,310.00
23	$ 3,310.00	$1,000.00	$ 4,641.00
24	$ 4,641.00	$1,000.00	$ 6,105.10
25	$ 6,105.10	$1,000.00	$ 7,715.61
26	$ 7,715.61	$1,000.00	$ 9,487.17
27	$ 9,487.17	$1,000.00	$ 11,435.89
28	$ 11,435.89	$1,000.00	$ 13,579.48
29	$ 13,579.48	$1,000.00	$ 15,937.42
30	$ 15,937.42	$1,000.00	$ 18,531.17
31	$ 18,531.17	$1,000.00	$ 21,384.28
32	$ 21,384.28	$1,000.00	$ 24,522.71
33	$ 24,522.71	$1,000.00	$ 27,974.98
34	$ 27,974.98	$1,000.00	$ 31,772.48
35	$ 31,772.48	$1,000.00	$ 35,949.73
36	$ 35,949.73	$1,000.00	$ 40,544.70
37	$ 40,544.70	$1,000.00	$ 45,599.17
38	$ 45,599.17	$1,000.00	$ 51,159.09
39	$ 51,159.09	$1,000.00	$ 57,275.00
40	$ 57,275.00	$1,000.00	$ 64,002.50
41	$ 64,002.50	$1,000.00	$ 71,402.75
42	$ 71,402.75	$1,000.00	$ 79,543.02
43	$ 79,543.02	$1,000.00	$ 88,497.33
44	$ 88,497.33	$1,000.00	$ 98,347.06
45	$ 98,347.06	$1,000.00	$ 109,181.77
46	$ 109,181.77	$1,000.00	$ 121,099.94
47	$ 121,099.94	$1,000.00	$ 134,209.94
48	$ 134,209.94	$1,000.00	$ 148,630.93
49	$ 148,630.93	$1,000.00	$ 164,494.02
50	$ 164,494.02	$1,000.00	$ 181,943.42
51	$ 181,943.42	$1,000.00	$ 201,137.77
52	$ 201,137.77	$1,000.00	$ 222,251.54
53	$ 222,251.54	$1,000.00	$ 245,476.70
54	$ 245,476.70	$1,000.00	$ 271,024.37
55	$ 271,024.37	$1,000.00	$ 299,126.81
56	$ 299,126.81	$1,000.00	$ 330,039.49
57	$ 330,039.49	$1,000.00	$ 364,043.43
58	$ 364,043.43	$1,000.00	$ 401,447.78
59	$ 401,447.78	$1,000.00	$ 442,592.56
60	$ 442,592.56	$1,000.00	$ 487,851.81
61	$ 487,851.81	$1,000.00	$ 537,636.99
62	$ 537,636.99	$1,000.00	$ 592,400.69
63	$ 592,400.69	$1,000.00	$ 652,640.76

Maria's 401(k) has grown to $2,876,529.23. In only four years the account has grown by almost $1 million. That is the power of compounding.

401(k) Age	Salary	Starting Value	Savings Amount	Ending Value
20	$ –	$ –	$ –	$ –
21	$ –	$ –	$ –	$ –
22	$ 34,000	$ –	$ 3,060.00	$ 3,060.00
23	$ 35,700	$ 3,060.00	$ 3,213.00	$ 6,579.00
24	$ 37,485	$ 6,579.00	$ 3,373.65	$ 10,610.55
25	$ 39,359	$ 10,610.55	$ 3,542.33	$ 15,213.94
26	$ 41,327	$ 15,213.94	$ 3,719.45	$ 20,454.78
27	$ 43,394	$ 20,454.78	$ 3,905.42	$ 26,405.68
28	$ 45,563	$ 26,405.68	$ 4,100.69	$ 33,146.94
29	$ 47,841	$ 33,146.94	$ 4,305.73	$ 40,767.36
30	$ 50,233	$ 40,767.36	$ 4,521.01	$ 49,365.11
31	$ 52,745	$ 49,365.11	$ 4,747.06	$ 59,048.69
32	$ 55,382	$ 59,048.69	$ 4,984.42	$ 69,937.97
33	$ 58,152	$ 69,937.97	$ 5,233.64	$ 82,165.41
34	$ 61,059	$ 82,165.41	$ 5,495.32	$ 95,877.27
35	$ 64,112	$ 95,877.27	$ 5,770.09	$ 111,235.08
36	$ 67,318	$ 111,235.08	$ 6,058.59	$ 128,417.18
37	$ 70,684	$ 128,417.18	$ 6,361.52	$ 147,620.42
38	$ 74,218	$ 147,620.42	$ 6,679.60	$ 169,062.06
39	$ 77,929	$ 169,062.06	$ 7,013.58	$ 192,981.84
40	$ 81,825	$ 192,981.84	$ 7,364.25	$ 219,644.28
41	$ 85,916	$ 219,644.28	$ 7,732.47	$ 249,341.18
42	$ 90,212	$ 249,341.18	$ 8,119.09	$ 282,394.39
43	$ 94,723	$ 282,394.39	$ 8,525.05	$ 319,158.87
44	$ 99,459	$ 319,158.87	$ 8,951.30	$ 360,026.06
45	$ 104,432	$ 360,026.06	$ 9,398.86	$ 405,427.52
46	$ 109,653	$ 405,427.52	$ 9,868.81	$ 455,839.08
47	$ 115,136	$ 455,839.08	$ 10,362.25	$ 511,785.24
48	$ 120,893	$ 511,785.24	$ 10,880.36	$ 573,844.12
49	$ 126,938	$ 573,844.12	$ 11,424.38	$ 642,652.91
50	$ 133,284	$ 642,652.91	$ 11,995.60	$ 718,913.79
51	$ 139,949	$ 718,913.79	$ 12,595.37	$ 803,400.55
52	$ 146,946	$ 803,400.55	$ 13,225.14	$ 896,965.74
53	$ 154,293	$ 896,965.74	$ 13,886.40	$ 1,000,548.72
54	$ 162,008	$ 1,000,548.72	$ 14,580.72	$ 1,115,184.31
55	$ 170,108	$ 1,115,184.31	$ 15,309.76	$ 1,242,012.50
56	$ 178,614	$ 1,242,012.50	$ 16,075.24	$ 1,382,288.99
57	$ 187,545	$ 1,382,288.99	$ 16,879.01	$ 1,537,396.90
58	$ 196,922	$ 1,537,396.90	$ 17,722.96	$ 1,708,859.55
59	$ 206,768	$ 1,708,859.55	$ 18,609.11	$ 1,898,354.61
60	$ 217,106	$ 1,898,354.61	$ 19,539.56	$ 2,107,729.63
61	$ 227,962	$ 2,107,729.63	$ 20,516.54	$ 2,339,019.13
62	$ 239,360	$ 2,339,019.13	$ 21,542.37	$ 2,594,463.41
63	$ 251,328	$ 2,594,463.41	$ 22,619.48	$ 2,876,529.23

The trust account has grown to $343,554.44.

Trust Account Year	Starting Value	Savings Amount	Ending Value
1	$ –	$5,000.00	$ 5,000.00
2	$ 5,000.00	$5,000.00	$ 10,500.00
3	$ 10,500.00	$5,000.00	$ 16,550.00
4	$ 16,550.00	$5,000.00	$ 23,205.00
5	$ 23,205.00	$5,000.00	$ 30,525.50
6	$ 30,525.50	$5,000.00	$ 38,578.05
7	$ 38,578.05	$5,000.00	$ 47,435.86
8	$ 47,435.86	$5,000.00	$ 57,179.44
9	$ 57,179.44	$5,000.00	$ 67,897.38
10	$ 67,897.38	$5,000.00	$ 79,687.12
11	$ 79,687.12	$5,000.00	$ 92,655.84
12	$ 92,655.84	$5,000.00	$ 106,921.42
13	$ 106,921.42	$10,000.00	$ 127,613.56
14	$ 127,613.56	$10,000.00	$ 150,374.92
15	$ 150,374.92	$10,000.00	$ 175,412.41
16	$ 175,412.41	$10,000.00	$ 202,953.65
17	$ 202,953.65	$10,000.00	$ 233,249.01
18	$ 233,249.01	$10,000.00	$ 266,573.92
19	$ 266,573.92	$10,000.00	$ 303,231.31
20	$ 303,231.31	$10,000.00	$ 343,554.44

Where They Should Be Investing

Now that Jackson and Maria need to use their investments to fund their living expenses, they need to reallocate their assets into the holy grail portfolio. The holy grail is the portfolio where their income alone from bucket 2 supports their distributions from bucket 1 (the live-off-the-income approach). Bucket 3 is there to help keep up with inflation and leave a financial legacy. In this case Jackson and Maria would map out their projected portfolio distribution adjusted for inflation and net of taxes. For the next two years, here is how much they would need in bucket 1, $692,045.45.

Age	Living Expenses	Taxes	Distribution Needed
60	$ 300,000.00	$ 40,909.09	$ 340,909.09
61	$ 309,000.00	$ 42,136.36	$ 351,136.36
		Total	$ 692,045.45

One year from now they will have spent their first year of living expenses, so they will need to replenish bucket 1 with $361,670.45, which is money they need when Jackson turns 62. This will ensure there is always at least two years in bucket 1.

Age	Living Expenses	Taxes	Distribution Needed
61	$ 309,000.00	$ 42,136.36	$ 351,136.36
62	$ 318,270.00	$ 43,400.45	$ 361,670.45
		Total	$ 712,806.82

The portfolio will have to generate a minimum yield of 6.36% from bucket 2 to produce enough income to generate $361,670.45. This income will be used to replenish bucket 1.

Category	Weight	Weight
Bucket | 1	$ 712,806.82	10.03%
Bucket | 2	$ 5,682,667.70	79.97%
Bucket | 3	$ 710,608.28	10.00%
Total	$ 7,106,082.80	100.00%

Given the current environment, we can produce more income from bucket 2 than the minimum requirement. We can produce $370,725.88 in income from this bucket. The following illustrates how we will accomplish it.

Bucket | 2	$ 5,682,667.70	79.97%	Yield	Income
AMLP	$ 511,440.09	7.20%	7.69%	$ 39,329.74
PFF	$ 568,266.77	8.00%	5.83%	$ 33,129.95
HYG	$ 568,266.77	8.00%	5.32%	$ 30,231.79
VNQ	$ 511,440.09	7.20%	3.76%	$ 19,230.15
NOBL	$ 1,420,666.92	19.99%	1.92%	$ 27,276.80
QYLD	$ 511,440.09	7.20%	12.94%	$ 66,180.35
HYIN	$ 511,440.09	7.20%	12.22%	$ 62,497.98
IDV	$ 568,266.77	8.00%	7.15%	$ 40,631.07
BIZD	$ 511,440.09	7.20%	10.21%	$ 52,218.03
			Total	$ 370,725.88

This process of determining the yield needed from bucket 2 will continue each year and we would make sure this bucket produces enough income to replenish the money needed in bucket 1.

Success!

There you have it—the power of two people working hard and consistently making the wealth-maximizing decisions has created by any definition an enviable amount of wealth and income. There is no doubt they will be able to comfortably enjoy their retirement and live a life they both love.

I hope you can take lessons from Jackson and Maria as proof that this information can also be applied to your own life.

Chapter 19
Case Study
Executive Summary

How do you stack up against Jackson and Maria detailed in the previous chapters?

Do you like what you saw by this power couple? As a quick guide to benchmark yourself against where you personally stand compared to Jackson and Maria, I have created an executive summary in this chapter for you to use as a guide. Check where you stand and your newfound information to get started.

Age 18 Executive Summary

You must save $1,859.99 annually at a 10% rate of return to accumulate $1,000,000 by age 60.

Current Account Value	$ –		
Rate of Return	10.0%		
Current Age	18		
Target Age	60		
Account Value Goal at Target Age	$ 1,000,000		
Annual Savings Needed	($1,859.99)		

Roth IRA			
Age	Starting Value	Savings Amount	Ending Value
18	$ –	$1,859.99	$ 1,859.99
19	$ 1,859.99	$1,859.99	$ 3,905.98
20	$ 3,905.98	$1,859.99	$ 6,156.57
21	$ 6,156.57	$1,859.99	$ 8,632.22
22	$ 8,632.22	$1,859.99	$ 11,355.43
23	$ 11,355.43	$1,859.99	$ 14,350.97
24	$ 14,350.97	$1,859.99	$ 17,646.05
25	$ 17,646.05	$1,859.99	$ 21,270.65
26	$ 21,270.65	$1,859.99	$ 25,257.71
27	$ 25,257.71	$1,859.99	$ 29,643.47
28	$ 29,643.47	$1,859.99	$ 34,467.81
29	$ 34,467.81	$1,859.99	$ 39,774.58
30	$ 39,774.58	$1,859.99	$ 45,612.03
31	$ 45,612.03	$1,859.99	$ 52,033.22
32	$ 52,033.22	$1,859.99	$ 59,096.53
33	$ 59,096.53	$1,859.99	$ 66,866.18
34	$ 66,866.18	$1,859.99	$ 75,412.78
35	$ 75,412.78	$1,859.99	$ 84,814.05
36	$ 84,814.05	$1,859.99	$ 95,155.45
37	$ 95,155.45	$1,859.99	$ 106,530.99
38	$ 106,530.99	$1,859.99	$ 119,044.08
39	$ 119,044.08	$1,859.99	$ 132,808.48
40	$ 132,808.48	$1,859.99	$ 147,949.31
41	$ 147,949.31	$1,859.99	$ 164,604.24
42	$ 164,604.24	$1,859.99	$ 182,924.65
43	$ 182,924.65	$1,859.99	$ 203,077.11
44	$ 203,077.11	$1,859.99	$ 225,244.81
45	$ 225,244.81	$1,859.99	$ 249,629.28
46	$ 249,629.28	$1,859.99	$ 276,452.20
47	$ 276,452.20	$1,859.99	$ 305,957.41
48	$ 305,957.41	$1,859.99	$ 338,413.14
49	$ 338,413.14	$1,859.99	$ 374,114.45
50	$ 374,114.45	$1,859.99	$ 413,385.89
51	$ 413,385.89	$1,859.99	$ 456,584.47
52	$ 456,584.47	$1,859.99	$ 504,102.90
53	$ 504,102.90	$1,859.99	$ 556,373.18
54	$ 556,373.18	$1,859.99	$ 613,870.49
55	$ 613,870.49	$1,859.99	$ 677,117.53
56	$ 677,117.53	$1,859.99	$ 746,689.28
57	$ 746,689.28	$1,859.99	$ 823,218.20
58	$ 823,218.20	$1,859.99	$ 907,400.01
59	$ 907,400.01	$1,859.99	$ 1,000,000.00

Age 24 Executive Summary

To be on target to save $1,000,000 by age 60, you must have a current account value of $14,350.97.

If you are behind:

- By 25% you must invest $2,230.76 annually
- By 50% you must invest $2,601.53 annually
- By 75% you must invest $2,972.30 annually
- By 100% you must invest $3,343.06 annually

Behind by	25%			Behind by	50%		
Current Account Value	$ 10,763.22			Current Account Value	$ 7,175.48		
Rate of Return	10.0%			Rate of Return	10.0%		
Current Age	24			Current Age	24		
Target Age	60			Target Age	60		
Account Value Goal at Target Age	$ 1,000,000			Account Value Goal at Target Age	$ 1,000,000		
Annual Savings Needed	($2,230.76)			Annual Savings Needed	($2,601.53)		
Age	Starting Value	Savings Amount	Ending Value	Age	Starting Value	Savings Amount	Ending Value
24	$ 10,763.22	$2,230.76	$ 14,070.31	24	$ 7,175.48	$2,601.53	$ 10,494.56
25	$ 14,070.31	$2,230.76	$ 17,708.10	25	$ 10,494.56	$2,601.53	$ 14,145.54
26	$ 17,708.10	$2,230.76	$ 21,709.66	26	$ 14,145.54	$2,601.53	$ 18,161.62
27	$ 21,709.66	$2,230.76	$ 26,111.39	27	$ 18,161.62	$2,601.53	$ 22,579.31
28	$ 26,111.39	$2,230.76	$ 30,953.29	28	$ 22,579.31	$2,601.53	$ 27,438.77
29	$ 30,953.29	$2,230.76	$ 36,279.38	29	$ 27,438.77	$2,601.53	$ 32,784.18
30	$ 36,279.38	$2,230.76	$ 42,138.07	30	$ 32,784.18	$2,601.53	$ 38,664.12
31	$ 42,138.07	$2,230.76	$ 48,582.64	31	$ 38,664.12	$2,601.53	$ 45,132.06
32	$ 48,582.64	$2,230.76	$ 55,671.66	32	$ 45,132.06	$2,601.53	$ 52,246.79
33	$ 55,671.66	$2,230.76	$ 63,469.59	33	$ 52,246.79	$2,601.53	$ 60,073.00
34	$ 63,469.59	$2,230.76	$ 72,047.31	34	$ 60,073.00	$2,601.53	$ 68,681.83
35	$ 72,047.31	$2,230.76	$ 81,482.80	35	$ 68,681.83	$2,601.53	$ 78,151.54
36	$ 81,482.80	$2,230.76	$ 91,861.84	36	$ 78,151.54	$2,601.53	$ 88,568.22
37	$ 91,861.84	$2,230.76	$ 103,278.78	37	$ 88,568.22	$2,601.53	$ 100,026.57
38	$ 103,278.78	$2,230.76	$ 115,837.42	38	$ 100,026.57	$2,601.53	$ 112,630.76
39	$ 115,837.42	$2,230.76	$ 129,651.92	39	$ 112,630.76	$2,601.53	$ 126,495.36
40	$ 129,651.92	$2,230.76	$ 144,847.87	40	$ 126,495.36	$2,601.53	$ 141,746.42
41	$ 144,847.87	$2,230.76	$ 161,563.41	41	$ 141,746.42	$2,601.53	$ 158,522.59
42	$ 161,563.41	$2,230.76	$ 179,950.51	42	$ 158,522.59	$2,601.53	$ 176,976.38
43	$ 179,950.51	$2,230.76	$ 200,176.33	43	$ 176,976.38	$2,601.53	$ 197,275.54
44	$ 200,176.33	$2,230.76	$ 222,424.72	44	$ 197,275.54	$2,601.53	$ 219,604.62
45	$ 222,424.72	$2,230.76	$ 246,897.95	45	$ 219,604.62	$2,601.53	$ 244,166.61
46	$ 246,897.95	$2,230.76	$ 273,818.50	46	$ 244,166.61	$2,601.53	$ 271,184.80
47	$ 273,818.50	$2,230.76	$ 303,431.11	47	$ 271,184.80	$2,601.53	$ 300,904.81
48	$ 303,431.11	$2,230.76	$ 336,004.98	48	$ 300,904.81	$2,601.53	$ 333,596.82
49	$ 336,004.98	$2,230.76	$ 371,836.24	49	$ 333,596.82	$2,601.53	$ 369,558.03
50	$ 371,836.24	$2,230.76	$ 411,250.62	50	$ 369,558.03	$2,601.53	$ 409,115.36
51	$ 411,250.62	$2,230.76	$ 454,606.44	51	$ 409,115.36	$2,601.53	$ 452,628.42
52	$ 454,606.44	$2,230.76	$ 502,297.85	52	$ 452,628.42	$2,601.53	$ 500,492.79
53	$ 502,297.85	$2,230.76	$ 554,758.39	53	$ 500,492.79	$2,601.53	$ 553,143.60
54	$ 554,758.39	$2,230.76	$ 612,464.99	54	$ 553,143.60	$2,601.53	$ 611,059.49
55	$ 612,464.99	$2,230.76	$ 675,942.25	55	$ 611,059.49	$2,601.53	$ 674,766.96
56	$ 675,942.25	$2,230.76	$ 745,767.23	56	$ 674,766.96	$2,601.53	$ 744,845.19
57	$ 745,767.23	$2,230.76	$ 822,574.72	57	$ 744,845.19	$2,601.53	$ 821,931.23
58	$ 822,574.72	$2,230.76	$ 907,062.95	58	$ 821,931.23	$2,601.53	$ 908,725.88
59	$ 907,062.95	$2,230.76	$1,000,000.00	59	$ 908,725.88	$2,601.53	$1,000,000.00

Behind by	75%			Behind by	100%		
Current Account Value	$ 3,587.74			Current Account Value	$ –		
Rate of Return	10.0%			Rate of Return	10.0%		
Current Age	24			Current Age	24		
Target Age	60			Target Age	60		
Account Value Goal at Target Age	$ 1,000,000			Account Value Goal at Target Age	$ 1,000,000		
Annual Savings Needed	($2,972.30)			Annual Savings Needed	($3,343.06)		

Age	Starting Value	Savings Amount	Ending Value	Age	Starting Value	Savings Amount	Ending Value
24	$ 3,587.74	$2,972.30	$ 6,918.81	24	$ –	$3,343.06	$ 3,343.06
25	$ 6,918.81	$2,972.30	$ 10,582.99	25	$ 3,343.06	$3,343.06	$ 7,020.43
26	$ 10,582.99	$2,972.30	$ 14,613.58	26	$ 7,020.43	$3,343.06	$ 11,065.54
27	$ 14,613.58	$2,972.30	$ 19,047.24	27	$ 11,065.54	$3,343.06	$ 15,515.16
28	$ 19,047.24	$2,972.30	$ 23,924.26	28	$ 15,515.16	$3,343.06	$ 20,409.74
29	$ 23,924.26	$2,972.30	$ 29,288.98	29	$ 20,409.74	$3,343.06	$ 25,793.78
30	$ 29,288.98	$2,972.30	$ 35,190.17	30	$ 25,793.78	$3,343.06	$ 31,716.22
31	$ 35,190.17	$2,972.30	$ 41,681.48	31	$ 31,716.22	$3,343.06	$ 38,230.90
32	$ 41,681.48	$2,972.30	$ 48,821.93	32	$ 38,230.90	$3,343.06	$ 45,397.06
33	$ 48,821.93	$2,972.30	$ 56,676.41	33	$ 45,397.06	$3,343.06	$ 53,279.83
34	$ 56,676.41	$2,972.30	$ 65,316.35	34	$ 53,279.83	$3,343.06	$ 61,950.87
35	$ 65,316.35	$2,972.30	$ 74,820.28	35	$ 61,950.87	$3,343.06	$ 71,489.03
36	$ 74,820.28	$2,972.30	$ 85,274.61	36	$ 71,489.03	$3,343.06	$ 81,980.99
37	$ 85,274.61	$2,972.30	$ 96,774.36	37	$ 81,980.99	$3,343.06	$ 93,522.15
38	$ 96,774.36	$2,972.30	$ 109,424.09	38	$ 93,522.15	$3,343.06	$ 106,217.43
39	$ 109,424.09	$2,972.30	$ 123,338.80	39	$ 106,217.43	$3,343.06	$ 120,182.24
40	$ 123,338.80	$2,972.30	$ 138,644.98	40	$ 120,182.24	$3,343.06	$ 135,543.53
41	$ 138,644.98	$2,972.30	$ 155,481.77	41	$ 135,543.53	$3,343.06	$ 152,440.95
42	$ 155,481.77	$2,972.30	$ 174,002.24	42	$ 152,440.95	$3,343.06	$ 171,028.10
43	$ 174,002.24	$2,972.30	$ 194,374.76	43	$ 171,028.10	$3,343.06	$ 191,473.98
44	$ 194,374.76	$2,972.30	$ 216,784.53	44	$ 191,473.98	$3,343.06	$ 213,964.44
45	$ 216,784.53	$2,972.30	$ 241,435.28	45	$ 213,964.44	$3,343.06	$ 238,703.95
46	$ 241,435.28	$2,972.30	$ 268,551.11	46	$ 238,703.95	$3,343.06	$ 265,917.41
47	$ 268,551.11	$2,972.30	$ 298,378.51	47	$ 265,917.41	$3,343.06	$ 295,852.21
48	$ 298,378.51	$2,972.30	$ 331,188.66	48	$ 295,852.21	$3,343.06	$ 328,780.50
49	$ 331,188.66	$2,972.30	$ 367,279.82	49	$ 328,780.50	$3,343.06	$ 365,001.61
50	$ 367,279.82	$2,972.30	$ 406,980.10	50	$ 365,001.61	$3,343.06	$ 404,844.83
51	$ 406,980.10	$2,972.30	$ 450,650.40	51	$ 404,844.83	$3,343.06	$ 448,672.38
52	$ 450,650.40	$2,972.30	$ 498,687.74	52	$ 448,672.38	$3,343.06	$ 496,882.68
53	$ 498,687.74	$2,972.30	$ 551,526.81	53	$ 496,882.68	$3,343.06	$ 549,914.02
54	$ 551,526.81	$2,972.30	$ 609,653.98	54	$ 549,914.02	$3,343.06	$ 608,248.48
55	$ 609,653.98	$2,972.30	$ 673,591.68	55	$ 608,248.48	$3,343.06	$ 672,416.39
56	$ 673,591.68	$2,972.30	$ 743,923.14	56	$ 672,416.39	$3,343.06	$ 743,001.10
57	$ 743,923.14	$2,972.30	$ 821,287.75	57	$ 743,001.10	$3,343.06	$ 820,644.27
58	$ 821,287.75	$2,972.30	$ 906,388.82	58	$ 820,644.27	$3,343.06	$ 906,051.76
59	$ 906,388.82	$2,972.30	$1,000,000.00	59	$ 906,051.76	$3,343.06	$1,000,000.00

Age 34 Executive Summary

To be on target to save $1,000,000 by age 60 you must have a current account value of $66,866.18.

If you are behind:

- By 25% you must invest $3,684.75 annually
- By 50% you must invest $5,509.51 annually
- By 75% you must invest $7,334.28 annually
- By 100% you must invest $9,159.04 annually

Behind by	25%		
Current Account Value	$ 50,149.63		
Rate of Return	10.0%		
Current Age	34		
Target Age	60		
Account Value Goal at Target Age	$ 1,000,000		
Annual Savings Needed	($3,684.75)		

Age	Starting Value	Savings Amount	Ending Value
34	$ 50,149.63	$3,684.75	$ 58,849.35
35	$ 58,849.35	$3,684.75	$ 68,419.04
36	$ 68,419.04	$3,684.75	$ 78,945.69
37	$ 78,945.69	$3,684.75	$ 90,525.01
38	$ 90,525.01	$3,684.75	$ 103,262.27
39	$ 103,262.27	$3,684.75	$ 117,273.25
40	$ 117,273.25	$3,684.75	$ 132,685.33
41	$ 132,685.33	$3,684.75	$ 149,638.61
42	$ 149,638.61	$3,684.75	$ 168,287.23
43	$ 168,287.23	$3,684.75	$ 188,800.70
44	$ 188,800.70	$3,684.75	$ 211,365.53
45	$ 211,365.53	$3,684.75	$ 236,186.83
46	$ 236,186.83	$3,684.75	$ 263,490.27
47	$ 263,490.27	$3,684.75	$ 293,524.05
48	$ 293,524.05	$3,684.75	$ 326,561.20
49	$ 326,561.20	$3,684.75	$ 362,902.08
50	$ 362,902.08	$3,684.75	$ 402,877.04
51	$ 402,877.04	$3,684.75	$ 446,849.50
52	$ 446,849.50	$3,684.75	$ 495,219.20
53	$ 495,219.20	$3,684.75	$ 548,425.87
54	$ 548,425.87	$3,684.75	$ 606,953.21
55	$ 606,953.21	$3,684.75	$ 671,333.28
56	$ 671,333.28	$3,684.75	$ 742,151.37
57	$ 742,151.37	$3,684.75	$ 820,051.26
58	$ 820,051.26	$3,684.75	$ 905,741.13
59	$ 905,741.13	$3,684.75	$1,000,000.00

Behind by	50%		
Current Account Value	$ 33,433.09		
Rate of Return	10.0%		
Current Age	34		
Target Age	60		
Account Value Goal at Target Age	$ 1,000,000		
Annual Savings Needed	($5,509.51)		

Age	Starting Value	Savings Amount	Ending Value
34	$ 33,433.09	$5,509.51	$ 42,285.91
35	$ 42,285.91	$5,509.51	$ 52,024.02
36	$ 52,024.02	$5,509.51	$ 62,735.93
37	$ 62,735.93	$5,509.51	$ 74,519.04
38	$ 74,519.04	$5,509.51	$ 87,480.46
39	$ 87,480.46	$5,509.51	$ 101,738.02
40	$ 101,738.02	$5,509.51	$ 117,421.34
41	$ 117,421.34	$5,509.51	$ 134,672.99
42	$ 134,672.99	$5,509.51	$ 153,649.80
43	$ 153,649.80	$5,509.51	$ 174,524.30
44	$ 174,524.30	$5,509.51	$ 197,486.24
45	$ 197,486.24	$5,509.51	$ 222,744.38
46	$ 222,744.38	$5,509.51	$ 250,528.33
47	$ 250,528.33	$5,509.51	$ 281,090.68
48	$ 281,090.68	$5,509.51	$ 314,709.26
49	$ 314,709.26	$5,509.51	$ 351,689.71
50	$ 351,689.71	$5,509.51	$ 392,368.19
51	$ 392,368.19	$5,509.51	$ 437,114.53
52	$ 437,114.53	$5,509.51	$ 486,335.49
53	$ 486,335.49	$5,509.51	$ 540,478.56
54	$ 540,478.56	$5,509.51	$ 600,035.93
55	$ 600,035.93	$5,509.51	$ 665,549.03
56	$ 665,549.03	$5,509.51	$ 737,613.45
57	$ 737,613.45	$5,509.51	$ 816,884.31
58	$ 816,884.31	$5,509.51	$ 904,082.26
59	$ 904,082.26	$5,509.51	$1,000,000.00

Behind by	75%		
Current Account Value	$ 16,716.54		
Rate of Return	10.0%		
Current Age	34		
Target Age	60		
Account Value Goal at Target Age	$ 1,000,000		
Annual Savings Needed	($7,334.28)		

Age	Starting Value	Savings Amount	Ending Value
34	$ 16,716.54	$7,334.28	$ 25,722.48
35	$ 25,722.48	$7,334.28	$ 35,629.00
36	$ 35,629.00	$7,334.28	$ 46,526.18
37	$ 46,526.18	$7,334.28	$ 58,513.07
38	$ 58,513.07	$7,334.28	$ 71,698.65
39	$ 71,698.65	$7,334.28	$ 86,202.80
40	$ 86,202.80	$7,334.28	$ 102,157.35
41	$ 102,157.35	$7,334.28	$ 119,707.36
42	$ 119,707.36	$7,334.28	$ 139,012.38
43	$ 139,012.38	$7,334.28	$ 160,247.89
44	$ 160,247.89	$7,334.28	$ 183,606.96
45	$ 183,606.96	$7,334.28	$ 209,301.93
46	$ 209,301.93	$7,334.28	$ 237,566.40
47	$ 237,566.40	$7,334.28	$ 268,657.32
48	$ 268,657.32	$7,334.28	$ 302,857.32
49	$ 302,857.32	$7,334.28	$ 340,477.33
50	$ 340,477.33	$7,334.28	$ 381,859.34
51	$ 381,859.34	$7,334.28	$ 427,379.56
52	$ 427,379.56	$7,334.28	$ 477,451.79
53	$ 477,451.79	$7,334.28	$ 532,531.24
54	$ 532,531.24	$7,334.28	$ 593,118.64
55	$ 593,118.64	$7,334.28	$ 659,764.79
56	$ 659,764.79	$7,334.28	$ 733,075.54
57	$ 733,075.54	$7,334.28	$ 813,717.37
58	$ 813,717.37	$7,334.28	$ 902,423.38
59	$ 902,423.38	$7,334.28	$1,000,000.00

Behind by	100%		
Current Account Value	$ –		
Rate of Return	10.0%		
Current Age	34		
Target Age	60		
Account Value Goal at Target Age	$ 1,000,000		
Annual Savings Needed	($9,159.04)		

Age	Starting Value	Savings Amount	Ending Value
34	$ –	$9,159.04	$ 9,159.04
35	$ 9,159.04	$9,159.04	$ 19,233.98
36	$ 19,233.98	$9,159.04	$ 30,316.42
37	$ 30,316.42	$9,159.04	$ 42,507.10
38	$ 42,507.10	$9,159.04	$ 55,916.85
39	$ 55,916.85	$9,159.04	$ 70,667.57
40	$ 70,667.57	$9,159.04	$ 86,893.37
41	$ 86,893.37	$9,159.04	$ 104,741.74
42	$ 104,741.74	$9,159.04	$ 124,374.95
43	$ 124,374.95	$9,159.04	$ 145,971.49
44	$ 145,971.49	$9,159.04	$ 169,727.67
45	$ 169,727.67	$9,159.04	$ 195,859.48
46	$ 195,859.48	$9,159.04	$ 224,604.47
47	$ 224,604.47	$9,159.04	$ 256,223.95
48	$ 256,223.95	$9,159.04	$ 291,005.39
49	$ 291,005.39	$9,159.04	$ 329,264.96
50	$ 329,264.96	$9,159.04	$ 371,350.50
51	$ 371,350.50	$9,159.04	$ 417,644.59
52	$ 417,644.59	$9,159.04	$ 468,568.08
53	$ 468,568.08	$9,159.04	$ 524,583.93
54	$ 524,583.93	$9,159.04	$ 586,201.36
55	$ 586,201.36	$9,159.04	$ 653,980.54
56	$ 653,980.54	$9,159.04	$ 728,537.63
57	$ 728,537.63	$9,159.04	$ 810,550.43
58	$ 810,550.43	$9,159.04	$ 900,764.51
59	$ 900,764.51	$9,159.04	$1,000,000.00

Age 44 Executive Summary

To be on target to save $1,000,000 by age 60 you must have a current account value of $203,077.11.

If you are behind:

- By 25% you must invest $8,349.15 annually
- By 50% you must invest $14,838.31 annually
- By 75% you must invest $21,327.46 annually
- By 100% you must invest $27,816.62 annually

Behind by	25%			Behind by	50%		
Current Account Value	$ 152,307.83			Current Account Value	$ 101,538.55		
Rate of Return	10.0%			Rate of Return	10.0%		
Current Age	44			Current Age	44		
Target Age	60			Target Age	60		
Account Value Goal at Target Age	$ 1,000,000			Account Value Goal at Target Age	$ 1,000,000		
Annual Savings Needed	($8,349.15)			Annual Savings Needed	($14,838.31)		

Age	Starting Value	Savings Amount	Ending Value	Age	Starting Value	Savings Amount	Ending Value
44	$ 152,307.83	$8,349.15	$ 175,887.76	44	$ 101,538.55	$14,838.31	$ 126,530.72
45	$ 175,887.76	$8,349.15	$ 201,825.69	45	$ 126,530.72	$14,838.31	$ 154,022.09
46	$ 201,825.69	$8,349.15	$ 230,357.40	46	$ 154,022.09	$14,838.31	$ 184,262.61
47	$ 230,357.40	$8,349.15	$ 261,742.29	47	$ 184,262.61	$14,838.31	$ 217,527.17
48	$ 261,742.29	$8,349.15	$ 296,265.67	48	$ 217,527.17	$14,838.31	$ 254,118.20
49	$ 296,265.67	$8,349.15	$ 334,241.39	49	$ 254,118.20	$14,838.31	$ 294,368.32
50	$ 334,241.39	$8,349.15	$ 376,014.67	50	$ 294,368.32	$14,838.31	$ 338,643.46
51	$ 376,014.67	$8,349.15	$ 421,965.29	51	$ 338,643.46	$14,838.31	$ 387,346.11
52	$ 421,965.29	$8,349.15	$ 472,510.97	52	$ 387,346.11	$14,838.31	$ 440,919.03
53	$ 472,510.97	$8,349.15	$ 528,111.21	53	$ 440,919.03	$14,838.31	$ 499,849.24
54	$ 528,111.21	$8,349.15	$ 589,271.48	54	$ 499,849.24	$14,838.31	$ 564,672.47
55	$ 589,271.48	$8,349.15	$ 656,547.78	55	$ 564,672.47	$14,838.31	$ 635,978.02
56	$ 656,547.78	$8,349.15	$ 730,551.70	56	$ 635,978.02	$14,838.31	$ 714,414.13
57	$ 730,551.70	$8,349.15	$ 811,956.02	57	$ 714,414.13	$14,838.31	$ 800,693.85
58	$ 811,956.02	$8,349.15	$ 901,500.77	58	$ 800,693.85	$14,838.31	$ 895,601.54
59	$ 901,500.77	$8,349.15	$1,000,000.00	59	$ 895,601.54	$14,838.31	$1,000,000.00

Behind by	75%			Behind by	100%		
Current Account Value	$ 50,769.28			Current Account Value	$ –		
Rate of Return	10.0%			Rate of Return	10.0%		
Current Age	44			Current Age	44		
Target Age	60			Target Age	60		
Account Value Goal at Target Age	$ 1,000,000			Account Value Goal at Target Age	$ 1,000,000		
Annual Savings Needed	($21,327.46)			Annual Savings Needed	($27,816.62)		

Age	Starting Value	Savings Amount	Ending Value	Age	Starting Value	Savings Amount	Ending Value
44	$ 50,769.28	$21,327.46	$ 77,173.67	44	$ –	$27,816.62	$ 27,816.62
45	$ 77,173.67	$21,327.46	$ 106,218.50	45	$ 27,816.62	$27,816.62	$ 58,414.90
46	$ 106,218.50	$21,327.46	$ 138,167.81	46	$ 58,414.90	$27,816.62	$ 92,073.01
47	$ 138,167.81	$21,327.46	$ 173,312.06	47	$ 92,073.01	$27,816.62	$ 129,096.94
48	$ 173,312.06	$21,327.46	$ 211,970.72	48	$ 129,096.94	$27,816.62	$ 169,823.25
49	$ 211,970.72	$21,327.46	$ 254,495.26	49	$ 169,823.25	$27,816.62	$ 214,622.20
50	$ 254,495.26	$21,327.46	$ 301,272.25	50	$ 214,622.20	$27,816.62	$ 263,901.04
51	$ 301,272.25	$21,327.46	$ 352,726.94	51	$ 263,901.04	$27,816.62	$ 318,107.76
52	$ 352,726.94	$21,327.46	$ 409,327.09	52	$ 318,107.76	$27,816.62	$ 377,735.16
53	$ 409,327.09	$21,327.46	$ 471,587.27	53	$ 377,735.16	$27,816.62	$ 443,325.30
54	$ 471,587.27	$21,327.46	$ 540,073.46	54	$ 443,325.30	$27,816.62	$ 515,474.45
55	$ 540,073.46	$21,327.46	$ 615,408.27	55	$ 515,474.45	$27,816.62	$ 594,838.51
56	$ 615,408.27	$21,327.46	$ 698,276.56	56	$ 594,838.51	$27,816.62	$ 682,138.98
57	$ 698,276.56	$21,327.46	$ 789,431.68	57	$ 682,138.98	$27,816.62	$ 778,169.50
58	$ 789,431.68	$21,327.46	$ 889,702.31	58	$ 778,169.50	$27,816.62	$ 883,803.07
59	$ 889,702.31	$21,327.46	$1,000,000.00	59	$ 883,803.07	$27,816.62	$1,000,000.00

Age 54 Executive Summary

To be on target to save $1,000,000 by age 60 you must have a current account value of $556,373.18.

  If you are behind:

- By 25% you must invest $33,796.84 annually
- By 50% you must invest $65,733.69 annually
- By 75% you must invest $97,670.53 annually
- By 100% you must invest $129,607.38 annually

Behind by	25%
Current Account Value	$ 417,279.89
Rate of Return	10.0%
Current Age	54
Target Age	60
Account Value Goal at Target Age	$ 1,000,000
Annual Savings Needed	($33,796.84)

Age	Starting Value	Savings Amount	Ending Value
54	$ 417,279.89	$33,796.84	$ 492,804.72
55	$ 492,804.72	$33,796.84	$ 575,882.03
56	$ 575,882.03	$33,796.84	$ 667,267.07
57	$ 667,267.07	$33,796.84	$ 767,790.61
58	$ 767,790.61	$33,796.84	$ 878,366.51
59	$ 878,366.51	$33,796.84	$1,000,000.00

Behind by	50%
Current Account Value	$ 278,186.59
Rate of Return	10.0%
Current Age	54
Target Age	60
Account Value Goal at Target Age	$ 1,000,000
Annual Savings Needed	($65,733.69)

Age	Starting Value	Savings Amount	Ending Value
54	$ 278,186.59	$65,733.69	$ 371,738.94
55	$ 371,738.94	$65,733.69	$ 474,646.52
56	$ 474,646.52	$65,733.69	$ 587,844.85
57	$ 587,844.85	$65,733.69	$ 712,363.02
58	$ 712,363.02	$65,733.69	$ 849,333.01
59	$ 849,333.01	$65,733.69	$1,000,000.00

Behind by	75%
Current Account Value	$ 139,093.30
Rate of Return	10.0%
Current Age	54
Target Age	60
Account Value Goal at Target Age	$ 1,000,000
Annual Savings Needed	($97,670.53)

Age	Starting Value	Savings Amount	Ending Value
54	$ 139,093.30	$97,670.53	$ 250,673.16
55	$ 250,673.16	$97,670.53	$ 373,411.01
56	$ 373,411.01	$97,670.53	$ 508,422.64
57	$ 508,422.64	$97,670.53	$ 656,935.44
58	$ 656,935.44	$97,670.53	$ 820,299.52
59	$ 820,299.52	$97,670.53	$1,000,000.00

Behind by	100%
Current Account Value	$ –
Rate of Return	10.0%
Current Age	54
Target Age	60
Account Value Goal at Target Age	$ 1,000,000
Annual Savings Needed	($129,607.38)

Age	Starting Value	Savings Amount	Ending Value
54	$ –	$129,607.38	$ 129,607.38
55	$ 129,607.38	$129,607.38	$ 272,175.50
56	$ 272,175.50	$129,607.38	$ 429,000.43
57	$ 429,000.43	$129,607.38	$ 601,507.85
58	$ 601,507.85	$129,607.38	$ 791,266.02
59	$ 791,266.02	$129,607.38	$1,000,000.00

Time to Act

Now that you have gone through this information and seen exactly where you stand, it's time to act. This cannot be the part of the book where you set it on the shelf and do nothing. No matter your age, how much or how little you have done to improve your financial position so far, and no matter your current resources, there are actions that you can take today. This will be a pivotal point in your life. You must decide right now if you are going to settle for a life of mediocrity and some discount version of what your life could be, or if you are going to take decisive action to live your best life.

I recommend now that you see where you should be based on your current life stage and then go through this book at least one more time. You will be approaching it this second time around with newfound knowledge, so the information will start to resonate even more than it did the first time.

When you go through the second time, take notes on how this information pertains to you. Specifically, start building an action plan utilizing where you currently stand within the age bands that we just reviewed and where you should be. Create a checklist. What have you already accomplished and what do you still need to do? Even if it's something as simple as starting a Roth IRA with $50 a month or investing $100 a month into starting your emergency account, there are things that you can do today.

Don't get overwhelmed if you looked at where you should be in these age brackets and realized you are behind. Most people are. What *most* people do, though, is absolutely nothing. They make excuses, procrastinate, and continue to do nothing. Your difference will be the actions that you take. You saw what simply acting did for Jackson and Maria. Procrastination will do the exact opposite.

Epilogue

The truth is that money makes things better, and, most important, it provides us with choice. Money gives you access to better healthcare, better neighborhoods, better schools, better experiences, and better relationships. Don't believe it? Money issues are a leading cause for divorce and create stress that most of us would love to have removed from our lives.

Money doesn't appear by chance or by mistake, though. Building wealth is an intentional commitment to continually making the right money choices day in and day out. Wealth comes from education, discipline, and perseverance. Money is as much a mind game as it is an academic and experience game. Your mindset and dedication to continually learn, improve, and take strategic action will determine the level of wealth you build and the impact it has on your life.

Money is certainly not everything, but I can tell you this: I have been poor, and I have been rich. There was never a situation that I faced where I preferred to be poor over rich. I'll take rich every time.

Money won't make you a good or a bad person, but it will probably magnify the person you already are today.

When I wrote this book, my goal was to help as many people as possible to upgrade their lives. I wanted to take the thousands of conversations that I have had over the years with all the families that I have helped to live their dreams and bring that knowledge to you in as simple of a manner as possible. I wanted to educate you but also provide you as much actionable information as I possibly could so that you could use this information to improve your life right now.

I wanted this book to be as close as possible to having me right there in your living room helping you to strategize and providing you with the answers to assist on every financial decision that you encounter. That is really my mission today. Through my Wealth Academy, where I educate my members each week, to my financial services firm Real Talk Holdings, where we have democratized high-quality financial advice and solutions, my YouTube and social media channels, where I provide free ongoing education, and now this book, everything I do now is about educating and helping people with no high fees, no account minimums, and meeting people where they are today in order to place and guide them on a path to continually make wealth-maximizing decisions. This information should be common knowledge, but sometimes it seems as though financial literacy is like chasing a leprechaun for his pot of gold at the end of the rainbow. That shouldn't be the case.

My team and I are very passionate about the work we are doing. Whether we are helping somebody purchase their first piece of real estate, make their first investment in the stock market, or start a profitable side hustle that morphs into a successful business, I am very inspired to continue to reach more people and watch the quality of their life improve.

I am extremely grateful to be in this position today and understand that it is a huge responsibility. My goal is to help at least one million people better their lives by increasing their financial IQ. I will be quite pleased if that becomes the professional legacy that I leave behind. I need your help, though. Please help me to execute my mission by having this change start with yourself. Please use this book, use my free services such as my website, my social media, and YouTube channel, to continue to stay informed and educate yourself and your family. Act on this information regularly and encourage others to do the same.

I want to hear your stories of success. Please share your stories by tagging me on social media and using the hash tag #closeyourwealthgap. Success is contagious. The more people can see others like yourself implementing these lessons and reaping the rewards that come through improving your financial life, the more they will want to join this movement. It's all about removing excuses, leveling the playing field, and providing access to the information, tools, and people that can help facilitate these changes. Now that you understand the core concepts that you need to begin building your own financial legacy, make sure that you take decisive action.

Don't wait another day to get started.

Appendix A
Resources

B efore we conclude, I will share some of the resources that I continually recommend to others and many times use myself. The key is lifelong education. I am a big believer in continuous learning. Change is the only constant, and staying updated and informed is an ongoing criterion of being the best possible version of yourself.

Risk and opportunities are dynamic. It's impossible to write a book with specific how-tos in any environment. That is because what may present a big opportunity today could very well become a big risk a year from now. For example, if there were a large decline in housing of, say, 15% plus, that would probably create a great buying opportunity for those who have been on the sidelines. But if prices rose 20% over the next year, and more inventory flooded the market, how could that still be the same opportunity? The answer is it wouldn't. There would be a far different risk and reward profile associated with buying real estate after it had such a huge run up and the supply and demand situation had changed. The same thing could be said for every major asset class out there.

There will be macro (large) economic moves that impact assets and micro (smaller) economic moves that are continually influencing what actions you should take with your money. In this book I taught you a lot more about ways to think and frameworks to help you than I did about exactly what to think or exactly what model to use. That would be nice if everything worked out by just setting and forgetting it. The truth is things will need to adapt.

There was some low-hanging fruit we discussed that will always be the wealth-maximizing decisions like making sure you get the highest rate for your savings, funding your emergency fund, tax minimization strategies, and other things that you will always benefit from doing. Most of financial literacy is about taking information that is dynamic and digesting that information in order to act on it in a way that is most impactful to your life.

Finding mentors, courses, and groups that share in the same thirst for knowledge and provide information will be essential. I have outlined resources to consider for more education and to stay informed. In full disclosure, I have economic gain in some of these resources, such as my Wealth Academy. From most I receive absolutely nothing.

This by no means is an exhaustive list. These just happen to be people I like, follow, and value their information. There are plenty of good resources that are out there but please just make sure they have been vetted by someone you trust because there is also a lot of garbage being sold that will hurt more than it will help you. Whatever you do though make sure you continue to stay informed and engaged in building your financial legacy and achieving your desired lifestyle. Building wealth is a lifelong commitment.

We also talked about upgrading your life. That will mean something different to everyone. What I wanted to do though is share my personal list of favorite things. Some small and some large luxuries that I personally enjoy, and some may be of interest to you. You will be able to find this along with your other resources on the books website www.closeyourwealthgaptools.com. I would love to hear your list as well. After all, I think that after freedom, new memories are the best things that money can buy. Share your experiences.

My Resources and Related

These are resources that I am involved with personally and from which I may receive monetary gain.

- **This book's official site** (www.closeyourwealthgaptools.com): Free calculators and updated information to improve on the information you learned in the book and to stay in touch with me.
- **The Rob Luna Wealth Academy** (https://robluna.com/wealth-academy): Lifelong learning and networking membership for investors and entrepreneurs.
- **The Lunatick Investor** (https://TheLunatickInvestor.com): Subscription service for publicly traded investment ideas that my team and I personally research and invest in.
- **My YouTube Channel** (www.youtube.com/lunarob): Check me out on YouTube.
- **Instagram** (@TheLunaRob): My Instagram account.
- **Twitter** (@TheLunaRob): My personal corner of Twitter.

Social Media Accounts

For now, I believe that Twitter is the premier social media platform for real-time and reliable investing information. The other platforms may have a resource here or there, but for the best financial content I would stick with Twitter. If you find accounts you like, check their other platforms to see if they resonate with you. Many also have free resources that you can sign up for via email.

Twitter Accounts

Twitter Personalities

- **Charles Payne** (@cvpayne): Charles is the host of *Making Money* on Fox Business; he is a champion for the retail investor. He provides amazing free content and has a subscription service for investors. This is a must-follow.
- **Kenny Polcari** (@KennyPolcari): Kenny is a great friend of mine who is a former NYSE floor trader. He is a current media personality and an amazing chef! Get amazing stock market info and recipes for the price of one follow!

- **Luis Galdamez** (@moneyluisG): My business partner. He holds the financial trifecta in designations—a CFA, CFP, and CMT—and is a brilliant dude. This guy is the biggest sleeper out there.
- **Peter Mallouk** (@PeterMallouk): Peter is the CEO of Creative Planning and provides some of the best charts that really educate and simplify things for investors.
- **Maria Bartiromo** (@MariaBartiromo): Maria is a legend. She has over one million followers on Twitter for a reason.
- **Aswath Damodoran** (@AswathDamodoran): Aswath Damodaran is a professor of finance at the Stern School of Business at New York University, where he teaches corporate finance and equity valuation. I have personally implemented a lot of his knowledge.
- **Mohamed A. El-Erian** (@Elerianm): The former investment manager of the Harvard Endowment fund, author, and currently the president of Queens' College, the University of Cambridge. If you want to follow one of the top brains in finance, this is the guy.
- **Elon Musk** (@elonmusk): Not necessarily a finance guy but he moves both the crypto and financial markets with his tweets. Need I say more?

Other Twitter Resources

- ***Wall Street Journal*** (@WSJMarkets): Real-time financial news data.
- ***Investor's Business Daily*** (@IBDInvestors): Great data on individual stocks and overall market trends.
- **Bloomberg** (@markets): With a handle like @markets you must follow them!
- **Federal Reserve** (@federalreserve): They control interest rates, and interest rates *really* matter!
- **FOX Business** (@Foxbusiness): Because your man is on there regularly!
- **MarketWatch** (@MarketWatch): They have over four million followers for a reason. Great market commentary and analysis.

- **StockTwits** (@StockTwits): A social platform for investors to share ideas. Do your own research, but it's great to have crowd sourcing new ideas for free.

Websites

- **Investopedia** (www.investopedia.com): A great free resource to get more information on financial terminology you may not be familiar with.
- **Yahoo Finance** (www.yahoofinance.com): An oldie but a goodie and one of the most reliable sources for information out there.
- **CNBC.com** (www.cnbc.com): Real-time stock market information.They have some paid features but a lot of great free resources here.
- **Chicago Board of Options** (www.CBOE.com): For those who may want to educate themselves on option trading, there is no better free resource out there.
- **Earnings Whispers** (www.earningswhispers.com): Find out what analysts and the street are really expecting when companies report earnings.
- **Bloomberg** (www.bloomberg.com): Great financial content and no BS.
- **Fox Business** (www.FoxBusiness.com): Real-time information and breaking news on everything business and investing.
- **Reuters** (www.reuters.com): Global business information to stay informed of what's going on around the world.
- **Side Hustle School** (www.sidehustleschool.com): We talked about getting your side hustle going. Check out their site and get on their podcast.
- *The Shawn Ryan Show* (www.shawnryanshow.com): Shawn is a patriot and the most underrated podcast host in America, in my humble opinion. This is hands-down my favorite podcast.

Appendix B
Glossary of Financial Terms

In this appendix, you'll find some of the most common financial terms you should know, from the Consumer Financial Protection Bureau at www.consumerfinance.gov/consumer-tools/educator-tools/youth-financial-education/glossary/. These are basic definitions you should understand.

I cannot explain every possible financial term because there are thousands; I just want to provide some of the most basic things you need to understand. If you want a robust list of terms, you can visit the Consumer Financial Protection Bureau website.

A

Annual return The profit or loss on an investment over a one-year period.

APR (Annual Percentage Rate) The cost of borrowing money on a yearly basis, expressed as a percentage rate.

Asset An item with economic value, such as stock or real estate.

B

Beneficiary Someone or something named to receive proceeds or benefits. In the insurance context, it's the person, charity, trust, or estate designated by the policyholder to receive the policy's benefits or payments.

Bond   A type of debt. When you buy a bond, you're lending to the issuer, which may be a government, municipality, or corporation. The issuer promises to pay you a specified rate of interest during the life of the bond and to repay the principal—also known as the bond's face value or par value—when the bond "matures," or comes due after a set period.

Budget   A plan that outlines what money you expect to earn or receive (your income) and how you will save it or spend it (your expenses) for a given period of time; also called a spending plan.

C

Capital gain   The profit that comes from selling an investment for more than you paid for it.

Capital loss   The loss that comes from selling an investment for less than you paid for it.

Credit   Borrowing money, or having the right to borrow money, to buy something. Usually it means you're using a credit card, but it might also mean that you got a loan.

D

Debt consolidation   Consolidation means that your various debts, whether they are credit card bills or loan payments, are rolled into a new loan with one monthly payment. If you have multiple credit card accounts or loans, consolidation may be a way to simplify or lower payments. But a debt consolidation loan does not erase your debt. You might also end up paying more by consolidating debt into another type of loan.

Deductible   The amount of expenses the insured must pay before the insurance company will contribute toward the covered item. For example, the amount you pay for covered healthcare services before your insurance plan starts to pay is your deductible.

Dividend   A portion of a company's profit paid to shareholders.

E

Earned income   Money made from working for someone who pays you or from running a business or farm. This includes all the income, wages, and tips you get from working.

Emergency fund   A cash reserve that's specifically set aside for unplanned expenses or financial emergencies. Some common examples include car repairs, home repairs, medical bills, or a loss of income.

Entrepreneur   Someone who organizes, manages, and assumes the risks of a business or enterprise.

F

Financial capability   The ability to manage financial resources effectively, understand and apply financial knowledge, demonstrate healthy money habits, and successfully complete financial tasks as planned.

Fixed expenses   Expenses, like bills, that must be paid each month and generally cost the same amount. Some fixed expenses, like a utility bill, may also be variable because the amount changes each month depending on usage.

G

Generational wealth   Wealth that is transferred from parents or relatives to children or other members of their family. This may take the form of cash, property, or anything else that has financial value, as well as investments in children's education, like paying for college or vocational training. Also referred to as intergenerational wealth.

Gross income   Total pay before taxes and other deductions are taken out.

I

Inflation   Inflation occurs when the prices of goods and services increase over time.

Interest   A fee charged by a lender, and paid by a borrower, for the use of money. A bank or credit union may also pay you interest if you deposit money in certain types of accounts.

L

Liability   Something that is a disadvantage, money owed, or a debt or obligation according to law.

Liquidity   A measure of the ability and ease with which you can access and use your money.

M

Moral hazard   The idea that you are less likely to be careful when you are shielded from the consequences of your actions.

Mutual fund   A company that pools money from many investors and invests the money in securities such as stocks, bonds, and short-term debt. The combined holdings of the mutual fund are known as its portfolio. Investors buy shares in mutual funds. Each share represents an investor's part ownership in the fund and the income it generates.

N

Net income   The amount of money you receive in your paycheck after taxes and other deductions are taken out; also called take-home pay.

O

Opportunity cost   The cost of the next best use of your money or time when you choose to buy or do one thing rather than another.

P

Prepaid card   A card on which you load money in advance to spend. While a prepaid card might look like a debit or credit card, there are differences. A debit card is linked to your checking account. When you use a credit card, you're borrowing money. A prepaid card is not linked to a checking account or credit union share draft account. In most cases, you can't spend more money than you have already loaded onto your prepaid card.

Prepayment   Payment of all or part of a debt before it comes due.

Principal   In the lending context, principal is the amount of money that you originally received from the lender and agreed to pay back on the loan with interest. In the investment context, it is the amount of money you contribute with the expectation of receiving income.

R

Rate of return   The profit or loss on an investment expressed as a percentage.

S

Secured loans   Loans in which your property (a thing you own) is used as collateral; if you cannot pay back the loan, the lender takes your collateral to get their money back. The lender can also engage in debt collection, can file negative information on your credit report, and might sue you.

Share   A unit of ownership, often in a company's stock or in a mutual fund.

Social Security   Provides benefits for retired workers and people with disabilities, as well as the unmarried children, surviving spouses, or former spouses (in certain cases) of both.

Stock   A type of investment that gives people a share of ownership in a company.

T

Tax credit   A dollar-for-dollar reduction in a tax. It can be deducted directly from taxes owed. Tax credits can reduce the amount of tax you owe or increase your tax refund, and some credits may result in a refund even if you don't owe any tax.

Tax deduction   An amount (often a personal or business expense) that reduces income subject to tax.

U

Unearned income   Income that people receive even if they don't work for pay. Can include things like children's allowances, stock dividends paid by corporations, and financial gifts.

Unsecured loan   A loan (such as most types of credit cards) that does not use property as collateral. Lenders consider these loans to be more risky than secured loans, so they may charge a higher rate of interest for them. If the loan is not paid back as agreed, the lender can also start debt collection, file negative information on your credit report, and might sue you.

About the Author

Rob Luna, MBA, is a wealth strategist and corporate advisor. He has 25 years of experience in private wealth management collaborating with successful executives, entrepreneurs, and professional athletes, managing everything from their real estate transactions and investment portfolios, to helping educate their families on being good stewards of wealth. Rob also has over 12 years of experience in corporate strategy consulting. He has consulted with some of the world's largest corporations such as Google, Microsoft, Amazon, Cisco, and Costco on strategic growth, capital raising, shareholder communication, and mergers and acquisitions (M&A).

He is an on-air contributor for Fox Business, where he can be seen weekly on the show *Making Money* with Charles Payne. He also appears regularly on *Mornings with Maria* starring Maria Bartiromo on Fox and has been featured in numerous publications such as the *Wall Street Journal* and *Barron's*. In 2021 and 2022 Rob was named a *Forbes* Best-in-State Wealth Advisor. Today, he works with a limited number of private clients on building multifamily and single-family office strategies, where his typical clients include successful entrepreneurs, senior executives, and professional athletes with a net worth greater than $25 million.

In January 2020, Rob sold a majority interest in Surevest, the wealth management firm he founded from a spare bedroom in 2002, to CI Financial, the largest nonbank publicly traded financial company in Canada, for an undisclosed amount. After the acquisition, Rob helped CI Private Wealth become the nation's fastest growing RIA firm collectively approaching $300 billion in assets.

Since 2020, Rob has transitioned his career and expanded his reach, creating new businesses including Rob Luna Enterprises, which includes the Rob Luna Wealth Academy, where he helps his members upgrade their life through personal financial education as well as personally coaching aspiring entrepreneurs to build multi-million- and billion-dollar businesses. At Real Talk Holdings LLC, Rob looks to democratize wealth management and disrupt both the financial services and insurance industries. He is also working on Real Talk tax, lending, and real estate solutions so that he and his team can improve everything that touches people's financial lives. All Rob's businesses combine to provide an ecosystem that supports the common theme of helping clients build, protect, and enjoy generational wealth so they can live a life they love.

In addition to his personal success as entrepreneur and over two decades of experience, Rob holds MBA degrees from the prestigious Anderson School at the University of California Los Angeles (UCLA) and Asia's top business school, the National University of Singapore (NUS), with an emphasis on global business management, international finance, economics, and strategy. An Ivy League alumnus of the Wharton School at the University of Pennsylvania, Rob graduated from the Wharton Advanced Management Program (AMP) in 2011 and served as a Wharton Fellow from 2011 to 2014.

Website: www.robluna.com
Instagram: @thelunarob
Twitter: @thelunarob
YouTube: www.YouTube.com/lunarob

Index